P9-EEP-129

AUGUSTANA UNIVERSITY COLLEGE
LIBRARY

CRITICAL PERSPECTIVES

The purpose of the works in this series is to provide the teacher and student with the most important critical and historic commentary on major authors, themes, and national literatures of the non-western world.

In a period when vast realignments of power and long overdue reassessments of the cultures of the third world are occurring, the documents and polemics reflecting and often speeding these changes should be readily available.

Senior Editors of the Series: D. Herdeck, Georgetown University, Washington, D.C., and B. Lindfors, University of Texas, Austin

Subjects of the first works in the Series:
1. Amos Tutuola
2. V. S. Naipaul
3. Nigerian Literatures
4. Cuba South—A Panoramic View of Caribbean Writing Havana to Cayenne

Future Volumes

Chinua Achebe
Wole Soyinka
Christopher Okigbo
Aimé Césaire
Léon Gontran Damas
Arabic Literatures 1930-1975
Contemporary Iranian Literature

CRITICAL PERSPECTIVES

ON

NIGERIAN LITERATURES

CRITICAL PERSPECTIVES

ON

NIGERIAN LITERATURES

Edited by

Bernth Lindfors

Three Continents Press: Washington, D.C.

FIRST EDITION

3&P

Copyright © 1976
Three Continents Press

The original essays collected in this Critical Perspectives appeared originally in *Research in African Literatures*, The University of Texas at Austin, except for "The Early Writings of Wole Soyinka" by Bernth Lindfors which appeared in the *Journal of African Studies* 2 (1975). Permissions to republish all the above gratefully received.

**Three Continents Press
4201 Cathedral Ave., N.W.
Washington, D.C. 20016**

Library of Congress Cataloging in Publication Data

Critical perspectives on Nigerian literatures.

(Critical perspectives; 3)
Includes bibliographical references.

CONTENTS: Vernacular literatures: Olajubu, O. Iwi Egungun chants. Owomoyela, O. Folklore and Yoruba theater. Adedeji, J. Trends in the content and form of the opening glee in Yoruba theater, Skinner, N., et. al. [etc.]

1. Nigerian literature—History and criticism—Addresses, essays, lectures. I. Lindfors, Bernth.

PL8014.N6C7   896'.33   75-27391

72029

ISBN 0-914478-27-3
ISBN 0-914478-28-1 pbk.

All rights reserved. No part of this book may be used or reproduced in any manner whatsoever without written permission except for brief quotations in reviews or articles.

Front cover design
by Patty Zukerowski

Acknowledgments

I wish to express my gratitude to all the authors included in this volume for allowing their essays to be reprinted; to Professor Boniface Obichere, editor of the *Journal of African Studies*, for permission to reprint my essay on Wole Soyinka; and to Professors Roger D. Abrahams and John Warfield, successive Directors of the African and Afro-American Studies and Research Center at the University of Texas at Austin, for their encouragement and enthusiastic support of *Research in African Literatures*.

Bernth Lindfors
Austin, Texas
August 13, 1975

AUGUSTANA UNIVERSITY COLLEGE
LIBRARY

CONTENTS

FOREWORD xi

VERNACULAR LITERATURES 1
   Iwi: Egungun Chants—An Introduction—Oludare Olajubu 3
   Folklore and Yoruba Theater—Oyekan Owomoyela 27
   Trends in the Content and Form of the Opening Glee in
      Yoruba Theater—Joel Adedeji 41
   Wakar Bushiya: A Hausa Satirical Poem—Neil Skinner *et al* 59
   The Dramatic Limits of Igbo Ritual—Michael Echeruo 75
   Early Fiction in Igbo—Ernest Emenyonu 87

LITERATURES IN ENGLISH 101
   The Narrative and Intensive Continuity: *The Palm-Wine
      Drinkard*—Robert P. Armstrong 103
   Cultural Norms and Modes of Perception in Achebe's Fiction—
      Lloyd Brown 131
   From Hausa to English: A Study in Paraphrase—Neik Skinner .. 147
   Plagiarism and Authentic Creativity in West Africa—
      Donatus Nwoga 159
   The Early Writings of Wole Soyinka—Bernth Lindfors 169
   The Role of the Publisher in Onitsha Market Literature—
      Don Dodson 195
   The Horn: What it Was and What it Did—W. H. Stevenson 215
   The "Communistic" African and the "Individualistic"
      Westerner—J. Z. Kronenfeld 243

NOTES ON CONTRIBUTORS 271

BIBLIOGRAPHY 275

FOREWORD

Foreword

Nigeria, one of Africa's wealthiest nations, is especially rich in verbal traditions. Generously endowed with oral and written literatures in a variety of languages, it has produced a number of remarkably talented creative artists who have become world-famous even while writing or performing primarily for their own people. Through these agents and their works, Nigeria has probably contributed more to international awareness of modern Africa's literary and cultural achievements than any other nation.

This book offers a sample of the scholarly attention that Nigerian literatures have received in recent years. Although it has not been possible to include essays on every significant topic or writer, the three major vernacular literatures—Yoruba, Igbo, Hausa—and the most important authors writing in English—are covered in some detail. All the essays but one originally appeared in *Research in African Literatures*, a journal which has been fortunate in attracting contributions from well-informed Nigerian scholars and critics as well as from Americans and Europeans who have lived and worked in Nigeria for a number of years. This collection may therefore serve as an introduction to Nigeria's newest verbal tradition—the tradition of academic discourse on Nigerian literatures.

VERNACULAR LITERATURES

IWÌ EGÚNGÚN CHANTS—AN INTRODUCTION

Oludare Olajubu

Iwì Egúngún,[1] a form of Yorùbá oral poetry, is an important genre of the traditional verbal art of the Ọ̀yọ́ Yorùbá.[2] In many ways it is very similar to ìjálá and rárà, two other genres of Ọ̀yọ́ Yorùbá verbal art. It is chanted exclusively by members of the Egúngún cult during the annual Egúngún festivals and during other Egúngún ceremonies and performances. Since iwì is closely linked with Egúngún and the Egúngún cult, some information about both is necessary for the understanding of iwì.

Egúngún[3]

Ancestor worship is an important feature of Yorùbá religion. The worship is based on the firm belief that the spirit of man never dies, but that after death, his spirit continues to influence the life of the community from another sphere. In times of crises or in the face of a challenge, the Yorùbá, like most Africans, summons and invokes the spirits of his ancestors. He swears by the name of his dead father. He ascribes all success in his human endeavors to the support he receives from his ancestors. Every year there is a festival in honor of the dead. During this festival, the spirits of the ancestors are reincarnated and materialized in the form of masquerades known as Egúngún.

The Egúngún appears under a costume known as agọ̀ or èkú, a big garment made of beautiful, bright-colored cloth which is worn to cover the head and body. Sometimes an allowance is made for sleeves. A net is fixed to the face to allow the wearer to see. He also wears a pair of trousers and a pair of shoes made of tough cloth. The edges of the shoes are sewn to the edges of trousers so that no part of the leg is exposed. Sometimes leggings of cloth are also worn on the trousers. The form of the agọ̀ varies from one type of Egúngún to the next. But what is essential is that an agọ̀ should be made to cover the entire body of the wearer. No part is left out.

The wearer of the costume is usually a man, never a woman. He always

3

carries a whip, and he speaks in a disguised voice, a coarse, croaky voice which resembles that of a frog. The wearer is usually a seasoned artist and is called an Ọ̀jẹ̀. He should not expose his face or any part of his body in public. His identity is usually kept a top secret. While everybody, male and female, knows that it is a living human being who wears the agọ̀ and is called Egúngún, he is regarded at the same time by the very same people as ará ọ̀rún—a being from heaven, one of the ancestors who has come to visit and bless the people. He is referred to as bàbá (father). Everybody in the society, old and young, pays him deep respect. It is believed that he can pray for the people to bring them good luck, cure their diseases, give children to the barren woman, and stop an abiku[4] from dying. In times of social crisis—drought, famine, epidemics—Egúngún is called upon to appear and carry away the ills of the people. Egúngún is also used to execute criminals and to expel dangerous people from the community. Though Egúngún is the reincarnation of the spirits of the dead ancestors, a particular Egúngún does not necessarily represent the spirit of any particular dead individual. Each Egúngún is symbolic representation of each and all the ancestors.

Egúngún performs various functions among the Yorùbá; apart from those enumerated above, the Egúngún also entertains people, dances, chants poetry and dramatizes. For this reason, there are different forms of Egúngún, each designed to perform specific functions. For instance, there is a form known as alabẹ̀bẹ̀ (the one with a fan) that dances; a type known as pààràká[5] (the one that goes about) that runs after children and young people flogging whomever he meets; another known as alágbo (the one with medicinal concoctions) who goes about praying for people; and yet another form variously known as onídán[6] (dramatist), alárìnjó[7] (one who dances as he walks) and agbégijó (one who dances with wooden masks) who combines dancing with poetry chanting and drama. But in whichever form, all egúngún are regarded as representatives of the ancestors and are therefore revered by the people.

Of all the various forms of Egúngún, the Egúngún onídán calls for special mention. While all the other forms of Egúngún appear and perform only during the festival periods, the onídán performs all the year round. Such performers go about in groups of six or eight with their children and wives and a troupe of drummers who are usually permanently attached to the group. At each town or village they visit, they stage public performances of dance, poetry chanting and acrobatic display. Because of this, the onídán performers become the greatest exponents of

Iwì Egúngún chants, and among members of the group and their wives and daughters can be found the best artists of Iwì Egúngún. They are motivated to sing well because members of the group supplement their living with earnings derived from the shows. Nowadays some groups of Egúngún *onídán* live entirely on the earnings of their performances.

During the shows, the onídán makes use of wooden masks which depict various characters in Yorùbá society which the *onídán* tries to caricature and satirize. The most popular characters include Tápà (the Núpeman), Aṣẹ́wó (the prostitute), the Policeman, Oyinbo (the white man), and Ìyá Ọmọ (a mother). As he wears the mask that depicts each character, the *onídán* dances in a funny manner and imitates some of the odd behavior for which the character is known. For example, the Oyinbo (white man) speaks through his nose in a way that makes it difficult for anyone to understand what he says. This is to ridicule the British and American expatriates in Nigeria whom most Nigerians, including some highly educated persons, find very difficult to understand. They just cannot pick up his words! It is the changing of the *onídán* into these masks that is called *idán* (wonders or magic). The audience would say "o ńpìdán" (He is performing wonders or "making scenes").

Apart from performing from town to town, the *onídán* also performs for important individual members of the society, either voluntarily or by invitation, on festive occasions.

At each show, iwì chanting plays a very major part. The onídán chants as he moves onto the open stage in the marketplace or under the shade of a tree, introducing all his dances and punctuating all his activities with iwì. He depends on these chants to move his audience to give him generous gifts. He also winds up his play with iwì before going home.

There is a secret organization charged with the responsibility of organizing the appearances of the Egúngún and keeping secret the identity of the wearer of the agọ̀. This organization is known as the Egúngún cult. It is essentially a male cult, and no women except an *ato*[8] can be admitted. New entrants into the cult usually undergo an initiation. Every member must swear on pain of death to keep the secrets of the cult and must assist in the effort to make people believe that the man under the costume is not an ordinary human being but one of the ancestors who has come from heaven. The cult is under a titled head known as Alágbàáà. He is assisted by other officials, among whom are Alápìnni, Eéṣọrun, Àreọ̀jẹ̀, Ọlópọndà, Alárǎn and Ọlójẹ̌.

The Egúngún festival comes up once every year between March and

June and lasts between a week and three months, the duration varying from place to place. During the festival various types of Egúngún appear in the streets in large numbers in their multi-colored dresses. Each is attended by drummers and surrounded by a large crowd of people made up mostly of wives and daughters of cult members and scores of whip wielding youths. Civic leaders and cult chiefs hold feasts for the Egúngún in rotation. During these feasts, the Egúngún and his followers entertain the patrons and the general public with music, dancing, poetry, drama, and parades in their colorful costumes. Each day of feast is preceded by an all-night iwì poetry chanting during which leading chanters compete for honors and distinction, and amateurs and apprentices try out their voices and skill.

Iwì and other Genres of Yorùbá Oral Poetry

All forms of Yorùbá oral poetry draw from a common source of oral materials for their composition. These oral materials include oríkì (praise names of persons, animals and other things), orílè (praise poems of various lineages and settlements in ancient Yorùbá kingdoms), ìbá (salutes to powers, natural and supernatural, that rule the Yorùbá world), proverbs, incantations, wise saying, clichés and prayers. These verbal formulae are set and cannot be altered or amended by individual artists. All artists are expected to memorize and chant them correctly during public performances. Members of the audience are always eager to reward correct renderings in cash and kind and to punish faulty renderings by way of cold reception and refusal to offer gifts.

Since all artists draw from this common source to compose the different genres, it follows that all the genres would have similar texts. In that case, what then distinguishes one genre from the other?

This brings up to the question of classification of Yorùbá oral poetry and the criteria for distinguishing one form from the other. Many Yorùbá scholars have written on this.[9] The main distinguishing features are as follows: each genre is chanted in a distinct tone of voice which is recognized by the audience; each is chanted by different types of people and on different occasions. For instance, ìjálá is chanted by hunters and devotees of Ògún (the Yorùbá divinity of iron and war) at their meetings and during festivals connected with Ògún. It is usually chanted by men only. Iwì is chanted by members of the Egúngún cult and their wives and daughters during the annual Egúngún festivals and during public performances of the Egúngún *onidán*. Rárà is chanted by professional beggars, minstrels and eulogists and can be chanted at all places and at all times by both male and female. But certainly the most important feature as far as the reader is concerned, since he is concerned with the printed texts, is the content of the texts of each genre. Each genre can be recognized by the type of information that dominates the text and by the order of arrangement of such information. The text can also reflect the nature of the audience, providing a clue to which genre it belongs. Therefore, though iwì shares some measure of similarity with other genres of Ọ̀yọ́ Yorùbá poetry, it is the special methods of composition and the special techniques of performance discussed below that distinguish it as a distinct genre of Yorùbá oral poetry.

Iwì is chanted exclusively by members of the Egúngún cult but not by every member of the cult because it is chanted in a special tone of voice which can only be achieved by talent, practice and skill. For instance, a chanter should be gifted with a sweet voice, and he should have a long repertoire of praise poems of the principal lineages in Yorùbáland. He should have a rich wealth of proverbs, wise sayings, incantations and jokes to draw from. Above all, he should have grown into the art by practice from childhood to adulthood. He should also be familiar with the principal personalities in the society.

There are two categories of chanters. The first category consists of the men who wear the agọ̀.[10] They are known as Ọ̀jẹ̀. Most of them belong to the onídán type of Egúngún. The second category consists of the talented members of the Egúngún cult who do not wear agọ̀. They are called Ẹlẹ́sà. A woman can also chant iwì if she is either a wife or daughter of a male member of the Egúngún cult and if she possesses the requisite talents and skill. During the annual Egúngún festivals, and during any Egúngún performance, it is usual for a crowd of men, women and children to accompany each Egúngún. During this time talented male and female members of the crowd chant iwì in praise of their ancestors, the Egúngún. This is the principal time when iwì is chanted. Iwì chanting is also an integral part of any public performance of an Egúngún onídán. Needless to say, in modern times iwì poetry can be chanted for entertainment during civic ceremonies like marriages, burial, and conferment of titles.

Iwì as a Poem: Composition and Performance Techniques

Iwì is a piece of verbal artistic creation having a beginning, a middle and a clear end. The beginning is made up of *ìbà* (homage or salute to powers that be) and other introductory chants. Such introductory chants include the signature tune of the chanter and his personal introduction. The middle is made up of salutes to individuals (oríkì), salutes to lineages (orílẹ̀), and comments on various aspects of Yorùbá life. The end is made up of the closing chants and the closing song. It is the duty of the artist making an iwì composition to harmonize the three parts of the iwì poem to produce a distinct form of oral poetry.

For the purpose of study, it is essential to view each iwì performance at a given social occasion to a given audience at a given time as one complete unit of iwì poetry. The length of such poetry can only be conceived in terms of the length of time employed in its performance. This ranges from two to ten hours, depending on the importance of the occasion, the size of the audience, the availability of refreshments and the ability of the artists. For instance, during the festival periods, iwì is chanted all night and all day, but only for few hours on other occasions. But whatever the length of an iwì performance, the structure of its text remains the same.

The iwì artist learns his chants by imitation. The art is usually a family art so that the artist grows into it, learning from the many public performances which his group gives every year. By the time he becomes a master artist, he should have in his repertoire the praise names of all members of the community, the praise poems of the important lineages, proverbs, wise sayings and incantations, all of which he has learnt by imitation over the years. He should also have learnt the sequence and technique of iwì performances. It is essential that he keep strictly to the traditional pattern and content of the chants in his public performances.

But the iwì artist is not a mere carrier of oral traditions or a mere performer reproducing by rote what someone else has composed. He is a creative artist—both a composer and a poet. His is a difficult job for he composes and performs at the same time. There is no time for rehearsal because his composition and performance are both conditioned by the circumstances of the performance.

Iwì is performed in the presence of large audiences in markets and public places. The audience is usually made up of chiefs, elders and nobles, craftsmen, farmers and traders. Some of them come early and stay till the end of the performance, while some leave early. But throughout the performance, people keep on coming and going. To the iwì artist, every member of the audience is important and worthy of his attention. Their patronage is the main impulse and motive behind the whole performance. The instability and variability of the audience, therefore, requires a marked degree of concentration on the part of the iwì artist. It also tests to the utmost his dramatic ability, his narrative skill and his ability to keep his audience for a long time.

Though the iwì artist has a set pattern or order of composing his poem, he must keep his eye on the audience, in composing and performing his chants. He must know the oríkì and orílẹ̀ of each member of the audience, the names of each member's wives, children and parents. He must be conversant with the current gossip, jokes and happenings. As each guest arrives or departs or offers a gift, so also must he react by singing the praise of the particular guest. In the process of doing this, he may remember a joke which we would like to make, a social misbehavior which he would like to satirize or a moral lesson which he would like to give. He would digress a little to include these. In the process, he may forget to return to his former topic and go on to new themes.[11]

The chant continues for as long as the audience is willing to stay and as long as the audience can sustain the performance by giving gifts of money and drinks to the artists.

The iwì text has a characteristic pattern. Every iwì chant opens with introductory chants which form the beginning of the poem; these consist of the ìbà and the self-introduction of the artist. The ìbà is a set of verbal salutes to the powers that rule the Yorùbá cosmos. To the iwì artist, these powers include the Olódùmarè (the almighty God, usually referred to in iwí as Ọlọ́jọ́ òní), the most important Òrìṣà, leaders of the Egúngún cult and the society in general, witches, veteran artists, medicine men and the artist's father.[12]

The body or middle of an iwì is the longest and most important part of the chant. It consists of salutes to members of the audience and their lineages (called oríkì and orílẹ̀), proverbs, fables, prayers, incantations, wise sayings, songs, and jokes. Pieces of these are woven together to form episodes and plots in the chant. Every plot or episode in the chant is directed at particular individual members of the audience to please, praise or amuse them.[13]

An iwì chant does not end abruptly. Every performance is rounded off with a valedictory note from the artist. The note, which usually includes prayers and thanks to the audience for the goodwill and gifts, is concluded with a fitting song.[14]

An iwì is rendered in two voice patterns. The first is a high tuned voice which is very near to that employed in song. This is usually used by the Egúngún onídán and the ẹlẹ̀ṣà so most performances of iwì are done in it; in fact, it is the only voice pattern known to many. The second voice pattern is a croaky voice, regarded by cult members as the real voice of the Egúngún. Anyone speaking in the second voice speaks only as an Egúngún and not as a human being. For this reason, the second voice pattern may not be uttered in public except under an agọ̀ by an Egúngún. This voice pattern is difficult to make; therefore, only specialists can chant iwì of any appreciable length with it. However, special talent, training and skill are required to produce any of the voice patterns.

An iwì is performed by a group of people who organize themselves into an orchestra or an ensemble. The orchestra consists of the solo, the chorus and the bàtá drummers. The solo is made up of men and women, usually two or three in each orchestra who have acquired specialization through long years of practice and have developed the longest repertoire. They alternate in singing the lead parts of the chant and from among them the leader of the orchestra is chosen.

The chorus is the group of chanters who sing the songs raised by the lead chanter. It consists of young boys and girls who are usually children or close relations of the lead chanters. Women who are wives or children of the lead chanters are also included.

Each iwì orchestra is homogeneous. Both the solo and the chorus belong to the same ẹbí.[15] The fathers, mothers or aunts become leaders— solo singers, while their sons and daughters serve as apprentices—chorus singers. When the leaders become too old to sing or when they die, their children take their places so that each member of the orchestra grows up and gains experience in performance. The drummers may not belong to the same ẹbí as the chanters but they must have permanent attachments with the chanters. The role of the drummers is to supply musical accompaniment to the songs raised in iwì. The chief drummer also aids the memory of the lead chanter by supplying him with hints and he encourages the lead chanter by shouting his praise names with his drum.

Every performance is opened by the leader of the orchestra and he chants the lead parts throughout the performance. He is however relieved and complemented by the other solo chanters at various stages of the chant. Sometimes the performance assumes the form of a dialogue among two lead chanters. At the end of each plot or episode in the chant, it is usual for the soloist to raise a song and for the chorus to sing the refrain. If the soloist likes, he can stretch the song for some time. Thus it can be seen that an iwì chant is the result of the joint effort of a team, every part of the team playing its part to build a single poem. This makes it unlike rárà which is a solo effort of an individual singer or ìjálá which is the work of rival artists each struggling to outclass the other.

Language

Iwì, being exclusively a verbal art of the Ọ̀yọ́ Yorùbá, is chanted in the Ọ̀yọ́ dialect and only Ọ̀yọ́ people or those who claim ancestry from Ọ̀yọ́ people chant it. This means that if there are Ìjèṣà or Ìjèbu who chant iwì, they must have descended from Ọ̀yọ́ stock, and such people chant their iwì in Ọ̀yọ́ dilect. Apart from this, there is nothing special about the language of iwì. It employs and enjoys all the known characteristics of the Yorùbá language such as tonal manipulation, lexical matching and lexical borrowing from other languages, particularly from Hausa and English. Above all, the iwì artist employs all the poetic devices of Yorùbá oral poetry—e.g., repetitions and ready-made expressions to fit into particular situations.[16] The situation of the performance of iwì chants and the varied and unstable nature of the audience impose on the iwì artist the temptations of digression and the inconveniences of interruption. The iwì artist, however, tackles all these problems within the framework of his chants. He devises ready poetic expressions with which he answers questions, checks noisemakers and wards off other interruptions without having to stop his chant.

Content

The content of iwì consists mainly of a sequence of praise poems about individuals, gods, and lineage groups, these being interspersed with incantations, benedictions and commentaries on various aspects of Yorùbá life. The content of two other related genres of Ọ̀yọ́ Yorùbá poetry—namely, ìjálá and rárà—is similar. A close examination will, however, reveal that the content of iwì is clearly different from that of other types of Yorùbá oral poetry. For example, apart from the praise poems about individuals, gods and lineages, ìjálá chants also include praise poems about birds, animals, and plants; relate the exploits of hunters in the bush; and devote much attention to Ògún—his praise, his might and his deeds. Rárà, on the other hand, is concerned mainly with the praise and flattery of particular individuals, with the sole aim of attracting gifts from the respective individuals who are the targets of the chants. Hence rárà is a sequence of vivid character sketches and profiles. But iwì is concerned solely with the praise of man—living and dead—and his society. It gives prominence to persons and interpersonal relationships and to attitudes and values derived from the chanter's conception of the world of the Yorùbá. Iwì also tells of the glorious days of the lineages, of heroes of past wars, and of current events and happenings. Unlike ìjálá, iwì is not concerned with animal and plant life nor does it put any particular emphasis on the praise of any particular òrìṣá. And unlike rárà, iwì is not concerned only with particular individuals in isolation but with man in relation to his total environment.

The content of iwì, therefore, consists mainly of salutes: salutes to the gods and the superior beings known as ìbà, salutes to lineages known as orílè, and salutes to individuals known as oríkì. The ìbà consists of salutes to the major òrìṣà like Ṣàngó, Ògún and Èṣù, salutes to the supernatural beings like mother witch and medicine men, and salutes to parents (ancestors), leaders of the cult and of the society, and the forerunners of the artist. The orílè consists of salutes to the major lineages or rather settlements of the old Ọ̀yọ́ Empire. Such lineages include Ìkòyí, Ìrẹsà Ògbojò, Ọ̀fà, Ìkìrun and Ẹ̀rìn. These salutes are made up of praise names and cognomens of the progenitors of the lineages, detailed descriptions of the general habitat of the original home of the lineages and narratives of major events in the history of each lineage. The oríkì (salute to individuals) consists of a series of character sketches and praises of certain individuals. These individuals include the artist himself, his parents, his patrons and members of his audience and of the society in general. Such individuals also include the dead and those who are not physically present at his performance. Each individual has a special poem formed around his person. The salute to an individual invariably ends up or leads to the salute of the lineage to which he belongs. Thus oríkì and orílè are closely related.

Oríkì and orílè have fixed contents. Though no two artists can chant a given oríkì and orílè the same way, yet there is a hard core or recurrent information running through each oríkì and orílè which is known to the artist and the audience.[17] All the artist has to do is to recite correctly each oríkì and orílè. No artist is expected to amend the known content of an oríkì or orílè. Such amendments are treated as errors on the part of the artist and are frowned on by the audience.

Oríkì and orílè form the largest and most important part of iwì. They are regarded by both the artist and the audience as the real chant. But the iwì artist punctuates the various oríkì and orílè, with another group of chants, the subjects of which are many and varied. They include prayers, songs, witty sayings, jokes and comments on Yorùbá life, and they come in at the end of long chants of oríkì and orílè, serving as interludes, asides and commentaries. They also afford the artist the opportunity to educate, amuse, thank and pray for his audience. One important feature of the content of this group of chants is that they are original compositions of the artist expressing his own independent views of life and representing his personal contribution to the content of his iwì chant. They are also evidences of his understanding of Yorùbá philosophy. The quality of an iwì artist is measured largely by the content of such compositions.

Though iwì is a form of traditional oral poetry, its content is not static or stereotyped. It keeps changing with different situations. For this reason, no artist can repeat verbatim a chant he has chanted before. Every performance yields a new poem, created on the spur of the moment to satisfy a new audience and a new situation.

Conclusion

Iwì is a distinct form of Ọ̀yọ́ Yorùbá oral poetry, not only because it is chanted exclusively by a special group of people in a special tone of voice but because of its distinct content and style of performance. Its distinctiveness also lies in its elaborate techniques of composition and performance, which blend the poetry with drum music. By employing all the known techniques and devices of Yorùbá oral poetry, iwì emerges as a highly artistic and rich genre of Yorùbá oral poetry.

FOOTNOTES

1 Iwì Egúngún is known by two other names: Ẹ̀sà and Ògbére. The word iwì should not be confused with *Ewì* which is the general term for all types of Yorùbá poetry.

2 Ọ̀yọ́ Yorùbá: a subtribe of the Yorùbá with headquarters at Ọ̀yọ́ and with Aláàfin as the paramount ruler. They inhabit the following administrative divisions: Ọ̀yọ́ North, Ọ̀yọ́ South, Ibàdàn, Ìbàràpá and Ọ̀sun, and in Modákẹ́kẹ́ and parts of Orígbó in Ifẹ̀ division, all in the Western State of Nigeria. They can also be found in Ọ̀fà and Ilọrin districts of Kwara State of Nigeria. Both the people and their language are known as Ọ̀yọ́.

3 There are two types of Egúngún connected with ancestral worship in Yorùbáland. The first, known as Egúngún Adó is that type of Egúngún found in Èkìtìland whose costume is a combination of cloth, palm fronds and feathers. The second, known as Egúngún Ọ̀yọ́, is that type of Egúngún found among the Ọ̀yọ́ people whose costume is made mainly of cloth. This paper refers exclusively to the latter.

4 In Yorùbúáland there is a belief that certain children are born to die, that such children keep coming to the same mother and dying. Any woman who loses her babies consecutively is said to be suffering from Abiku. Such children are given special names—like, Igbékòyí, Dúródolú, and Kòsọ́kọ́. See R. C. Abraham, *Dictionary of Modern Yoruba* (London: University of London Press, 1958), pp. 7–8, and A. B. Ellis, *The Yoruba-speaking Peoples of the Slave Coast of West Africa* (London: Chapman and Hall, 1894), pp. 111–14.

5 Meaning, literally, one who roams or wanders about—i.e., one who parades the streets.

6 A magician in the sense that the Egúngún is believed to be able to metamorphose into various characters—e.g., ape, royal python, crocodile, policeman, Tapa and prostitute. The idán (magic) is achieved by the Egúngún putting on masks and costumes that would make him look like caricatures of these characters.

13

[7] Meaning, literally, "one who dances as he walks or travels"—i.e., a member of a travelling theatre group.

[8] Name given to the third of the triplets, if female. She is dedicated to the Egúngún and has the privilege of knowing Egúngún secrets. But since women who know Egúngún secrets usually go barren, most Ato wait till menopause before they avail themselves of this privilege.

[9] Cf. Ulli Beier and B. Gbadamọsi, *Yoruba Poetry* (Ibadan: Government Press, 1959); S. A. Babalọlá, *The Content and Form of Yoruba Ijala* (Oxford: Clarendon Press, 1966), p. 23; E. L. Laṣebikan, "Tone in Yoruba Poetry," *Odu*, No. 2 (1956), p. 35; and Ọlátúndé Ọlátúnjí, "Classification of Yoruba Oral Poetry," (Paper at the Weekend Seminar of Yoruba Language and Literature, Institute of African Studies, University of Ife, December 13–16, 1969).

[10] Also known as ẹ̀kú—the Egúngún costume.

[11] See Appendix II below.

[12] For an example of ìbà, see Appendix I below.

[13] For an example of the middle of an iwì chant, see Appendix II below.

[14] For an example of the end of an iwì chant, see Appendix III (a) and (b) below.

[15] Blood relation.

[16] Cf. Adébóyè Babalọlá, "The Poetic Characteristics of Yoruba Ìjálá Chants," (Seminar paper, Institute of African Studies, University of Ife, Ibadan, 1964); Ọlátúndé Ọlátúnjí, "Tonal Counterpoint in Yoruba Poetry," (Paper presented at the 8th Annual Conference of the West African Linguistic Society, Abidjan, March 1969); E. L. Laṣebikan, op. cit., pp. 35–36, and "The Structure of Yoruba Poetry," *Presence Africaine*, 8, 10 (1955), 43–50.

[17] Cf. Babalọlá, *The Content and Form of Yoruba Ijala*, p. 25.

Appendices
To
Iwì Egúngún Chants

APPENDIX I

Ìbà o o o ò ò ò.
Mo ríbá lóní, mo ríbàa bòge.
Babàa mi ibà,
Mo ríbà Eṣu, mo ríbàa Ṣàngó.
Mo ríbàa pélébé owó.   5
Mo ríbàa pèlèbè esè.
Mo ríbà àtélesé tí ò hurun.
Tó fi dé jogbolo itan.
Ìbà ìyáa mi òṣòròṇgà.
Apamáránkú olókìkí oru,   10
Afínjú àdàbà tí í jẹ lárìn ásà.
Afínjú eyẹ tí í jẹ ní gbangba oko.
Ìbà omo afòrurìn.
Ibà Èṣù Láaróyè aràgbó,
Láfián omo élébo tí i jorí eran.   15
Òkàkà tí í ṣobìrin yàngìyàngì.
Èṣù dákun má ṣe mi lóde ilè yí láéláé.
Mo wá ríbà ríbá.
Mo wá ríbàa babaà mi.
Òlójó òní mo ríbà lódò rẹ,   20
Kí n tó máwo ṣe.

ORIN

Òjè: Mo ríbà o
        Mo ríbà a.
        Ātawo àtògbèrì
        Mo ríbà a.
Ègbè: Mo ríbà o, mo ríbà a
        Ātawo àtògbèrì mo ríbà a.

APPENDIX II
EXAMPLE OF THE MIDDLE OR BODY OF AN IWÌ CHANT

ÒJÈ KÍNÍ:
        O ṣé láyé Omo Abílódeṣú.   *Signalling his take-over*
        O ṣé láyé o ó gbádùn ara.
Ara yíò gbădùn rẹ.
Bóyìnbó ti ṣe gbádùn-un bàtà   ⎤
Báwon alágbàṣé ṣe gbádùn ilè tó bá kún. ⎦ *A witty saying.*   5
Bẹ́ẹ̀ lèmí í ṣe e polódùmarè mi.
Adéyẹmí Omo lóógun.
Ākànjí Àgbé, oba asòlùdérò.
Ākànjí tó gbárèmo rè Bàdàn   *Salute or*
Tó gbákìrun bò wá núu lé.   *praise to*   10
Adéyẹmí lo Ámólàóyè.   *Adéyẹmí, the*
Òmo Erínjogúnolá Ojomu odẹ.   *Oba of*
Omo àpèwáàjoye láti wájú o   *Ìkìrun*
Ākànjí nlẹ́ omo ojà obì.   *(Akìrun)*
Adéyẹmí oko Ṣègilolá   15
Òkánjúàa ṣòbìyà, in ṣá lĀkànjí.

16

APPENDIX I
EXAMPLE OF THE BEGINNING OF IWÌ-ÌBA

Homage!
I pay homage today, I pay homage to Bòge
Homage to you my father.
I pay homage to Èṣù and to Ṣàngó
I salute the flatness of the palm.   5
I salute the flatness of the feet.
I salute the sole of the feet that grows no hair,
Till the smooth fat part of the thigh.
Homage to, Oṣoronga, my Mother,
Who kills without sending for death. The famous one of the night.   10
An elite of a dove that feeds among hawks.
An elite of a bird who feeds in the open farmland.
Homage to the offspring of the one who walks in darkness
Homage to Èṣù Láaróyè Aràgbó,
Láfian, child of the offerer of a sacrifice who eats the head of the sacrificial animal.   15
Òkàkà that makes a woman rather restless.
Èṣù, please never use me in this town.
I again pay homage.
I again pay homage to my father.
Ruler of today, I pay homage to you,   20
Before I embark on my art.

SONG

Òjẹ̀:   I pay homage,
          I pay homage.
          Both the initiated and the uninitiated,
          I pay homage.   25
Chorus: I pay homage,
          I pay homage.
          Both the initiated and the uninitiated,
          I pay homage.

APPENDIX II

FIRST ÒJẸ̀:
Thank you offspring of Abilodeṣu.
Thank you, may you enjoy your body.
May your body enjoy you
As the white man enjoys his shoes,
As the laborer enjoys very weedy farmland.   5
That is how I salute my Lord.
Adéyẹmí, offspring of the brave one.
Àkànjí Àgbé, the king who brings peace to the town.
Àkànjí, who went to Ibàdàn as an Arẹmọ,
Who came back home as an Akinrun.   10
Adéyẹmí, Amọla-Oye, has gone.
Offspring of Erínjógunọlá, the Ojọmu of the hunters.
Offspring of the one who was invited from afar to take a title.
Hello Àkànjí, offspring of the owner of the kolanut market.
Adéyẹmí husband of Sègilọlá.   15
A covetous guinea worm, that was Àkànjí,

17

Tí ńdá mọ lórùn ẹsẹ̀.
Ọmọ Oníkòkò.
Babaa wọn àgbà,
Ló gbé kòkò dénú igbó tán.
In náá ló dirúnmalẹ̀ tí ńgbé Kìrun   *Oríkì orílẹ̀*   20
Nílé ọmọ Erínjogúnọlá ojọmu ọdẹ̀.   *Ìkìrun.*
Àgùntonílàá ọmọ ọjà obì.
ỌJẸ̀ KEJÌ:
E má jẹ́ ó ju méjìméjì lọ
Àlàbí oníbàtáá mi.
Bààmú–ọwọ́–òsì–tẹ́ẹ́rẹ́ baba Kàrímù.   *Personal*   *Salute to*   25
Ọmọ Igbólẹ́rù atìdímu.   *Oríkì*   *Àlàbí*
Òmọ Igbólẹ́ké ojúupa.
Ọmọ èyọ̀ọ, mi èyọ̀.
Ọmọ èyọ̀ tó ti mú Kìrun dòkun   30
Ọmọ èyọ̀ tó ti mu Kìrun dọ̀sà.
Ọmọ èyọ̀ tó ti mú Kìrun dùn gbọ́ngbọ́n.   *Salute or*
Aláìsí ewúrẹ́.   *praise to*
Wọ́n sọgbà síloro.   *Àlàbí my*
Àìsí àgùtàn,   *Bàta Drummer.*
Wọ́n sọgbà á yàrà.   *Orílẹ̀ Ìkìrun*   35
Àìsínlé Inálowúwà
Wọ́n sọgbà Ṣóńtokí
Lánùmí, mọ oníkẹmbẹ tí í légún-ún lọ.
Mo gbàào n ò sebẹ́ nisàlẹ̀ Isán.
ỌJẸ̀ KÌNÍ
Òótọ́ ni bẹ́ẹ̀ náà ni.   *Signalling his take-over*
Bẹ́ẹ̀ ni mo ṣe ńpe Adé'ẹmí,
Àkànjí àgbé.   *More salutes to*
Ọba díẹ̀ k'Ákirun.   *Adeyemi the Ọba*
Ọmọ oníkeníirin   *of Ikìrun* (Akirun)   45
Àgbà àgùntonílàá ọmọ rọjà obì.
Alóólódù ọkọ Ṣẹ̀gi.
Adéyẹmí ọmọ lóógun.
Àkànjí àgbé ọba asọ̀lúdẹ̀rọ̀.
ỌJẸ̀ KEJÌ
Ẹ má jẹ́ ó ju méjìméjì lọ.   *Signalling his take-over.*   50
Òkété-ṣa-bi-ó-le-gbé Adédìjí.   *Oríkì of his grandfather Adédìjí*
Babaà mi àgbà ló kọ́ mi lọ́fọ̀ kan àjímọ́ọ̀rọ́.
Ẹ tún wá bi mí ẹ ní kí ni?
ỌJẸ̀ KÌNÍ
Bó bá ti rí o làdí ẹ̀ han ni.   *Introducing an*
                                    incantation.
ỌJẸ̀ KEJÌ
Wọ́n ní, alóló alòló.   55
Àtiròrun àkàlà.
Ojú ro wọ́n tòkí.
Ló dífá fún olómitútù   *Incantation*
Tí ńsobìrin Àgbọnìrègún.   *and*
Èdìdì àlọ̀.   *Prayer*   60
Ifá ò ní polómitútù kó pupa.
Ẹ è ní bá wọn kúkú ọ̀wọ́wọ̀ láéláé.

That attacks one on the ankle.
Offspring of the owner of the Pot.
Their grandsire
Carried pots to the forests.   20
Which later became spirits that lived at Ìkìrun.
In the household of Erínjogúnọlá, Ọjọmu of the hunters.
Àgùntọnílàá, offspring of the owners of the kolanut market.
SECOND ỌJẸ́:
Don't let it exceed two at a time.
Àlàbi my bàtá drummer,   25
One with a mark across the left cheek father of Kàrimù
Offspring of the dreadful forest.
Offspring of Igbólẹ́kẹ́
Offspring of Ẹ̀yọ̀, my Ẹ̀yọ̀
Offspring of the Ẹ̀yọ̀ that turns Ìkìrun to an ocean.   30
Offspring of the Ẹ̀yọ̀ that makes Ìkìrun very sweet.
Without goats,
They made a fence across the lane,
Without sheep,
They made a fence across the ravine,   35
Because Inalowura was absent,
They made a fence across Ontoki
Lámùmí, offspring of the one with big trousers that pursues an army.
I hired a fireplace, I made no soup down there at Isàn.
FIRST ỌJẸ́:
It is true, so it is,
That is how I salute Adé'ẹmí
Àkànjí Àgbé.
Akìnrun is no little king
Offspring of possessor of both plastic and iron.   45
Àgùntọnílàá, the old one, offspring of the owners of the kolanut market.
Owner of both money and safe husband of Sègi
Adéyẹmí son of the brave one
Àkànjí Àgbé, the king who restores peace to the town.
SECOND ỌJẸ́:
Don't let it exceed two at a time.   50
Adediji, a rodent who selects its own abode.
It is my grandfather who taught me an incantation, useful for daily recitation.
Now ask me, say, what is it?
FIRST ỌJẸ́:
Explain how it is.
SECOND ỌJẸ́:
They say, alóló alòló   55
When the àkàlà was to go to heaven
It was very painful to them.
That was the divination that came for Olómitútù
Who was wife to Agbọnìrègún.
Èdìdì àlọ̀.   60
Ifá will not kill Olómitútù and make it red
You will never die of smallpox.

ỌJẸ KĬNÍ
Èmi gàan ó máa ṣàmín àṣẹ
Mo ní, nítorí péyín téégún fí í jobì
Abẹ́ aṣo ló ńgbé.   65
Eyín tókèté fi í pakurọ.   *Commentary*
Ọmọ rẹ̀ ní í fi í hàn.
Eyín tí babaà mí fí í jobì,
Mé fí han-ẹnì kan.
Àkànjí Àgbé mọ Ìrán-dùn-tó-tó-ó-jó.   70
ỌJẸ KEJÌ
Ọmọ Abílódeṣù máa gbọ́ wàsíì mi.   *Announcing his take-over.*
Wọ̀nrànwọnràn ní òṣùká
Ọmọ àyán-án-fílù-ọ̀tẹ̀-pẹ̀   *His personal Oríkì*
Bí kò bá sí ikú,
Àdìsá, máa gbọ́ wàsíì mi.   75
Ẹni mẹ́ta ni ìbá pe'raarẹ̀ l'Ọ́lọ́run ọba.   *Introducing an Epigram; note the dialogue style.*
Ẹ wá bi mí, ẹ ní ta ni?
ỌJẸ KĬNÍ
Eléwo ni
Bó bá ti rí o làdí ẹ̀ han ni.
Torí àṣípayá lóbìnrínn í ṣílẹ́kùn éémọ.   80
ỌJẸ KEJÌ:
Olówó ìbà pe'raarẹ̀ l'Ọ́lọ́run Ọba
Olóògùn ńkọ́?
Ibá pe'raarẹ̀ l'Ọ́lọ́run Ọba.
Àlùfáà ńlá ìbá pe'raarẹ̀ l'Ọ́lọ́run Ọba.   *An epigram.*
Níjọ́ ikú ó bǎ polówó.   85
Owó ò ní ṣiṣẹ́.
Níjọ́ ikú ó polóògùn,
Agádágodo ni,
Gbètugbètu ni,
Àkáábá ni,   90
Àbà ni;
Àní gbogbo ẹ̀ nií ó mà wọmi.
Ijọ́ ikú ó pààfáà ńlá,
Ẹ̀fúùfù lèlẹ̀ a máa gbé tákààdá ẹ lọ.
ỌJẸ KĬNÍ:
Òótọ́ ni bẹ́ẹ̀ náà ni.   95
Ikú pa babaláwo,
Bí ẹni tí ò kọ́ Ifá.
Ikú polóògùn
Bí ẹni tí ò lóògùn.
Ikú ló pààfáà ńlá,   100
Bí ẹni tí ò ké s'Ọ́lọ́run Ọba.   *Wise saying.*
Mo wòkè,
Mo wòsàlẹ̀.
Mé è rọ́ba méjì tí í j'Ọ́lọ́run Ọba.
Kò ṣọ́ba bíi Bàlárátù tí í jóńṣẹ́ ńlá.   105
ỌJẸ KEJÌ
Òótọ́ ni bẹ́ẹ̀ náà ni.
Ẹ má jẹ̌ ó ju méjì-méjì lọ.   *Signalling his take-over.*

20

FIRST ỌJẸ̀

I too will say "amen so let it be"
I say this because the teeth with which the masquerade eats kolanut
Abide under the mask.   65
The teeth used by rodent to break the palm
It is to its child it will reveal them.
The teeth used by my father to eat kolanuts
I don't reveal it to anyone.
Àkànjí Àgbé, offspring of the grand show that befits one's participation.   70

SECOND ỌJẸ̀:

Offspring of Abílódeṣù, listen to my words.
One with disordered head pad.
Offspring of one who the drums hail with rebellious strains.
But for death,
Àdìsa, listen to my sermon.   75
Three persons would have designated themselves, God the King.
Now ask me, say, who are they?

FIRST ỌJẸ̀:

Who are they?
However it may be, explain it
Because a woman will always open wide the door of the feared one.   80

SECOND ỌJẸ̀:

A rich man would have designated himself, God the King.
What of the medicine man (the Doctor)?
He would have designated himself, God the King
The great priest, would have designated himself, God the King.
On the day death would kill the rich man   85
Money would be of no avail
On the day death would kill the medicine man
The charm that locks up man's intentions,
The one that stupefies one
The one that makes one look like a fool   90
The one that arrests one's movements.
Indeed, everything will perish.
On the day death will kill the great priest,
Gentle winds will carry off all his papers.

FIRST ỌJẸ̀:
                                                                                                      95
It is true, it is perfectly so,
Death kills a herbalist
As if he learns no Ifá
Death kills the medicine man
As if he possesses no charms.
Death kills a great priest   100
As if he does not cry unto God the King.
I look up
I look down below
I see no two kings known as God the King.
No king like Bàlárátù who is called the doer of great deeds.   105

SECOND ỌJẸ̀:

It is true, it is perfectly so.
Don't let it exceed two at a time

21

Ó dorí Rááji Àjàlá ọmọ ewé ojúmọ́lá.
Ǹlẹ́ Olóbùró òdodo
Èdè ilé Òbùró mọ gbẹ̀bìọ̀kúnọ́là,   110
Ọmọ agbẹ̀bí ile gbẹ̀bí òde.
Mọ agbẹ̀bí ẹranko gbẹ̀bí èèyàn.   *Oríki*
Ọmọ ọ̀sán pọ́n ganríngánrín.   *Orílẹ̀*   *Salute to*
Kẹ́ni má kò tòde àwọn lọ.   *Olóbùró*   *Rááji Àjàlá*
Ọmọ oòrún kan tàrí gbọ̀ngbọ̀ngbọ̀n   115
Kẹ́ni má gba t'Àágberí.
Kìkì iwọ, Kìkìi jìnjinni,
Ní m̀bẹ, lode Àágbérí.
Ẹ má mà fi jìnjìnnì kàn mí.
Ẹ sá jẹ n kú tìkáàmi.   120
Èdè tilẹ́ Òbùró mọ agbẹ̀bí ò kún ọ́là.
ỌJẸ̀ KÍNÍ:
O ṣé láéláé o ó gbǎdùn ara.   *Signalling his take-over.*
O ò máa gbọ́ nítorí Àládòkun.
Àjàlá onílùu Dòkun ni ṣe.   *Oríki*   125
Onílùu Dòkun ni o, awó-lé-nù,   *An Orílẹ̀*
Oníjàrẹ́, mọ awólénù lọna Àrè.
Àyàndá lọmọ wólé,   *Salute or Praise*
Ọmọ túnlémọ.   *to Àládòkun—a*
Àdìsá lọmọ tàkáararẹ̀ mọlé ẹyẹlé   *Oríki*   *popular magician.*
Àyàndá la bálágbèdẹjà   130
Tó fa ọmọ owú ẹ dá.
Ṣebí núu lée bàbáà rẹ ni.
Oníjàrẹ́ mọ awọ́lénù lọnà Àrè.

APPENDIX III
EXAMPLES OF THE END OF IWÌ

a. Un ó ṣe
   Un ó relé
   Ọdẹ́ ńṣe gbérèé apó ńlé.
   Àgbẹ̀ ńṣe gbérèé òjò
   Iyáa mí ńṣe gbérèéè mi.   5
   Wọ́n ńṣe gbérèéè mi nínúu lée wa.
   Àgùnbẹ́ onílẹ̀ obì.
   Ọmọ iṣú jinná n sán bọnu,
   Òwè ṣe rẹ̀rẹ̀ gbilẹ̀ n'Isàn.
Orin
   Ọ̀jẹ̀: A ó lọ,   10
         Kẹ́ ẹ mọ́ pá ò dá-gbére mọ́.
   Ègbè: A ó lọ,
         Kẹ́ ẹ mọ́ pá ò dá-gbére mọ.
   Ọ̀jẹ̀: A ó lọ o.
         Kẹ́ ẹ mọ́ pá ò dá-gbére mọ.   15
   Ègbè: A ó lọ.
         Kẹ́ ẹ mọ́ pá ò dá-gbére mọ.
   Ọ̀jẹ̀: Akérébúrú ọmọ Jálugun
         Ijó inú ẹ̀kú, ẹrù niyọ̀
         Ọ̀jẹ̀ tí í jó bí alágbàálẹ̀.   20

22

It is now the turn of Rááji Àjàni offspring of a certain leaf.
Hello Olóbùró the true one
Knowledgeable one of Òbùró who takes child deliveries free.   110
Offspring of one who takes child deliveries both at home and outside the home.
Offspring of one who takes child deliveries for both man and animal.
When the sun is high up in the sky,
Let no one walk across the front of their house.
When the sun is directly at the center of the head,   115
Let no one pass through Aágberí.

All poisons, all maladies,
Exist at Aágberí,
Do not afflict me with any malady,
Just let me die on my own   120
The knowledgeable one of Òbùró offspring of the one who takes child deliveries free.
FIRST ỌJẸ̀:
Thank you very much, may you enjoy yourself.
Now listen for the sake of Àládòkun.
Àjàlá, he is Dòkun's drummer.   125
He is Dòkun's drummer, one who broke down houses.
Oníjàrẹ offspring of one who broke down houses at Àrè.
Àyàndá is the offspring of one who broke down houses.
Offspring of one who rebuilt houses.
Àdìsá is the offspring of one who on his own built a nest for pigeons   130
Àyàndá is the one who fought with the blacksmith,
And broke his hammer.
I think it is in your father's household.
Oníjàrẹ one who broke down houses at Àrè.

APPENDIX III
EXAMPLES OF THE END OF IWÌ

Ọjẹ̀:   I will now be done.
           I will go home.
           The hunter longs for the quiver at home.
           The farmer longs for the rain;
           My mother longs for me.   5
           They all long for me in our household.
           Agunbẹ, offspring of the owner of kolanut plantation.
           Offspring of the place where one waits for the yam to be done before eating it.
           Bean leaves blossom green at Iṣan.

Song:
Ọjẹ̀:   We will be going,   10
           Lest you say we have not bade you goodbye.
Chorus: We will be going,
           Lest you say we have not bade you goodbye.
Ọjẹ̀:   I say we will be going,
           Lest you say we have not bade you goodbye.   15
Chorus: We will be going.
           Lest you say we have not bade you goodbye.
Ọjẹ̀:   Akereburu son of Jalugun
           Dance inside Ẹku, the ponderous one.
           An Ọjẹ̀ that dances as one who has received an advance payment.   20

23

Ègbè: A ó lọ.
     Ké ẹ mọ́ pá ò dá-gbére mọ.
Ọ̀jẹ̀: Iwọ̀n-ọ̀n lú là á ṣèlú,
     Akéréburú, bá a bá ti lówó sí,
     Leégún fi í jó fún ni í mọ.   25
     Mo níjó ọlọ́jà lọ́tọ̀.
     Ké ẹ mọ́ pá ò dá-gbére mọ́.
Ègbè: A ó lọ,
     Ké ẹ mó pá ò dá-gbére mọ́.
b. Ọ̀jẹ̀: Aláré mo júbà o
     Iǹlé o Àjèjé
     N ó máa fèyí ṣè lọ
     Kò búrú kò bàjẹ́
     A ò ní féégún eléyì ṣàṣemọ   5
     Ìpé tá a pé rèwerèwe
     Ìpò tá a pọ̀ ní mọ̀gbà
     Idùnmú la á kàn a à láburú ú rí
     Èmi Ọ̀jẹ̀ Àkànó mọ jìngín-là-á-gbọ́wọ́ọ-jó.
     N ó jéré délé   10
     Gbogbo yín ẹ ó jèrè délée tẹ̀yin
     N ó jéré délé tẹ̀yin
Ègbé   N ó jèrè délée tèmi
Ọ̀jẹ̀:   Èmi rábẹsá okọ Adédoyin
     Ọ̀jẹ̀ tí í sọ dídùn baba ọ̀rọ̀   15
     N ó jèrè délé
Ègbé: N ó jèrè délée tèmi
Ọ̀jẹ̀:   Èmi jìnnìjìnni l'Ágbé mọ Wòírà
     Nílé ọmọ abélépopọ́n
     Nílé ọmọ abélépopọ́n
     N ó jèrè délé   20
Ègbè: N ó jèrè délée tèmi.

Chorus: We will be going.
   Lest you say we have not bade you goodbye.
Ọ̀jẹ̀: The affairs of a town are managed according to its size.
   Akereburu, it is according to the strength of one's purse.
   That an Egungun performs for one.   25
   I have a special dance for the village head
   Lest you say we have not bade you goodbye.
Chorus: We will be going,
   Lest you say we have not bade you goodbye.
Ọ̀jẹ̀: I pay homage to you singers
   Hello Ajeje,
   I will be going with this.
   It is neither bad nor ill.
   This egungun festival will not be our last.   5
   As we gather here as youths,
   As we are many here as elders,
   It is gladness we shall meet, we have nothing evil to see.
   I, Akano the Ọ̀jẹ̀, offspring of one who gracefully raises his hand in dance
   I will reach home with blessings.   10
   All of you will reach your homes with blessings
   I will reach home with blessings.
Chorus: I will reach my home with blessings.
Ọ̀jẹ̀: I, the plain-faced one, husband of Adedoyin
   The Ọ̀jẹ̀ who says sweet things, the best of words.   15
   I will reach my home with blessings.
Chorus: I will reach my home with blessings.
Ọ̀jẹ̀: I, the feared one of Agbe, offspring of Woira
   In the household of one whose complexion is like palm oil.
   I will reach home with blessings.   20
Chorus: I will reach my home with blessings.

FOLKLORE AND YORUBA THEATER

Oyekan Owomoyela

The purpose of this essay is not merely to apply a generally accepted opinion—that theater and folklore have a specially close relationship, one to the other—to the Yoruba situation. We know, for instance, that the ancient Greek dramatists relied heavily on folklore for their material, that Shakespeare found European folklore useful, and that the theaters of the East—Japanese, Chinese or Indonesian—also make extensive use of folklore. While in this essay an attempt will be made to show that what was, and is, true of the theaters cited is equally true of Yoruba theater, more importantly, an attempt will be made to disencumber Yoruba theater of the religious and ritual deadweight that threatens to become grafted on to it.

Taking their cues from a certain school of thought that advocates a ritual origin of drama (since Aristotle has supposedly proved this fact with reference to Greek theater), certain writers have claimed that Yoruba theater is a bequest of Yoruba religious instinct. Typical are the following statements by a Yoruba scholar, Joel A. Adedeji:

> Religion is the basis of dramatic developments in Yoruba as in most cultures of the world; disguise is its means, and both depend on artistic propensities for their fulfilment.[1]

> The worship of Ọbàtálá [the Yoruba arch-divinity] has important consequences for the development of ritual drama and, finally the emergence of the theatre.[2]

He further says that "the human instinct for impersonation and ritualistic expression . . . leads to 'developmental drama'."[3]

Another Nigerian, poet-dramatist John Pepper Clark, has earlier written:

> As the roots of European drama go to the Egyptian Osiris and the

Greek Dionysus so are the origins of Nigerian drama likely to be found in the early religious and magical ceremonies of the peoples of this country.[4]

He goes on to cite the *egúngún* and *orò* of the Yoruba as "dramas typical of the national repertory."[5]

It is not difficult to see that the views quoted borrow credence from the fact that Aristotle, the first systematic theater historian, had seemingly proved the religio-genic nature of Greek theater and, by implication, of all theater. But the question should be asked whether Aristotle in fact intended to say that the dramatic instinct of the Greeks, or indeed of any other people, resulted from religion. A careful reading of the *Poetics* leads one to believe that Aristotle was primarily concerned with one specific form of theatrical expression—Greek tragedy—which had benefited from the performers and performances associated with the Dionysiac revels. That he would not subscribe to such views as that "Religion is the basis of dramatic developments" is indicated by the following words from the *Poetics*:

> As to the *general* origin of the poetic art, it stands to reason that two causes gave birth to it, both of them natural: (1) Imitation is a part of man's nature from childhood, (and he differs from other animals in the fact that he is especially mimetic and learns his first lessons through imitation) as is the fact that they all get pleasure from works of imitation. . . . and (2) melody and rhythm also. . . , at the beginning those who were endowed in these respects, developing it for the most part little by little, gave birth to poetry out of the improvisational performances.[6]

Thus, two thousand years ago, Aristotle recognized that imitation and impersonation are part of human nature. Whether religion is part of human nature or not is definitely open to debate; what is certain is that the mimetic instinct develops in man very much earlier than any evidences of religious inclination, and before religious indoctrination. Thus, long before children can make any sense of religious beliefs and practices, they evince a sense of mimesis by playing house, and cops and robbers—apart from performing those mimetic activities associated with the learning process.

The evidences adduced by the scholars who believe in a ritual origin of drama to support their claim come in the main from festivals that, while purporting to be religious, incorporate theatrical performances. Depending on the circumstances, the festival cited could be that of Dionysus, or that of *egúngún* among the Yoruba. In any case, the fact that religion and drama can be seen hobnobbing in certain festivals can be very easily explained.

Festivals are social institutions by means of which men satisfy their fun-seeking instincts. They generally take place when the commodities that will ensure their success are in abundance (for example, when the harvest is in) and also when the festivals will not prejudice the performance of activities vital to the life of the community. It follows, therefore, that festivals are generally associated with holidays and periods of community-wide relaxation.

At the end of a hunt, the participants delight to wind down with a feast and a ball; so, at the end of a working season, the community delights to let its collective hair down and have a festival. It can be stated, without the need for a supporting argument, that theatrical sketches are just some of the accretions that festivals incorporate from time to time as they become more elaborate.

The supernatural powers become involved in festivals simply because of man's desire to placate them before and during the revels so that the revellers would be left in peace. To this end, "insurance" sacrifices are offered to the gods at the beginning of the festivals, and at the end, the grateful men return with thanks offerings. Moreover, during the revels, the participants decide to elect their favorite divinity as patron for the same reasons that long ago, certain players elected the King, the Chamberlain, or the Admiral as their patron and called themselves "The King's Men," "The Chamberlain's Men," or "The Admiral's Men." The men in question did not perform plays because they were in the first instance associated with King, Chamberlain, or Admiral, association with whom entailed the performance of plays. Rather, they associated themselves with the notables because they wished to perform plays and thought they could best do so if they enjoyed the protection of such powerful personalities. If the players later included plays about their patrons in their repertoires, that would still be consistent with their strategy.

Therefore, if among the Yoruba we encounter festivals whose designations suggest that they are "in honor of" certain divinities, we should not allow the evidence of the name to befuddle our minds to such an extent that we become unable to determine the relative importance of different festival aspects.

In the Yoruba theater of today (which is often referred to as "folk opera"), we see the culmination of a socio-political development which began around the middle of the nineteenth century in Lagos. It was in 1851 that the British conquered Lagos and put its affairs in the hands of a ruler who would put an end to the hitherto flourishing slave trade. Two years later, a British Consul arrived to take up residence there. With the establishment of British presence, the town became so secure that it began to attract European missionaries, European commercial agents, well-educated freed slaves from the Sierra Leone and the Americas, and ambitious native Africans from the nearby areas. Favored by its situation on the Atlantic coast and by its command of a vast rich hinterland, Lagos soon became a flourishing cosmopolis the direction of whose affairs rested in the hands of a cosmopolitan *élite* class.

The introduction of drama into the city around 1880 was a means of providing evening diversion on the European model for the Lagos *élite*, made up, as we have seen, of expatriates and westernized Africans.[7] As one would expect, the theatrical fare was strictly European, featuring such dramatists as Molière and Gilbert and Sullivan.

In those days, one had to be a practising Christian to be socially acceptable. In fact, the prestige of the Christian establishment was such that the city's life revolved mainly around the different mission houses.[8] It was, therefore, no wonder that the performing groups were invariably connected with one Christian mission or the other. This connection must have eased some practical difficulties because the most readily available performance places were the schoolrooms that were all owned by the missions. The students of certain schools, recognising the social advantages and financial possibilities of theatrical entertainment, had themselves formed dramatic societies either for the purpose of raising money, or just for the love of diversion.[9]

The profound changes that occurred in Lagos after the European powers had divided the continent of Africa among themselves at the 1885 Berlin Conference proved significant for the development of Yoruba theater. In the past, the Europeans in Lagos were there for limited purposes—commerce, or the conversion of heathens—and they were not averse to treating Africans as equals. But now, the emphasis shifted to colonization and the attitude of the resident Europeans underwent a change. They now saw themselves as masters and the Africans as clients and they behaved accordingly. African church officials felt the change most traumatically because the Church was one institution in which native personnel had been put in the fore-front of the campaign, obviously because the European missionary bodies recognized the wisdom of making use of African converts who could function in the inhospitable climate and communicate with the natives. Now, their European colleagues took steps to put all authority in their own hands.

As a result of the friction generated, African groups seceded from the European and American Churches and founded protestant African Churches. The first of these groups broke off under David B. Vincent from the American Baptist mission in 1888.[10]

What is more important is that the Africans began to react against the rigorous suppression of all facets of African culture by the European Christians. They now looked to their culture for reassurance, and as something they could take pride in. According to E. A. Ayandele,

> From 1890 onwards useful researches were made into Yoruba mythology, philosophy of religion and metaphysics of *Ifá* [the Yoruba system of divination]. In 1896 appeared the Reverend Moses Lijadu's *Yoruba Mythology* in which *Ifá* and the legend of creation. . . were examined. . . . Studies of indigenous religion led to the foundation on 12 April, 1901 of "The West African Psychical Institute Yoruba Branch," for the purpose of encouraging the study of comparative religion, philosophy and science, especially the psychic laws known to *Babaláwos* (*Ifá* priests) and secret societies.[11]

As early as 1882, a correspondent of the *Lagos Observer* had made a strong plea for discarding "borrowed plumes" in the form of European or Europeanesque literature in favor of "the legends connected with our race, and . . . the brilliant exploits of our ancestors as handed to us by tradition." By the turn of the century, the African amateur dramatists, mainly drawn from the ranks of the secessionist churches, were performing works mainly on local themes and in the native language—Yoruba.

It was not until 1945 that a professional Yoruba theater group came into existence, and then it came as an offspring of one of the African churches. Ulli Beier has described its development in the following words:

> Theatre in the Yoruba language is mostly a kind of opera, in which the songs are rehearsed, while the dialogue is improvised. In the late twenties and thirties this form was developed in the so-called African Churches, the Apostolic Church and the Cherubim and Seraphim. The bible stories and moralities performed by these church societies soon gave way to profane plays, social and political satires which were played by professional touring companies.[12]

31

In 1944, Hubert Ogunde presented to the public an expanded version of what he had written as a devotional Service for the Church of the Lord in Lagos. It was a dramatization of the biblical story of the Garden of Eden, the action was simple, and all the lines were sung by dancing performers to the accompaniment of a competent off-stage band. The church had already realized that divine worship enlivened by drumming, clapping, and dancing was more satisfying to the African than the austere and sedate services that characterized "European" worship. The same proved true in the sphere of entertainment, as the enthusiastic public acceptance of Ogunde's "opera" proved. In the next year, he turned professional and gave Nigeria her first professional theater company—the Ogunde Concert Party.

The fact that he called his company a "concert" party is proof that Ogunde acknowledged that he was continuing a tradition that had been long in existence rather than creating something entirely new. (The nineteenth century theatrical activities were often billed as "concerts" because they often formed part of long programs that included songs, duets, magical displays, and such like.)

Moreover, since the missionary schools began presenting plays to parents and friends in the early years of theater, the tradition grew stronger and stronger until it became a fixed part of school activities. In most schools today, "dramatization" is always one of the items on the program of the end-of-year exercise, and Duro Ladipọ, one of the present masters of Yoruba theater, told me he began his career as a dramatist in such end-of-year activities at school. Apart from occasional biblical plays, the fare on these occasions was predominantly extracted from the Yoruba wealth of folk stories. It is not surprising, therefore, that in 1936, a school teacher—E. K. Martin—wrote, "As a means of general entertainment our folklore is never lacking. Folk stories may be . . . dramatized and the songs accompanying them practised and sung in the vernacular."[13] It was precisely this type of dramatization that bridged the gap between the turn of the century when, for several reasons, the theatrical flowering of the late nineteenth century fizzled out, and the time of Hubert Ogunde.

The dependence of Yoruba theater on Yoruba folklore is easily explained. First, it was nationalistic. Reaction to foreign oppression meant, in this instance, return to the native culture. James Coleman wrote:

The special grievances of the westernized elements [in Nigeria] were crucial factors in the awakening of racial and political consciousness. Much of their resentment, of course, was the inevitable outcome of the disorganization following rapid social change. The desire to emulate Europeans tended to separate them from their traditional milieu. Had they been accepted completely and unconditionally as dark-skinned Englishmen—as, in fact, certain members of the first generation were accepted—and had they been permitted to achieve a social and economic status that was both psychologically meaningful and materially satisfying, the course and the pace of Nigerian nationalism would most likely have been quite different. This did not happen, however, mainly because of the attitudes of many of the European residents and the policies of the British administration in Nigeria.[14]

It was as part of the reaction to those attitudes and policies that the Lagosians gave up trying to emulate Europeans and began to look askance at European theatrical fare which they eventually replaced with African material. It was to their credit that they did not discard theater wholesale but merely adapted it to suit the new mood.

Secondly, Yoruba theater has depended on folklore as a matter of expediency. Folklore is a vast treasury of theater material. The tales furnish a wealth of plots, the proverbs and such eulogistic poems as *oríkì, ìjálá* and *ewì* provide rich examples of ornamental dialogue, and if we include folkways in folklore, the physical actions connected with certain festivals give to dramatists action ideas that are effective on stage.

Lastly, it is logical that an alien institution that is introduced into a society should, in the course of time, be influenced by the native institution that is its parallel. Theater, being a form of evening pastime, naturally looked to the traditional evening story-telling session for material, the more so because of the political and nationalistic incentives that have already been mentioned.

Today, an accommodation has been effected between the native and the foreign elements of Yoruba experience, and it has resulted in a hybrid civilization at one polar fringe of which is maintained a more or less foreign, and at the other, a more or less native, complexion. Applied to evening entertainment, this situation means that on the one hand, there is a theatrical tradition that is for all practical purposes alien European (as typified by Wọle Ṣoyinka), and on the other hand, there is the continuing tradition of storytelling, particularly in areas that have not been drastically affected by modernization. In the middle of these is the Yoruba "folk opera" of Hubert Ogunde, Kọla Ogunmọla, and Duro Ladipọ.

Wọle Ṣoyinka's drama is world famous and, therefore, there seems to be no reason to dwell on it in this short essay. The uses of folklore among

33

the Yoruba do not differ in essence from those of other traditional societies, and, as a result of international tours by the "opera" artists, their art
form is becoming better known internationally.[15] However, to make it
easy for readers to compare the traditional evening amusement and the
new theater of the Yoruba, I will briefly describe each in its appropriate
setting.

For the evening storytelling session, we go to a compound in a ward
of Ibadan where we find an extended family that has not been wholly
caught up by creeping modernization. Apart from such concessions to
progress as the use of electricity, pipe-borne water, and the Rediffusion
box that brings a fixed radio program by wire from a local transmitting
station, the household remains a redoubt of tradition. After the evening
meal, the members of the family gather on a porch and if there is moon-
light, the younger members gather in the courtyard to play games like
hide and seek.

On the porch, the entertainment begins with riddles. What dines with
an *ọba* (paramount chief of a community) and leaves him to clear the
dishes? A fly. What passes before the *ọba's* palace without making
obeisance? Rain flood. On its way to Ọyọ its face is towards Ọyọ, on its
way from Ọyọ its face is still towards Ọyọ. What is it? A double-faced
drum.

After a few riddles, the tales begin. A member of the gathering announces the story of a certain man called *Àwòdọ́run*. He lived in a far-
gone age when men had eyes on their shins and cracked nuts with their
behinds. This man—*Àwòdọ́run*—was so nosey that whenever he saw two
people conversing or arguing he went and stood by them so that nothing
they said would escape him. His parents and friends warned him against
such behavior, but all to no avail.

On a certain day, while on his way to the market, *Àwòdọ́run* came upon
two men arguing spiritedly. As usual, he hurried to where they stood and
listened intently. Before long, the two men decided to press their points
by resorting to blows. This new development proved even more exciting
to *Àwòdọ́run* who urged them on with encouraging shouts. The com-
batants fought so hard that soon both fell and died from exhaustion.

At first, *Àwòdọ́run* was alarmed but soon his alarm gave way to anger
that the contestants dared die on him and thus deprived him of the benefit of knowing who had won the argument. Deciding that it could not be
dismissed as a stalemate and that the two men would, in all probability,
continue their argument on their way to heaven, he threw himself down

and died, the better to follow them. He would have stayed dead too but for his relatives who came and squeezed the juice of certain leaves into his eyes and thus revived him.

The next tale is of a certain young and beautiful girl who would not accept any man as her husband. Her parents became so angry and worried that they warned her they would turn her out of their home if she did not agree to marry someone soon. She, however, replied that she had not yet seen any man who appealed to her.

On a certain day, she went, as usual, to the market to sell some oil. As soon as she got there, she saw an exceptionally handsome man and immediately decided that she would be his wife. She abandoned her oil and approached the man who told her it was impossible for him to accept her offer. She would not be refused, and she followed him on his way home. As they went, the man sang to her:

Man	El'épo d'ẹ̀hìn o	Oil seller, please go back,
	Méè ṣ'ọkọ̀ rẹ.	I cannot be yours.
Response	D'ẹ̀hìn o méè d'ẹ̀hìn.	Go back? Not I!
Man	B'ó ò bá d'ẹ̀hìn wa d'ódò aró.	If you don't
		You'll cross an indigo river.
Response	D'ẹ̀hìn o méè dẹ̀hìn.	Go back? Not I!
Man	B'ó ò bá d'ẹ̀hìn wa d'ódò ẹ̀jẹ̀.	If you don't
		You'll cross the river of blood.
Response	D'ẹ̀hìn o méè d'ẹ̀hìn.	Go back? Not I!
Man	El'épo d'ẹ̀hìn o	Oil seller, please go back,
	Méè ṣ'ọkọ̀ rẹ.	I cannot be yours.
Response	D'ẹ̀hìn o méè d'ẹ̀hìn.	Go back? Not I!

As he sang, the young man cast off, piece by piece, the beautiful clothes he wore and, in the end, even his flesh, until he was nothing but a skeleton. The girl saw it all as a trick and still followed him across both the indigo and the blood rivers. Then the young man became a boa constrictor and proceeded to swallow her. Only then did she panic and yell for help. Luckily for her, a hunter heard her cries and came to her aid. He killed the boa and released the girl who there and then agreed to be the hunter's wife.

Many such stories are told until, when it is very late, the gathering disperses to sleep and take up the storytelling tradition the next evening.

For a performance of a Yoruba "folk opera," we need not go outside the city of Ibadan. The Arts Theatre of the University of Ibadan has hosted Ogunmọla's *Palmwine Drinkard* in the past, and it can be re-created here.[16]

The story is of *Lànké* an incurable drunk who follows his dead tapster —*Àlàbá*—to the town of the dead in order to persuade him to come back to earth and resume his palmwine tapping. The "opera" opens on a drunks' carnival hosted by *Lànké*. He exhorts his drunkard friends:

Ẹmu, ẹmu, ẹmu, ẹmu!
Ẹ jẹ́ k'á m'ẹmu à mu k'ára!
Mo l'ẹ́rú mo n'íwẹ̀fà,
Mo l'áya mẹ́fà, mo bí mọ méjọ!
Mo l'ówó l'ọ̀wọ́, mo ti kọ́'lẹ́.

. . . .

Asán ni gbogbo ẹ̀ l'ójú mi.
Ẹmu, ẹmu, ẹmu, ẹmu!
Ẹ jẹ́ k'á m'ẹmu à mu k'ára.

Palmwine, palmwine, palmwine, palmwine!
Let's all drink palmwine with all our might!
I have slaves, I have bondsmen,
I have six wives, I have eight children,
I have money, I have a house.

. . . .

That's all vanity to me.
Palmwine, palmwine, palmwine, palmwine!
Let's all drink palmwine with all our might.

The party continues with riddles from the guests. What can you see on the sea but not on land? The moon and stars. What drops into water and makes no sound? Needle. A large rock lives in a stream and still complains of thirst? The tongue. What is the two-cent wife that chases a hundred-dollar wife out of the house? Palmwine, of course! *Lànké* then recites the *oríkì* of palmwine:

Ẹmu!
Ẹmu ògidì pọnbé!
A bá 'ni w'ọ̀ràn b'á ò rí dá.

Ògùrọ̀ ogidì.
Tí kì í jẹ́ k'ẹni ó mọ̀'ṣẹ́ ara ẹni.
Ìyàwó o kọ́bọ̀-kan àbọ̀.
Tí ńlé onígba-òkẹ́ s'ígbó.
Akúwáńpá
Ab'itọ́ funfun l'ẹ́nu.
Àkíìkà!
Ẹni t'áwọn àgbá kì kì kì tí wọn ò le è kì tán,
Wọ́n l'ó sọ baálé ilé
D'ẹni tí ńyọ kóńdó
Lé ọmọ ọl'ọ́mọ kiri.

Palmwine!
Pure undiluted palmwine!
It finds you trouble when trouble is scarce.
Undiluted palmwine!
It screens your mind from pressing problems.
The two-cent wife that chases
The hundred-dollar wife into the bush!
Epileptic
That froths at the mouth.
Truly,
The elders, unable to find your ultimate *oríkì*,
Say you turn a landlord into a raving maniac
That chases children around
With a cudgel.

Soon, the supply of palmwine is exhausted and *Lànkẹ́* sends *Àlàbá* posthaste to the top of the palmtree for more palmwine. Unfortunately, the tapster falls from the tree and dies. *Lànkẹ́* cannot live without palm-wine and there is no tapster like *Àlàbá*. *Àlàbá* must return, so *Lànkẹ́* throws himself down and dies and thus begins his pilgrimage to the town of the dead.

Along the way, *Lànkẹ́* has many adventures, including an encounter with a white god who asks him to go and capture Death in a net (a feat he successfully accomplishes). But more pertinently, he is instrumental in rescuing a young and beautiful girl from some wicked Spirits determined to kill her. Her name is *Bísí*, and *Lànkẹ́* is drinking palmwine at her market stall when her father comes to tell her that complaints have reached him to the effect that she has sent every man who proposed to her away with insults. He warns her that she had better find herself a husband soon, and leaves. A little while later, a well-dressed young man arrives and asks the way to the fish stall. *Bísí* sees him and jumps at him. She has found the man she will marry, she says. The man protests but *Bísí* will not listen. She will follow him home.

On his way home, the man sings to her:

On'íyán d'ẹ̀hìn l'éhìn mi, tẹ̀tẹ̀ d'ẹ̀hìn o.
Ninikúnni.
On'íyán d'ẹ̀hìn l'éhìn mi, tẹ̀tẹ̀ d'ẹ̀hìn.
Ninikúnni.
B'ó ò bá d'ẹ̀hìn o ó d'ódò aró!
Ninikúnni.
B'ó ò bá d'ẹ̀hìn o ó d'ódò ẹ̀jẹ̀ ò ò!
Ninikúnni.

Foodseller leave me and go back home,
Ninikúnni.
Foodseller leave me and go back home,
Ninikúnni.
If you don't you'll cross the indigo river,
Ninikúnni.
If you don't you'll cross the river of blood,
Ninikúnni.

As he sings, he discards his clothes and his flesh, but *Bísí* follows him across the indigo river and the river of blood. They are now in a land inhabited exclusively by all sorts of grotesque Spirits who make it a point to kill any human who discovers their abode and their secrets. *Bísí* is tied up and would have been killed but for *Lànkẹ́* who arrives to put a spell on the Spirits and cut her loose.

The "opera" continues until *Lànkẹ́* has contacted *Àlàbá* who, even though he cannot leave the town of the dead and return to earth, gives *Lànkẹ́* a magic egg that will turn water to palmwine. He returns home with the egg only to wake up and find that his adventure was all a dream. The "opera" ends as it began with the exhortation:

Ẹmu, ẹmu, ẹmu, ẹmu!
Ẹ jẹ́ k'á m'ẹmu à mu k'ára!

Palmwine, palmwine, palmwine, palmwine!
Let's all drink palmwine with all our might!

When Ogunmọla's *Palmwine Drinkard* is considered in the light of the description of a family evening entertainment provided earlier, it is easy to see that his form of theater is, essentially, Yoruba folklore in a dress more compatible with a new milieu. The *Palmwine Drinkard* may not be typical in all respects of Ogunmọla's work or of the other Yoruba dramatists', but it will not be difficult to take any work by any of the dramatists and prove the same points that this essay has sought to prove.

A more detailed examination of the Yoruba "operas" will undoubtedly reveal borrowings from aspects of Yoruba culture other than the folklore. But that is only to be expected in a work of art whose nature is to pretend to be real life. The cornerstone of Yoruba theater is story, and Yoruba folklore has been, and remains, the most useful and the most important quarry of the dramatists.

REFERENCES

1. Joel Adeyinka Adedeji, *The Alárìnjó Theatre: The Study of a Yoruba Theatrical Art from its Earliest Beginnings to the Present Times* (Ph.D. Thesis, University of Ibadan, 1969), p. 32.
2. Ibid., p. 39.
3. Ibid., p. 66.
4. John Pepper Clark, "Aspects of Nigerian Drama," *Nigeria Magazine*, 89 (June 1966), 118.
5. The *egúngún* are fully masked figures that are supposedly the embodied spirits of dead ancestors. There is an annual festival around June, when the *egúngún* materialize out of secret groves and join humans in a feast during which some of them perform tricks and satirical sketches. Some funeral ceremonies also feature some *egúngún* that represent the deceased at funerary processions. *Orò* is a god of the night that must not be seen by non-initiates and never by a woman. This institution supposedly came into being early in Yoruba history as a means of preserving Yoruba culture and mysteries in the face of alien influences.
6. *Poetics*, 1448b, 4–24; Gerald F. Else, *Aristotle's Poetics: The Argument* (Cambridge, Massachusetts: Harvard University Press, in cooperation with the State University of Iowa, 1963), p. 124.
7. The first dramatic group was P. Z. Silva's Brazilian Dramatic Association formed in 1880. See Lynn Leonard, *The Growth of Entertainments of Non-African Origin in Lagos from 1866–1920 (with Special Emphasis on Concert, Drama, and the Cinema)* (M.A. Thesis, University of Ibadan, 1967), p. 25.
8. J. F. Ade Ajayi, *Christian Missions in Nigeria, 1841–1891: The Making of a New Elite* (London: Longmans, 1965), ch. 5.
9. Leonard, pp. 19, 23.
10. E. A. Ayandele, *The Missionary Impact on Modern Nigeria, 1842–1914: A Political and Social Analysis* (London: Longmans, 1966), p. 200.
11. Ibid., pp. 264–265.

12. Ulli Beier, "Introduction," in Ọbọtunde Ijimere, *The Imprisonment of Ọbàtálá and Other Plays,* English adaptation by Ulli Beier (London: Heinemann, 1966).
13. E. K. Martin, "The Importance of Our Folklore," *The Nigerian Teacher,* 8 (1936), 14.
14. James S. Coleman, *Nigeria, Background to Nationalism* (Berkeley: University of California Press, 1958), 145.
15. In 1964 and 1965, Duro Ladipọ participated in the Berlin Theatre Festival and the Commonwealth Festival in Britain respectively, Kọla Ogunmọla participated in the 1969 Festival of Negro Arts at Algiers, and Hubert Ogunde toured Britain from 1968–1969.
16. See Kọla Ogunmọla, *The Palmwine Drinkard,* translated and transcribed by R. G. Armstrong, Robert L. Awujọọla and Val Ọlayẹmi. Occasional Publication No. 12 (Ibadan: Institute of African Studies, University of Ibadan, 1968).

YORUBA "OPERAS" IN TRANSLATION

1. Ijimere, Ọbọtunde. [Duro Ladipọ and Ulli Beier] *The Imprisonment of Ọbàtálá* and *Everyman (Èdá)* in Ọbọtunde Ijimere. *The Imprisonment of Ọbàtálá and Other Plays.* English Adaptation by Ulli Beier. (African Writers Series.) London: Heine-mann, 1966.
2. Ladipọ, Duro. *Ọba Kò So.* Transcribed and translated by R. G. Armstrong, Robert L. Awujọọla and Val Ọlayemi. (Occasional Publication No. 10.) Ibadan: Institute of African Studies, University of Ibadan. 1968.
3.—————. *Three Yoruba Plays.* [*Ọba Kò So, Ọba M'Órò, Ọbá W'Àjà.*] Ibadan: Mbari Publications, 1964.
4. —————. *Mórèmí.* In *Three Nigerian Plays.* Introduction and notes by Ulli Beier. London: Longmans, 1967.
5. Ogunmọla, Kọla. *The Palmwine Drinkard.* Transcribed and translated by R. G. Armstrong, Robert L. Awujọọla and Val Ọlayẹmi. (Occasional Publication No. 12.) Ibadan: Institute of African Studies, University of Ibadan, 1968.

TRENDS IN THE CONTENT AND FORM OF THE OPENING GLEE IN YORUBA DRAMA

J. A. Adedeji

Introduction

This article* will trace the origin and development of the Opening Glee as a theatrical art form and account for those factors which have brought about changes in the content and form of presentation. These changes will also be linked in general terms to changes in Yoruba society. Examples of Yoruba drama will be drawn from the theatrical presentations of the Yoruba Masque Theatre (Alárìnjó or Eégún Aláré) and the Yoruba Operatic Theatre (the Travelling Theatre Parties). These are the two theatrical developments in Yorubaland which are indigenous and are products of Yoruba cultural history. Both are professional theatres with travelling troupes or companies which developed from religious rites.

The Opening Glee

The Opening Glee is a theatrical form which, like the classical "prologus," is an entrance song or chant that precedes a play. In the traditional Yoruba theatre, the Yoruba Masque Theatre, the prologue or entrance song was called the Ìjúbà. This was a ritualistic opening scene between the leading or chief actor and the chorus. The Ìjúbà contained a pledge and was a form of salute. As a theatrical form it is believed to have been first used by Ẹ̀sà Ògbín, the foremost Yoruba masque-dramaturg and professional entertainer, as a tribute to Ológbin Ológbojò, the "father" of the traditional theatre.

The Yoruba Masque Theatre emerged as a Court entertainment from the egúngún (masquerade) rites about the early part of the seventeenth century at the instance of Ológbin Ológbojò, an official at Court at Ọyọ Igbòho.[1] By the eighteenth century, it had become the people's theatre, with troupes plying the towns and villages of the Old Ọyọ empire. The theatre survived the collapse of the empire, but its existence has been

* This article is a revised version of a paper read at the conference on "Yoruba Language and Literature" held at the University of Ife, Nigeria, December 13th–16th, 1969.

41

marked by vicissitudes as a result of the onset of Western European culture in Yoruba society.

The following is an example of the traditional entrance song of the Yoruba Masque Theatre as presented by the Agbégijó troupe at Ọtta (recorded on tape February 16, 1965).

CHIEF ACTOR:

>Mo júbà, kí ibà mi ṣe.
>Ìbà ni ngó kọ́ jú ná, aré mi d'ẹ̀hìn.
>Mo rí'bà, mo ri'bà Baba mi Àjànkoro Dùgbẹ̀.
>Òun l'eégún Aláré, a-bi-kókó l'étí aṣọ.
>Afínjú Ọjẹ̀ tí í dún kòokò lórí Eégún.
>Baba mi má a gbóhùn ẹnu mi,
>Mo rí'bá, mo rí'bà.
>Jẹ́ k'óde òní yẹ mi o.

>Mo júbà pẹtẹ́ ọwọ́,
>Mo júbà pẹtẹ́ ẹsẹ̀,
>Mo júbà àtélẹsẹ̀ tí kò hu'run tó fi de gbògbòlò itan.
>Ará iwájú mo túúbá,
>Jànmáâ mo bẹ̀bẹ̀ ẹ̀hìn.
>Ibà ẹnyin Iyàmi Òṣòròngà,
>Ẹiyẹ a-bọ́wọ́ winni,
>Ẹiyẹ a-bẹsẹ̀ winni,
>Afínjú ẹiyẹ tí í jẹ láârín òru,
>Mo júbà o, k'óde òní ó yẹ mí.
>Mo tún júbà Èṣù Láâlú Ọkùnrin ọ̀nà,
>Ò ṣa' mọ l'ọgbẹ́, gún'mọ l'ọbẹ.
>Èṣù Láâlú mo juba o,
>Mo júbà j'óde òní ó yẹ mí.

CHORUS:

>Ojú Aiyé pé! (4 times)
>Ẹ wá wo gbẹ̀du àwa.
>Ojú Aiyé pé!
>Ẹ wá wo eégún àwa;
>Eégún àwa nfọ Tápà, ó nfọ 'Jẹ̀ṣà.
>Ojú Aiyé pé!
>Ìta pé!
>Ará pé!
>E wá wo gbẹ̀du àwa.

Ò-ṣèré l'Adélọwọ.
Ò-ṣèré l'Odìgbo.

CHIEF ACTOR:

Olóde àgò o!
Òkúta àgò o!
Ẹnyin Olóde!
Ẹ bùn wá l'óde o
K'áwa ó rí bi jó.
Ó d'ọwọ́ Ìrèlè.
Ó d'ọwọ́ Ìtá,
Ó d'ọwọ́ Òsanyìn,
Ó d'ọwọ́ Ògbojò tó l'eégún.
Nítorí Ogèdèngbé ló d'ójè 'lè,
Sọungbé ló ti kọ́ awo ó ṣe.

SONG:

"Ibi ẹ rí, ẹ kí' gbe mi lọ,
Ibi ẹ rí o ẹ kí' gbe è mi lọ. (2 times)
Emi Adélọwọ̀ ọmọ 'Ṣábí,
Ibi ẹ rí o ẹ kí' gbe mi lọ,
Ẹní ba ṣè l'aiyé mú. O-ṣèré l'Adélọwọ."

CHORUS:

Ojú Aiyé pé!
Ita pé!
Ará pe!
Ẹ wá wo gbẹ̀du àwa.
Ojíkí orúkọ
Ìyàmi Òṣòròngà.

SONG:

"Ẹ̀mú Aiyé!
Ẹ má mà mú wa.
Ẹmú Aiyé o!
Ẹ má mà mú wa!
Ẹní bà ṣè l'Aiyé mú,
O-ṣèré l'Adélọwọ."

43

CHIEF ACTOR:

I submit my pledge, may my pledge be fulfilled.
It is the pledge I will first submit, my performance comes
    at the end.
I behold a pledge, the pledge is to my father,[2] Ajankoro
    Dugbe.
He is the masque-actor, with a concealed knot at the hem
    of his garment.
The scrupulously neat masque-histrione who is a threat
    to the existence of other masquerades.
My Father, hearken to my voice,
Behold the pledge,
Let me become worthy of this outing.

I pledge to you my open hand,
I pledge to you my flat foot,
I pledge to you the underfoot that grows no hairs, even
    as far as knee-high.
To you who have passed before me, I humbly bow.
From you my companions, I beg for courage.
The pledge is to you,
Iyami Oşoronga,[3]
A "bird" with divers hands,
A "bird" with divers legs,
The scrupulously neat "bird" whose sorties are at
    midnight.
I hereby submit my pledge;
Let me become worthy of today's outing.

My pledge is also to you Eşu Laalu who patrols the road,
Who slashes and inflicts wounds.
Eşu Laalu, behold my pledge.
I submit the pledge,
Let me become worthy of this outing.

CHORUS:

The eyes of the World are set!
Come and see our "gbèdu."[4]
The eyes of the World are set,

44

Come and see our masquerade;
Our masques speak Tapa, they speak Ijẹsha.
The eyes of the World are set
Ìta (the open)⁵ is complete!
Brethren are assembled!
Come and see our "gbẹ̀du."
Adelọwọ is a player;
Odigbo is a player.

CHIEF ACTOR:

You owner of the Open, make way!
You owner of the Open, give us a space,
A space to put on our show.
We consign ourselves to the deity Irẹlẹ;
We consign ourselves to the deity Ìtá;
We consign ourselves to the deity Ọsanyin;
We consign overselves to Ologbojo, the owner of the
    masquerade.
Because of Ogedengbe,⁶ he introduced masque-drama-
    turgy.
He first learnt the secret at Sọungbe.

SONG:

"Shout my name, wherever you may,
Shout my name wheresoever you may. (2 times)
I am Adelọwọ, son of 'Ṣabi,
Shout my name, wherever you may.
It is he who offends that the World catches.
Adelọwọ is but a player."

CHORUS:

The eyes of the World are set!
Ita is complete!
Come to see our "gbẹ̀du."
"Early homage" is your name Mother-Superior, Ọsọ-
    ronga.

SONG:

"You catcher of the World, do not catch us.
You catcher of the World, do not catch us!

45

It is he who offends the World catches.
Adelowo is only a player."

Modern Yoruba society has witnessed the emergence of a new form of entertainment, the Operatic Theatre.[7] It developed from the "Native Dramas" popularized by guilds and societies of the Secessionist Churches in Lagos in the early part of the twentieth century. Later, encouraged by its popularity and success as a theatrical art form, some of the Choirmasters involved with the production of the "Opéra," as it was then called, organized their own drama groups outside the Church and held public performances at the Lisabi Hall, Ebute Metta and the Glover Memorial Hall, Lagos. With developing interest in concerts and amateur theatricals growing out of the remnants of the Variety Shows or the so-called Concerts of the 1880s, the organizers of the Yoruba Opera began to operate with artistic modifications that derived from traditional and foreign sources.

It was the Lagos Glee Singers, an established group of prominent Lagosians and veteran performers of European Operettas,[8] who were the first to use the "Opening Glee" to describe its entrance song. The term was later adopted and popularized by the Operatic Theatre in their operations in Lagos and the provinces. But what is most significant in the early examples of the Opening Glee was its focus on departure from the traditional ijuba. The following example is that of the Ogunmola Travelling Theatre in the late forties:[9]

CHORUS:

Eré dé, eré o.
Eré tó gbámúṣén,
Eré tó lárinrin,
À-rí má le è.lọ,
À-wò-pádà-sẹ́hìn.
Ẹ f'ara ba'lẹ̀ kẹ́ rí ran o e!

CHIEF ACTOR:

Alága wa o, àti 'gbákejì,
Ẹnyin ìyáa wa,
Ẹnyín bàbáa wa,
Kí a tó má a b'ére wa lọ,
Bí babaláwo bá jí,
A júbà l'ọ́wọ́ Ifá.

46

B'oníṣègùn bá jí o,
A júbà l'ọ́wọ Ọsanyìn.
Onígbàgbọ́ tó bá jí o,
A f'ìbà f'Ọlọ́run.
Ọba ọrun, ar'áiyé-rọ́run,
Awá mà júbà l'ọ́wọ Rẹ o.

CHORUS:

Òní a dá'jọ́ eré,
Òla a f'ọkàn s'ọnà.
Ọjọ́ tí a dá pé l'óni o,
Ẹ f'ara balẹ̀,
K'ẹ f'ara balẹ̀ wò ran l'ójọ́ òní o.
Agbe t'ó l'aró, Kì í rahùn aró.

Alùkò t'ó l'osùn,
Kì í rahùn osùn.
Lékeléke t'o l'ẹfun, Kì í rahùn ẹfun.
Kí ẹ má rahùn owó,
Kí ẹ má rahùn ọmọ,
Ohun t'ẹ́ ó jẹ, t'ẹ́ ó mun
Kó má wọn nyín o.

Òní a dá'jọ́ eré,
Òla a f'ọkàn s'ọnà.
Ọjọ́ tí a dá pé l'oni o
Gbogbo ènià.
L'ọ́wọ́ ikẹ́kùn Aiyé,
L'ọ́wọ́ ikẹ́kùn Èṣù,
L'ọ́wọ́ alákobá Aiyé o
Abáni-wá-kún-tẹni,
Èdùmàrè kó gbà wá o.

Àwa l'elére Ilẹ̀,
Àwa l'elére omi,
Egbére, Òṣùpà, Ilẹ̀, ilè aiyé o. (2 times)
Bí're ló bá mọ̀ ọ́ ṣe,
Ko múra o kíkan-kíkan.
Bí'bi ló bá mọ̀ ọ́ ṣe a,
Ko múra o kíkan-kíkan.
A, Páradísè la ó ti ṣè 'dájọ́,

47

A, Párádíse!

CHORUS:

We are here to present our play.
This is the time for the play,
A play that is gripping,
A play that is entertaining,
A play that one would see and would not like to leave,
A play that one would like to see backwards.
Be patient and see a real show.

CHIEF ACTOR:

Our Chairman and his supporter,
Our mothers,
Our fathers,
Before we go on with our play, when the priest of the
    Ifa cult awakes,
He places his pledge in the hands of Ifa.
When the physician awakes,
He places his pledge in the hands of the deity Ọsanyin.
The Christian, when he awakes pledges to God,
King of Heaven, One who oversees earth and heaven,
This is our pledge to Thee.

CHORUS:

Today we announce the date of our performance,
Tomorrow we look forward to it.
But today completes the announcement,
So be patient to see our show this day.
The bird "agbe,"[10] who is the possessor of the indigo,
    never lacks the dye.
The bird "aluko," who is the possessor of the "osun,"[11]
    never lacks the dye.
The cattle-egret who is the possessor of the chalk,
    never lacks the color.
May you not lack money,
May you not lack children,
May you never be short of what to eat and what to drink.

Today we announce the date of our performance,
Tomorrow we look forward to it.

48

But today completes the announcement
To all people.
From the snare of the World,
From the snare of "Eṣu,"[12]
From the World's troubleshooter who increases one's misfortunes,
May the Almighty deliver us.

We are the players on the Land.
We are the players on the Waters,
You Spirits, Moon, Land, of this World.
If doing good is your accomplishment,
Be steadfast at it.
If evil-doing is your accomplishment,
Be steadfast at it.
It is in Paradise that we shall face judgement.
Yes, in Paradise!

Hubert Ogunde, regarded as the "father" of the Yoruba Operatic Theatre, popularized the Opening Glee at the early part of his professional career. It was his remarkable and spectacular entrance song that became the model for many others who came after. But as time went on, his Opening Glee acquired more foreign characteristics and sloughed off its traditional elements. Recently, the tendency has been to replace the entrance song with an improvised "curtain-raiser" which has nothing to do with the total performance. Other contemporary practitioners have even abandoned it.

In his plays of the fifties, Ogunde used the Opening Glee as a commentary on the action of the play in performance or sometimes to tell the story of the play. The following is an extract from the Opening Glee of his play, *Journey To Heaven*:[13]

Aráiyé ẹ wá k'awá k'ọrin ọ̀go s'Olúwa.
Angélì ẹ bọ̀ k'awá k'ọrin iyìn s'ókè o. (2 times)
Ará aiyé ẹ gbọ́ mi, ará ọ̀run ẹ gbọ́ mi.
Ọmọ l'ẹ̀hìn-ìwà, ọmọ l'òpó ilé.
Èdùmàrè fún wa l'ọ́mọ,
Tí yí o gbẹ̀hìn tún ẹ̀hìn ṣe o. (2 times)
Ẹni ọmọ́ sin l'ó bí'mọ, ọmọ ò l'áyọ̀lé,
Ẹni ọmọ́ sin l'ó bí'mọ o, ọmọ ò l' áyọ̀le o.

49

Èdùmàrè àwá mbẹ ọ́ o dáríjì àwọn apànìa.
Aiyé l'ọjà, ọrun n'ilé,
Aiyé l'ọjà, ọrun n'ilé o.
Ẹ̀nyin tí mbẹ l'áiyé,
Ẹ kú ọjà aiyé o,
Ẹ̀nyin tí mbẹ l'áiyé, ẹ kú ewu ìrìnajò, etc.

O come, mankind, for us to sing a song of glory to the
    Lord.
O come, angels, for us to sing a song of praise to the
    Highest. (2 times)
Dwellers on earth hear me,
Dwellers in heaven hear me,
Child is after-life, child is the post that sustains a house,
May the Almighty give us children who will succeed us
    and clear up after us. (2 times)
He has children, whoever is buried by his children.
Until this happens, it is futile to put one's hope on them.
Indeed, he has children, whoever is succeeded by his
    children since their life is so uncertain.
Almighty we beseech Thee to forgive murderers.

The World is the market, Heaven is home.
Those of you in this market-like World, we greet you.
Those of you living in this World accept our greetings
    on the occasion of your pilgrimage.

In the entrance song of his play, *Yoruba Ronu* (1964),[14] however,
Ogunde returns to the traditional role of the Yoruba dramatist. In it he
offers a supplication:

SOLO:

Olúwa ló ni iṣé aiyé.
Ènìà mà ni 'ránṣẹ rẹ̀,
Èdùmàrè t'ó rán mi ní ṣé aiyé
Ọ ní 'ngbó o, o ní 'ntọ́ o.
Ọ ní 'ndẹ̀ bè 'tàn s'éhìn.
Ẹ̀bẹ mo bẹ̀ aiyé, Ẹ ma dàamú mi.
Ẹ mà jẹ njẹ́ṣẹ́ Ẹlẹ́dà rán mi o.

CHORUS:

Ẹní bá m'aiyé yío j'ogún aiyé.

50

Ẹni kò bá m'aiyé, Ẹ mà kú iyà ò.
Aiyé ni kọ̀rọ̀, aiyé ni gbangba òde.
Aiyé l'okùnkùn, aiyé yi ni'mọ́lẹ̀.
Àwa ò mọ bi aiyé mí lọ.
Ẹnìkan ò mọ bi aiyé ti ńbọ̀ o,
Ṣùgbọ́n a mọ bi a gbé ti bẹ̀rẹ̀.

SOLO:

Ìjì Aiyé bẹ́ni k'iṣu ẹni má jiná.
Ìjì ọmọ ènià b'ẹ́ni k'ọbẹ̀ ẹni má sọkalẹ̀.
Ẹlẹ́da mi ní irọ́ni.
Ó ní orí mi kò gbà ibi,
B'ẹ́ni àiyà mi kò gbẹ̀bọ̀dè.
Aiyé l'odò, odò l'aiyé.
Aiyé bí ẹ bá d'agbọ́n, Ẹ má ta mí,
Bí ẹ bá d'odò, Ẹ má mà gbé mi lọ.
Bí ẹ bá d'àgbàlá igbò, Ẹ má ṣe kàn mí.
Mo ti bá wọn ṣ'awo de'lé Olókun.
Gedegede l'ọwọ́ 'yọ ju orí.
Iṣẹ́ku ọrun p'ẹ̀hìndà;
Ẹ mà jẹ́ njíṣẹ́ Ẹlẹ́da rán mi o.

CHORUS:

Olúwa ló rán mi.
Èmi a jíṣẹ́ Ẹlẹ́da rán mi
Ògàràmilálẹ̀ o!

SOLO:

The works of this World is the Lord's.
Mankind is His Messenger.
The Almighty who has sent me on errand to this World
Says I must grow to old age, says my life must endure,
Says I must prosper and leave a record behind.
I beseech the World not to worry me;
Allow me to deliver the message of my Creator.

CHORUS:

The one who knows the World will inherit the World.
You who do not know the World accept my
    condolences on your suffering.

The World is the hidden places, the World is the
open places.
The World is darkness, the World is the light.
We do not know whither the World is going
No one knows from where the World is coming.
But we know from where we set out.

SOLO:

If the World could have a wish, no one would wish
one's yam properly cooked.
Human beings never wish that one's stew is
properly cooked.
But my Creator says nay:
He says my head will withstand any evil
designs that can harm me;
He says my heart will resist any conspiracy
that can damage me.
The World is the lower layer of the Universe.
The lower layer of the universe is the World.
O World, if you become a wasp, do not sting me;
If you become a ram in a stampede, do not attack me.
I have joined them at the Olokun shrine for initiation,
I have sacrificed to the denizens of the Earth.
The hands outstretched project beyond the head.
You the ghost-mummer from Heaven turn your back;
Allow me to deliver the message of my Creator.

CHORUS:

It is the Lord who has sent me.
I will deliver my Creator's message.
Behold my humble pledge!

In both the traditional and modern Yoruba theatre, the entrance song
is significantly a theatrical device of social consequences. An analysis of
its content and form yields evidence of its relevance to and consistence
with the Yoruba ideational system.

The traditional Yoruba theatre (the Aláìnjó or the Masque Theatre)
is a social institution with an indirect regulative function. It has two basic
dramatic genres: the spectacle and the revue. The dramatic spectacles are
designed to meet religious objectives and are based on Yoruba myths and

totems. The revues are sketched out as comments on the state of or happenings in Yoruba society. In both types satire is a theatrical element.

In view of his role, the traditional Yoruba dramatist sees himself as one who has a sacred duty. To this extent, therefore, his entrance song or opening glee has an integrative function. His ijuba (pledge) is a social obligation, and it is his responsibility to open his show with it as a formal salute. In relating this practice to the social context, the ijuba is seen as a functional attribute of the performer.

The traditional Yoruba dramatist uses his art to explain his knowledge of the world through satirical representations. In this act he needs a sensitive participation of his spectators in the reality of his art. The spectators are an assortment of people who crowd round the arena of play to see the dramatist's performance. The arena of play, in fact, is an open space encircled by them. It is therefore the first duty of the performer to create an atmosphere that will rouse congenial feelings and to capture the necessary mood that will ensure friendly responses in his spectators. By design, the entrance song has a sense of beauty and is endowed with efficaciousness. The performer is aware that the Yoruba universe is sustained and animated by certain vital forces. Therefore his entrance song must inspire confidence, and at best, find an echo in the mind and sensitivity of his spectators.

The entrance song of the Aláṛinjó or the Yoruba Masque Theatre, apart from clarifying the role of the dramatist in society, reveals the relationship between the performer's art and the import of what he communicates. The performer makes certain acknowledgements. His first pledge is to his "baba" (father) who is his source of inspiration. In the Yoruba social structure "father" is a classificatory rather than a descriptive term. The art of the Masque Theatre belongs to the Ọ̀jẹ̀ (a guild of histriones). Ológbojò, who is the acknowledged founder of the guild, is addressed as "baba" (father), likewise all his descendants. Since acting started as a lineage profession, the present dramatist is likely to have trained under his own late father.

During performance, the performer is confronted by the Yoruba cosmos which is believed to be inhabited by certain vital forces. Since his theatrical arena is an open space, the dramatist is obliged to acknowledge the presence in it of certain "unseen higher powers":

"Iyami Oṣoronga" is the Mother Superior who is head of the guild of witchcraft. According to Pierre Verger,[15] "Odù Ọ̀sá Méjì" describes the important position of womanhood in Yoruba society and says that Ifa has decreed as follows:

> Ó yẹ kí a má a f'ìbà f'óbirin,
> Nítorí ọgbọ́n aiyé ti wọn ni.

> It is fitting that we should give our pledge to women,
> Because the wisdom of the world is theirs.

Èṣù Láàlú is believed in Yoruba theology to be the lieutenant of Olo-dumare and acts as "a special relations officer between heaven and earth, the inspector-general who reports regularly to Olodumare on the deeds of the divinities and men, and checks and makes reports on the correct-ness of worships in general and sacrifices in particular."[16] The dramatist is anxious that he does not get into trouble through the agency of Èṣù. The deity is needed more for his benevolence and protection than for his capabilities in mischief-making.

Apart from his pledge, the dramatist seeks the cooperation of certain other deities and the express permission of the owner of the open space. The Yoruba universe in divided into three spheres: Ọ̀run (Heaven), Aiyé (World) and Ilẹ̀ (Earth). Ọ̀run is the seat of Olódùmarè or Ọlọ́run (High God or owner of Heaven). In Yoruba cosmology, Aiyé is an ordered structure whose stability is maintained by certain elements and vital forces. Its inhabitants are diverse and include human beings, animals and "ẹbọra" or visitors from the other spheres, namely, Ọ̀run and Ilẹ̀. Ilẹ̀ is believed to be the creation of Ọbàtálá, the arch-divinity, but its worship is enshrined in the rites of the Ògbóni cult. Onílẹ̀ is the earth-god. Both Ọlọ́run and Onílẹ̀ maintain a kind of surveillance over Aiyé through their emissaries and agents.

The Aiyé is a collective, and the traditional theatre is a functional insti-tution within it. The dramatist submerges his own personality even as he uses his art to work for its stability and continuity. By informing and ex-posing certain deviant behaviors in society in an entertaining way, the dramatist is indirectly using his art to regulate the norms of society. Drama, whether as a presentational or representational art, is larger than life. In the acts of performance, it is not unlikely that the dramatist's de-signs become distortions of actuality and therefore offensive. Thus, he may incur the ire of his spectators, both humans and deities, as the case may be. His entrance song, therefore, is a pledge that ensures his safety.

In the modern Yoruba theatre (the Operatic Theatre), on the other hand, the content and form of the entrance song show evidence of modi-fications which are the direct consequences of westernization in the

Yoruba society. The style and form of any theatrical art must reflect the sensibilities of the people with whom it communicates. In spite of its traditional links, the Yoruba Opera is a form of entertainment which developed as a result of Christian education and the influence of Western culture in the Yoruba society. Even though the traditional role of the dramatist has not changed, his world-view as well as his attitudes have. As a Christian, his concept of the universe is that which is dominated by the biblical Ọlọ́run (Lord of Heaven) and filled with angels who serve Him as messengers.

The place of performance is a playhouse, an enclosed physical structure, with a stage or a raised platform on one end and an auditorium on the other. The spectators comprise those who fulfil the necessary conditions of admission to see a show. At the head of the assemblage is a chairman whose duty is to oversee the orderliness of the spectators and the smooth running of the program. He is even allowed to make a speech and announce his donation.

The dramatist in his entrance song recognizes the category of peoples assembled before him and in anticipation of their gifts pays tribute to them. He does not stand in awe of his spectators and the consequences of the effect of his drama. He is aware that everyone has to give an account of his stewardship to God on the day of judgement.

But the attraction and prospects of Christian education and Western culture have not changed the personality of the Yoruba dramatist completely. The entrance song of Ogunde's *Yoruba Ronu*, as an illustration, represents the ambivalence of the "transitional man" in a changing society whose Christian faith is sometimes submerged by his apparent recognition of the existence of other forces in his universe. In it, in spite of his faith in God, Ogunde appeals to the vital forces and the elements who are the inhabitants of Aiyé (the World) to assist him in his mission to deliver his Creator's message:

> Olúwa ló rán mi;
> Èmi a jíṣẹ́ Ẹlẹ́da rán mi.

> It is the Lord who has sent me;
> I will deliver my Creator's message.

The modern dramatist believes God to be his only source of inspiration. His art is a product of missionary activities and westernization. He has not descended from a long line of traditional artists and attributes his success to doing God's will. He works with a view to creating a new dimension in society and relies on the esthetics and theatricality of a foreign form and style for accomplishment. But in spite of his faith, his new art form, and the security of his playhouse, the dramatist still entertains a nagging fear of Aiyé. It is this dynamic, yet complex phenomenon of the Yoruba cosmos that brings both the traditional and the modern dramatists to the same level of humanity.

Conclusion

The form of an art is affected by its function. The Opening Glee is a technique of approach, and it functions for the purpose of identification. Its content and form reveal that the role of the Yoruba dramatist, in spite of his creativity, is to communicate a message which he believes to be transcendentally inspired. However, in recognition of the nature of certain vital forces which exist within the Yoruba cosmos the dramatist pledges himself to them as a guarantee that while his performance lasts, he is safe. By using word and gesture, music and dance, as well as the means of the theatre, the dramatist evokes the image and rhythm which are the basic characteristics of performance.

In order to analyze the significant trends in the content and form of the Opening Glee, it has been necessary to discriminate between function and meaning in order to relate the value of the artistic form to its social context. Analyzing the data, there is evidence of the overriding concern of the dramatist, both traditional and modern, about Aiyé (the World). The role of the dramatist in the Yoruba society shows the importance of the theatre as a regulative institution. It seems probable that the dramatist originally designed the Opening Glee to serve an integrative function, but its concept and esthetic effect are found to be theatrically effective.

FOOTNOTES

[1] See J. A. Adedeji: *The Alarinjo Theatre: The Study of a Yoruba Theatrical Art From Its Origin to the Present Times*, Ph.D. Thesis, University of Ibadan, 1969.

[2] The reference to "father" is conventional. It is an implied recognition of the person who was the actor's source of inspiration and tutor. "Father" may, in fact, be the lineage-head from whom the actor has descended, acting being a lineage profession.

[3] She is "Mother Superior," the head of the guild of witchcraft.

[4] The expression is rhetorical. A pageant is implied and not the royal drums.

[5] It is not the "open" that is being referred to but the owner of it, sometimes called Olóde (the Lord of the Open or the god Ṣọ̀npọ̀ná). The expression is to the effect that the god's presence has made the open whole.

6 Ògèdèngbé is one of the attributive names of Olúgbèrè Àgan, the first Yoruba mummer or masked actor.

7 This theatrical art is erroneously called the "Folk Opera."

8 See advertisement in *Lagos Standard*, May 4, 1910; May 31, 1911; and also the *Times of Nigeria*, October 9, 1917.

9 Ogunmola used this "Opening Glee" for all his shows in the late forties and early fifties before he modified the form.

10 "Agbe" is the Blue Touraco Musophagidac of the Cuckoo family.

11 "Osùn" is the African camwood which yields a dye used as cosmetics.

12 "Èsù" in this reference is the biblical devil, Satan or Lucifer. He is thought of as the malignant supernatural being capable of malevolent acts.

13 Hubert Ogunde, *Journey to Heaven* (Lagos: Sore-Masika Press, n.d.), pp. 1-2.

14 Hubert Ogunde, *Yoruba Ronu* (Yaba: Printed by the Pacific Printers, n.d.), pp. 5-6.

15 Pierre Verger, "Grandeur et Decadence du Culte de Iyami Osoronga," *Journal de la societe des Africanistes*, 35 (1965), 200-218.

16 Bolaji Idowu, *Olodumare, God in Yoruba Belief* (London: Longmans, 1962), p. 80.

WAƘAR BUSHIYA: A HAUSA SATIRICAL POEM BY ISA HASHIM

NEIL SKINNER, TOM ALLEN and CHARLES N. DAVIS

Introduction

Hausa poetry composed in the regular Arabic meters is usually concerned with major religious and social themes: the improvement of religious practices, the vanity of things temporal, the rewards and punishments of the next world, various conspicuous sins and heresies, the lives of the great and the uplifting of the nation. It has been less preoccupied with the expression of individual joy or frustration, which have either gone unexpressed or have been poured out in less formal song. But some of the younger intellectuals, whose knowledge of modern Arab—and indeed other—literature suggests to them a wider use of the vehicle, have experimented with more personal topics. One such poet is Na'ibi Wali, whose Waƙar Damina ("Song of the Rains") has been translated and discussed in Arnott (1968). In that poem the theme was joy—joy in the life, abundance and greenery of the rainy season. In the poem that follows, in contrast, the theme is one of frustration and resentment against unfair treatment by a man placed in authority over the poet.

Waƙar Bushiya ("Song of the Hedgehog") was composed in 1955 or 1956 by Isa Hashim, now a senior civil servant in the Kano State Government. He was born in 1933 and belongs to a Fulani Kano family, whose ancestor Jamo, he tells us, preferred at the time of the Fulani jihad to let his younger brother Dabo be emir and found the new dynasty, while he remained a scholar and teacher (Hausa mālam). Apparently there have been no notable poets in the family, but poetry has often been a sideline to scholarship (mālanci). Isa trained first at the Kano Judicial School, but his father did not wish him to be a mufti "learned in the law," so he later joined the Kano Native Administration service and worked in several departments, before transferring to the Northern Regional service in Kaduna. He says he has composed poetry

AUGUSTANA UNIVERSITY COLLEGE
LIBRARY

from time to time, in both Arabic and Hausa, ever since he was at the Judicial School. Among others, in 1952 he wrote *Raihāna*, a brief poem to his cat, and in 1953 a poem to welcome back the first Kano mission to the Middle East. In the same year he won third prize in a competition for a poem on the death of the Emir of Kano, Abdullahi Bayero. Two others of his poems are on themes popular with modern Hausa poets— *Mu Yāki Jāhilci* ("Let Us Fight Ignorance"), in support of the campaign for literacy and enlightenment which the regional government was conducting; and, in 1954, *Juyin Zamani* ("The Times Are A-Changing"), the theme of which was "we are all at sixes and sevens. May God help us to straighten ourselves out." All these poems, as so much of Hausa poetry, remain unpublished. In recent years, as a busy official, he has had less time to compose, but in 1968 he was a member of the panel of judges for the competition to award a prize for a poem on the Federal Army during the Civil War. This prize went to Akilu Aliyu for his *Wakar Soja*.

The poet did not say who was the object of his resentment that occasioned this poem, but at the time it would have been clear to any of his friends who heard him sing it. This is normal for a poem in the genre of *habaici* or *zambo* "personal satire." Such a genre is more commonly employed by *maroka*, the traditional bards, than by writers of learned poetry. *Maroka* praise lavishly, provided they are lavishly rewarded, but are apt to turn to *zambo*, if the subject of their song is insufficiently generous. Among the Arab poets too, especially those of the pre-Islamic *jāhiliyya* days, *hijā'* was a common theme, stemming either from personal or intertribal feuds. But in Hausa learned poetry, whose main focus has been religion, the denunciation of heretics and backsliders has been open and forceful. Doubtless poems of *zambo* were composed in the nineteenth century, but they would not be the ones chanted by the beggers to solicit alms from the Faithful and thus passed on and preserved. One poem from early in this century that is full of *zambo* is *Tābar Koko*, by Aliyu dan Sidi, Emir of Zaria, and there is still reluctance to publish it, for fear of hurting the feelings of the relatives of those satirized.

The *zambo* strain was much in evidence in the political conflicts of the years 1955–1966, and powerful, bitter poems inspired by the NPC–NEPU clash, and themselves fuelling that struggle, were composed and circulated, many of them reaching print. With the end of "politics" and establishment of the Military Government in 1966, this phase passed, but doubtless we shall see the satirical strain again as the need arises. In fact, *Wakar Soja*, while mostly *yabo* "eulogy" of the Federal soldiers, also gives the poet an opportunity to indulge in some powerful *zambo* at the expense of Ojukwu. Perhaps one may make a distinction between *zambo* and *habaici* at this point, and suggest that the former tends to be more open and direct, while the latter uses innuendo and metaphor, so that only those in the know get the full message. This, of course, given the lapse of a generation since the composition of a *habaici* poem, creates difficulties of interpretation, especially for the foreign scholar.

Isa relates that he composed *Bushiya* at a time when he was feeling very frustrated. At that time he was a young man, newly moved into a home of his own, the product of a strict Muslim upbringing. Sitting at home at night and nursing the resentment he felt against his senior officer, he would hear immigrant workers in the streets outside singing a particular tune, with somewhat obscene words, as they courted the *kāruwai* "ladies of the town." It was to this tune, one of *bēge* "longing," slow and plaintive, that he fitted his words. It seems that one of the chief features of this work is just this contrast, between the violent abuse of the words, conventionally fitted into a religious frame, and the sad, pensive, almost feline quality of the tune. The tune dominates the words to the extent that on many occasions vowels are shortened or, more frequently, lengthened to suit its rhythm. A particularly noticeable feature is the pause before the last three or four syllables of the couplet.

Bushiya—Bish da Kàya

1. Na gode Maɗaukaki, Mai Girma, Mataimaki,
   Sarki wanda yai halitta don sonsa, Haliƙi,
2. Samammen da ba rashi, Mai Ikon da ba ya shi.
   Wani ba shi ba tarkace, bari roƙonsa—bai da shi.
3. Allah dinga gaisuwa, mai tsarki da ƙaruwa
   gun manzommu wanda ba wani bayansa, Muhammadi.
4. Allah ni fa kai nake roƙo, don ko kai ka ce
   kome in ba kai ba ba wani mai yinsa, bare ya yi.
5. Kai ka yiwo ni, kai ka san kome nawa. Kar ka san
   shashancin da zai hana min bautaŕka, Raziƙi.
6. Taimaki masu taimako, maƙiya ko ka dandaƙo,
   can asalinsu tumɓuke har saiwarsa, ka ya da shi!
7. Duk wani wanda ke zato zai cuta gare ni, to,
   Allah zai tsare ni. Shi ko ƙaryarsa, ja'iri.

8. Ikon dandaƙe rashi, ko ko rabon tagomashi
   ba shi da shi daɗai, ba zai kuma samo ba shagili.

9. In ko ya ce yana da shi ya riƙe, zai ga bai da shi.
   Ni ko Rabbu zai kwararo baiwarsa, ta tad da ni.

10. Malam, kai ka ce da ni ka san kanka tun tuni.
    In da ka sani, ba ka zama shangai ba, furar tsaki.

11. Yanzu taho ka bayyanan halayenka, kar ka ban
    dungu. In ko ka ƙi, to, ai na gane ka, wagili.

12. Yanzu ashe mutum yana sane ya kama ƙoƙuna
    ya fasa don ganin akwai gyartai? Kaitonsa, shagili.

13. Kai wofi, masha giya, yai gori da tutiya.
    Banza bunsuru abokin 'ya'yansa—wadai da shi!

14. Ka riƙa babu hankali, tsohon dandi, jahili.
    Daga zancenka za'a gane wautarka, fajiri.

15. Mai zina me kake zato Allah zai da kai? Fito!
    Ka ji, banza marar rabon yau har gobe, fasiƙi.

16. Kai, daina ka tuba, tun ba ka faɗa a tasku ɗin
    da abokinsa ko kaɗan bai tsira. Tuba, kar ka ƙi!

17. Mai ɗaga kai da taƙama, mai homa da fankama,
    Mene ne ya ƙarfafe ka kake gāma da izgili?

18. In ilminka ne ya sa ka zaton yanzu ka isa
    ka yi kome ka keta kowa, kaitonka ja'iri!

19. In mulki kake gani ka samu a kan wani,
    ka tuna wanda yai ka shi ne ya yiwo shi, Zahiri.

20. In kuma dukiyarka ce ta sabauta ka karkace,
    ka tuna zaka bar ta yanda ka same ta, makiri.

21. Ga Shaiɗanu ya ɓace, ga kuma Fir'auna ya wuce,
    ga Karuna ya nutse—ka tuna sun fi ka tanadi.

22. Huɗuban nan, da Ahmada yai ran hijjatul wida,
    ta nuna wa Ɗan Adam bin Allah ne abin a yi.

23. Tuna wa'azi da gargaɗi da nasihar da an faɗi
    Lukuman yai wa ɗansa. Kada ka sake, malam, ka sau jiki.

24. Asali, inda duk ya kai, bai fisshe ka, don ko kai
    ba ka kai Faɗima ba 'yar Manzon Allah, bare ka fi.

25. "Fadima, tsarci Rabbana" in ji babanta, "kin shina
    gun Allah ba zan tare maki kome ba." Ta ko yi.

26. Magagin da duk muke, lalle zamu wartsake.
    San da mutum ya karɓi amfanin aikinsa, za ya ci.

27. Surar Inshiƙaƙi ta faɗi zancen, ka gaskata.

Duba cikinta, ka ga yanda abin zai faru zahiri.

28. Ya Allahu Rabbana, Isa Hashimi yana
neman taimakonka tare da baiwarka da agaji.

29. Ko wani za ya tambaya, ce sunanta "Bushiya—
Bish da Ƙaya." Ku kyautata mata fatanku, kar ku ƙi.

Hedgehog—Hedge of Prickles

1. I thank the Exalted One, the Great One, the Helper,
   the King who made creation at His will, the Creator,

2. Who exists and dies not, whose power has no peer.
   Every other is insignificant. Do not invoke them for they are
   powerless.

3. God, may Your pure blessings, ever increasing
   be upon our Messenger, he who has no successor, Muhammad.

4. God, I pray to You, for You have said
   that nothing is created but by You. No other may attempt it,
   much less achieve it.

5. It was You who made me, You know me through and through. Do
   not lead me into foolish ways that will prevent me serving You,
   Giver of all things.

6. Assist those who give assistance, but crush those who refuse it;
   extirpate them from their very beginning, their roots, and cast
   them out.

7. Every man who hopes to wrong me will find that
   God will protect me. His hopes will be given the lie, shameless
   fellow.

8. The power to crush those who are weak or to hand out favors
   is not, and will never be, his, stupid creature,

9. And if he thinks that he has it securely, he will find he is wrong.
   But as for me, the Lord will pour out His gifts, to light on me.

10. Malam, long ago you told me that you knew what you were about,
    but had you really known, you wouldn't have acted so stupidly,
    fura of coarse flour.

11. Come now and tell me all about yourself—and don't try
    to deceive me. If you refuse—well, in any case I see through
    you, weak fool.

12. Will a man in his senses really pick up small calabashes
    and smash them, just because he knows there are calabash-
    menders? Poor fellow, head-in-clouds!

13. Useless fellow, drunkard whose capacity mocks the flagon!
    Billy-goat who joins with his own children in depravity, ac-
    cursed!

14. Adult, but without sense! Old profligate! Ignoramus!
    Your talk betrays your stupidity, depraved fellow.

15. Fornicator, what do you expect God will do to you? Come on out!
    Do you hear? Useless one, destined to fail now and always, prof-
    ligate.

16. Cease and repent in time, before you end in the place of torture
    which your friend has in no way escaped. Repent, do not refuse!

17. Strutting along with your head up, boasting and insolent,
    what makes you so confident with your swollen head and scorn-
    ful ways?

18. If you think that your learning is sufficient now
    for you to do what you like, harm whom you will, you're to be
    pitied, shameless fellow.

19. Or if it is the authority you see you have over another,
    remember that He who made you, the Conspicuous One, made
    him too.

20. Or again if it is your wealth that has led you astray,
    remember that just as you acquired it, so you will lose it, crafty
    scoundrel.

21. Satan disappeared; Pharaoh is no more;
    Karuna has passed below. Remember these were richer than you.

22. The sermon that Muhammad gave on the Farewell Pilgrimage
    taught man that his duty was to obey God.

23. Remember the solemn words of warning and the good advice it
    was said Luqman gave his son. Don't relax, malam, don't
    slacken!

24. Nor will birth, however noble, save you, for you
    are not so noble as Fatima, the Prophet's daughter—certainly not
    nobler!

25. "Fatima, fear our Lord" her father said, "and understand
    that before God my help will avail you nothing." And she
    obeyed.

26. We are all in a daze and shall indeed be scattered.
    Then a man shall receive the fruit of his works and consume it.

27. The Chapter called Inshiqāq has said it and you must believe it;
    look there and you will see clearly stated how it will be.

28. Oh God, our Lord, Isa Hashim
    craves Your help, Your inspiration and Your aid.

29. And if any ask the name of this poem, say it is "Hedgehog
    Abristle with Spines." Let it have your good wishes, do not re-
    ject it.

Notes on Text and Translation

Acknowledgements for help must be made, first to the poet himself; to
the American Philosophical Society and the Social Science Research
Council for support; and to faculty and students at Abdullahi Bayero
College, especially Dr. Kabir Galadanci and M. Ibrahim Mukoshy.

Summary: couplets 1 thru 6, invocation to God for help; 6 thru 9, the
poet and his enemies; 10 thru 17, poet's *bête noire* abused; 18 thru
27, *bête noire* warned of his mortality and the Judgement; 28 and 29,
concluding appeal to God for help and the audience for sympathetic
attention.

Title: *bish* which occurs only in this phrase, which is the *kirāri* "praise
epithet" of the hedgehog, is perhaps an ideophone, emphasizing sharp
and bristly. The title suggests that the writer may appear insignificant,
but that if you touch him, you will hurt yourself.

2. *bai da shi* = *ba shi da shi* or *ba ya da shi*. Poets commonly elide *ya*
   "he" and *yi* "do, make," two very frequent words, to *y* to fit
   their meter.

3. *gaisuwa*: a Hausa word, instead of the Arabic-derived *salla* which
   is usual in this context of praying for God's blessings on the
   Prophet.

5. *Kar ka san* = *Kada ka sa ni*
   min = *mini*

8. This couplet was omitted in the recorded version of the poem, but
   subsequently supplied by the poet.
   rashi "lack," i.e., those who lack.

10. *furar tsaki: fura* is made from balls of flour usually eaten with
    milk, the normal morning meal. *Tsaki* is the more coarsely
    ground flour, usually made from bulrush-millet and so an in-

ferior food, metaphorically applied to the subject of the poem.

11. *bayyanan* = *bayyana mini*, a usage found especially in Kano.
kar ka ban dungu = *kada ka ba ni dungu* "don't give me the stump."
This comes to mean "don't deceive me" from a situation where, instead of a man offering a sound hand to another to shake, he reveals only a stump, a poor substitute.

12. The poet describes his subject as initiating futile—and also destructive—activities, like digging holes to have them filled in. The insignificance of the work is underlined by the fact that the occupation of calabash-mender is traditionally a very humble one, like the charcoal-burner in the English tales.

13–15. The poet reaches a climax of abuse in these lines, using very forceful words in accusing his enemy of drunkenness and incest. But the melody continues, plaintive and slow as always.

13. *Kai . . . . yai*: rapid change of person, in this case from addressing the subject of the poem to addressing the listener, is common in Hausa poetry. Often a poet will make yet another change, turning to invoke God, all within a few lines. This imposes difficulties on the translator.
yai gori da tutiya: "mocks the flagon," because he holds more liquor than it does. Cf. Prince Henry's calling Falstaff a "tun."
tutiya "large, metal container."

15. *marar rabon*: someone who lacks *rabo* or *arziki*, in Hausa Muslim thinking, is not merely "unfortunate" or "under-privileged" or "ill-fated," he is someone frowned on by God and therefore evil and to be avoided. In fact, the probable subject of this poem was very wealthy.

16. Again the change of person from direct address (*Kai*) of the subject of the poem to address of the listener (*–sa*).
bai etc. has been rendered by the perfect tense in English, though there is only a single negative in Hausa. But this may be uncompleted action, with *bai tsira* = *ba ya tsira* "he is not escaping" or even "he will not escape."

17. The poet piles on six nominals indicative of boastful pride.

21. This is the common *memento mori* theme, beloved of Hausa poets proclaiming the frailties and fleeting nature of the delights of this world. Perhaps Satan represents worldly knowledge, Pharaoh power and Karuna wealth. For a typical example of this

zuhudu theme, see Usuman dan Fodio's poem quoted in Robinson (1896) at p. 76. For Karuna (Qārūn), see *Koran* 28, verse 76, etc. He revolted against Moses, being led astray by his wealth.

22. The Farewell Pilgrimage (*hijjatul wadāᶜi*) is described in Robson (1963), p. 544, etc.

At this point in his performance, the poet repeated each of three verses twice, perhaps because he was not satisfied with the way he had rendered them on the first occasion, perhaps to help him remember what came next.

23. *Lukuman*: for Luqman's advice to his son, see *Koran* 31, verse 12, etc., in particular verse 18—"surely God does not love any self-conceited boaster."

sau jiki = *saki jiki.*

25. There is reference to a similar conversation with A'isha in Robson (1963). She asked the Prophet ".... Will you remember your family on the day of resurrection?" and he answered "There are three places where no one will remember anyone" and detailed the three stages of the Judgement.

26–27. *Surar Inshikaki*: *Koran* 84 *Al Inshiqāq* "The Bursting Asunder" is said to be one of the earliest revelations and contains, like many other early ones, apocalyptic descriptions of the Judgement and the contrasting rewards of the virtuous and the wicked. 26 seems to be a translation from Arabic, but does not come from the Sura referred to.

28–29. The epilogue, containing the name of the poet and the name of the poem, with an appeal to God for blessing and to the listener for his favorable consideration. Traditionally, in addition, a poet might add the number of verses and the date it was written. The latter would be contained in a *ramzi*, a word made up of Arabic letters whose numerical values added up to the date of the Muslim year. Even today most Hausa poetry does not reach print and thus such an epilogue serves an obvious practical purpose.

Rhyme

In traditional Arabic terms, this is irregular in that it is the final vowel, here –*i*, that is the recurring element. The norm for written poetry is to make CV the rhyme, leading in Hausa verse to a sometimes monotonous repetition. Here the poet, by giving himself more freedom, has been able to reduce repetition, though there are some occurrences, e.g., *ja'iri* in 7 and 18; *da shi* in 2, 6, 13; *shagili* in 8 and 12; *zahiri* in 19 and 27. In the first two couplets, there is internal rhyme between the first and second hemistitch, but thereafter only occasionally and probably not by design.

Meter

Basically this seems to be the Arabic *ṭawīl*, which can have the form ∪ − −|∪ − ∪ − repeated twice for each hemistich, giving 28 syllables to the line, thus:

∪ − −|∪ − ∪ −|∪ − −|∪ − ∪ −|| ∪ − −|∪ − ∪ −|∪ − −| ∪ − ∪ −

However in this poem, the poet makes − − − the norm for the three syllable foot, and also not infrequently resolves one of the first two of these three syllables into two shorts; but rarely does so more than once in any one foot. So we have, e.g., in 2 ∪ ∪ − − *wani ba shi* and in 5 − ∪ ∪ − *kai ka yiwo*, while in 23 there is an example of two resolved syllables in one foot, viz. *Tuna wa'azi* ∪ ∪ ∪ ∪ − . However, in the first foot of either hemistich, the third syllable is never resolved and remains long throughout. As for the last syllable of the third foot, in about a fifth of its occurrences, there is a redundant syllable added. So in 3, there is *wani bayansa* ∪ ∪ − − ∪ . Note that this feature is not usually resolution, though in 17, exceptionally, the poet chants it as if it were: *ka kake gama* ∪ ∪ − ∪ ∪ . However, as lexically *gama* is [gāmà], this may have been an error in performance.

In contrast with the three syllable feet, the four syllable feet are seldom varied: the second foot only once, at 23 *wa dansa. Ka* ∪ − ∪ ∪; the fourth foot not at all. This last statement presumes that the redundant syllable just described belongs to the third, rather than the fourth foot. As already said, in recitation there is a very clear pause before the last foot or, often, before the last three syllables of that foot; the choice usually being governed by the sense.

Tune

The scale used here is D pentatonic (as recorded it is D^b pentatonic, but for the sake of clarity and readability, it has been transcribed as D). Thus the notes employed are:

the five notes

The B♭ in parentheses, though not in the scale itself, is used once or twice, preceding an A. Other non-scale tones employed, such as an occasional F♮, A♭ or E♭, should not be considered as altering the nature of the scale, but as variations due to the performer's freedom of expression.

As for the melody, there are three elements which, with some variation, are found in every verse. Skeleton structures of each of these are:

In addition there is a refrain at the end of each couplet. This refrain is one of the most important unifying elements in the piece and the most significant motif in that it is repeated each time in the same form and always with a clear pause preceding and following it:

To show how these motifs occur in actual performance, here is a verbatim transcription of couplet 2, as recorded on August 14, 1968 in Kano by the poet for Neil Skinner:

Here, A, B, C and D mark the beginnings of each of the fully-formed melodic elements described. Note the sustaining of a syllable and the moving of its pitch downward, found at the end of A and C (and throughout the poem). Note also the rhythmic combinations: the triplets in the first hemistich going to 8ths and 16ths ♩♫ in the second hemistich, and returning to triplets in the refrain—

The rhythmic figures used are as follows:

triplet rhythms, giving a bouncy effect, a basic characteristic of the piece

duple walking and running rhythms

a drawn-out "winding," walking effect.

As observed above, the triplet figures alternate with the 8th and 16th rhythms, giving composite results such as

In addition, the length of time given to different beats (a quarter note getting one beat) differs. So may be longer on one occasion than on another. This phenomenon might be represented graphically as follows:

where the lengths of the heavy black lines represent different quantities of time per beat. Thus it can be seen that a time signature implying a steady progression of beats would be misleading. Moreover, there would be no set number of beats.

Many hemistiches have within them phrases sung in one breath and set off by pauses or holds. An example from couplet 5 will illustrate. Commas and fermatas $\left(\underset{\cdot}{\frown}\right)$ indicate, respectively, pauses and sustained notes.

Kai ka yi wo ni kai ka san ko mai na wa kar ka san

Usually such pauses are justified by the sense of what is being said.

Summing up the tune in general, we may say that its structure can be found at four levels. These are: (1) couplet, ending in the refrain; (2) hemistich, ending on the tonic note; (3) phrase, ending with a hold or pause, and (4) beat. The poem is intended to be heard in terms of phrases and couplets, i.e., meaning units. Since beats and phrases are irregular in length, it is only by listening for meaning units that a hearer can pace his listening. In fact, anyone who listened with an ear for temporal structure such as is found in Western music would be frustrated. To elucidate this point it is perhaps relevant to introduce a brief discussion of this aspect of Western music.

Traditionally in this music, we are accustomed to having rhythmic and harmonic structure which lets us anticipate. As soon as we hear the first two or four measures, we expect some resolving effect. A good example of this type of structuring is sonata form. To quote Donald Francis Tovey, British musicologist and composer:

> Two types of form are . . . common to the . . . sonata style . . . The terms "binary" and "ternary" have been chosen for these . . . A binary melody falls into two portions, of which the first ends away from the tonic, and the second ends on the tonic. *Barbara Allen* . . . is an exquisite example on the smallest possible scale. A ternary melody, such as *The Bluebell of Scotland*, has a complete first clause (*i.e., ending on tonic*), a second clause not as complete (*ending on dominant*), and a third clause consisting of the first over again; a form conveniently symbolised as A B A (Italics are ours.)

In *Bushiya*, on the other hand, the absence of such resolution can be observed, by reference to couplet 5, quoted above. However, one genre of music that a hearing of *Bushiya* to a certain extent recalls is that of Blues, as composed and performed by American Blacks, and the common African background makes it interesting to look a little more closely for the common traits. In particular, there seem to be two of these. Firstly, the scales used in Blues are largely pentatonic, often with the 5th flatted, or employing both flatted and natural fifths; and often employing seconds and non-scale tones. This poem keeps closer to the pentatonic than Blues does, but both vary from the scale to suit the wish of the performer. Secondly, as with Blues, the theme of *Bushiya* is complaint, an expression of frustration. But it is worth noting too that Blues has more of a tone of resignation, of somehow finding one's way in circumstances that seem hopeless. Take, for example, these lines quoted by Richard Wright:

Whistle keeps on blowin' an' I got my debts to pay.
I've got a mind to leave my baby, and I've got a mind to stay.

Whereas Isa Hashim is calling the wrath of God down on his enemy and his tone is confidently aggressive—as a Blues singer would never be. Such a difference may reflect that between the background of a member of a ruling Fulani family—whose ancestors had acquired and owned slaves—and the circumstances of American Blacks a hundred years ago or more.

On the other hand, so far as concerns beat and structure, *Bushiya* differs markedly from Blues. The latter always has a strong beat (being, in fact, given by some people the credit of being the source for Rock and Roll). Whereas, as described here, this is lacking in this poem. Secondly, Blues is highly structured. Twelve bar Blues is always built as follows:

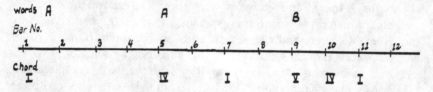

We can see here by the regularity with which the chords change at 2 and 4 bar intervals that for Blues, as for Tovey's examples, rhythmic and harmonic structure go together. In addition, the first line of words is repeated in bars five through eight, bringing textual structure into conjunction with rhythmic and harmonic.

Summing up the tune of this poem, it is fair to say that it is a simple one, borrowed, as noted above, by the poet as a device for the artistic amplification of what he has to say. It is, in general, secondary to the words, but freely prevails on many occasions over lexical vowel length and tone.

Conclusion

We have seen how a young Hausa intellectual—Hausa in speech, but of Fulani descent—suffering from a strong sense of injustice done him by someone set above him in the modern hierarchy, gives expression to his feelings. He takes the melody of a popular song of love and longing and sets his own words to it. He uses, with a few variations, a classical Arabic meter in the tradition of Hausa learned poetry and—inevitably —includes a number of recondite loanwords from Arabic as well as common, vigorous Hausa expressions. He then chants the poem thus composed to a small group of friends, who understand who the subject of the poet's abuse is, even though no name is mentioned. They appreciate too the various contrasts of the performance: solemn religious references and violent satire; slow, sensual melody and invocation of hellfire; God's generosity and the shabbiness of one particular man; and through it all the haunting tune with its repetitive, inevitable refrain.

BIBLIOGRAPHY

Arnott, D. W. 1968. "The Song of the Rains": A Hausa Poem by Na'ibi S. Wali. *African Language Studies* 9: 120–47.

Robinson, Charles Henry. 1896. *Specimens of Hausa Literature*. Cambridge.

Robson, James. 1963. *Mishkāt al Maṣābīḥ*, translation of Ibn al Farrā'. Lahore.

Skinner, Neil. 1971. "The Slattern—a Theme of Hausa Poetry." In *Afrikanische Sprachen und Kulturen—ein Querschnitt* (Festschrift Lukas), ed. Veronika Six et al. Hamburg.

Tovey, Donald Francis. 1956. *The Forms of Music*. Meridian, New York.

Wright, Richard. 1963. Foreword. In Oliver, Paul, *The Meaning of the Blues*. New York.

THE DRAMATIC LIMITS OF IGBO RITUAL

Michael J. C. Echeruo

Introduction   This paper is a very tentative statement of a view which I have held for some time but which I have hesitated to advance because more extensive field research than I have been able to undertake seemed required for its full validation. I present it now because this seems to me as good an opportunity as one could ever want for securing the reaction of those who have been engaged in Igbo and related studies for a much longer time than myself.* I should hope, in any event, that my argument will be found not only valid for the study of Igbo traditional literature but also helpful to our creative writers who may wish to exploit our traditions for contemporary uses.

My approach has been inevitably determined by my interest in myth-criticism, that is in the archetypal meaning derivable from the structure of ideas and action in a given work of art. Accordingly, I have tended to look at the Igbo festival in gross, as an event whose structure has meaning in itself. Drama lends itself very naturally to this critical approach because its outlines of action are usually clear and the sequence of its events invariably of a deliberate kind.[1] For this reason, also, I have not concerned myself at this stage with the language of the festivals, nor with Igbo dramaturgy—that is with the Igbo *style* of presenting action. These are important aspects of the subject which, for me, follow only after the more general and theoretical argument has been established.

African Drama   It is generally agreed these days that drama is an important element in traditional African culture. In this country (Nigeria), the Yorubas, Ijaws, and sometimes the Efiks, are usually singled out as illustrating this contention.[2] In these studies, attention is drawn to the elements of song, dance, and costuming which, in various combinations, have resulted in such dramatic forms as heroic drama, burlesque, satire and

* This paper was read to the Seminar on Igbo Language and Literature organized by the Institute of African Studies, University of Nigeria, Nsukka, November 24–27, 1971.

75

ribald comedy. "The Ijaws, perhaps more than any other people in Nigeria," one writer has argued, "have developed over the centuries a form of dramatic art which is religious in purpose but which has become weighted heavily on the side of skilful performance and artistic values."[3] Similar studies have not been carried out in detail among the Igbo, but from the evidence already in print, indications are that the same conclusions are likely to be reached with regard to the place of drama in Igbo culture.[4] It will also be found that the Igbo do not lack adequate mythologies, that they have a keen sense of stylized representational action, and that they certainly do not lack a feeling for ceremony.

While asserting this, we should not lose sight of the argument recently advanced by Ruth Finnegan that "it would be truer to say" that "there are certain dramatic and quasi-dramatic phenomena to be found" in African traditional festivals. This is important, she holds, in view of what she regards as the absence of "linguistic content, plot, represented interaction of several characters, specialized scenery," etc. in these indigenous dramas.[5] Her argument is borne out, in part, by statements made by some of those who champion the idea of a fully-developed indigenous drama. Writing of the *Ekine* dramas, for example, Robin Horton says that "the masquerade is not intended as the enactment of verbal narrative. Its dominant symbols are those of rhythmic gesture, dictated by the drum; and in so far as its verbal commentaries have a use, it is one of directing attention to the broad area in which the meaning of the dance gestures lies . . . it is left to the language of dance to fill in the detail which makes the masquerade rich and satisfying to its audience."[6] If this is true, then, there is reason to re-examine our use of the word "drama" to describe these events, since for example, the "recitation" and "performance" of epic poetry in chorus can also have most of the characteristics of the indigenous festival and still not be drama.

Drama and Society   Drama, in its very many manifestations, including its ritual manifestations, is very specifically communal in character. More than any of the other arts, it requires a group audience at all stages of enactment; quite often, in fact, it demands the participation of the audience in the action or song. For this reason, some theorists have argued, quite convincingly, that drama flourishes most in a society that has developed a strong consciousness of itself *as a community*.[7] We should, however, add that drama flourishes best in a community which has satisfactorily transformed ritual into celebration and converted the mythic structure of action from the religious and priestly to the secular plane.

On the level of theory, this is the explanation often advanced for the development of Greek drama. It is maintained that the plays depended on the identification of Greek civilization with its common religious and cultural roots and the transformation of that identity from its strictly Dionysian or Apollonian origins to the equivalent secular experience which, nevertheless, still retained something of the original religious implications.[8] Where this happens, drama becomes the ideal festival, a communal feast which features reenactment and rededication for every individual in the community. In Greek and similar societies, drama, as festival, reinforces common values, shared bonds and common taboos. It reestablishes links with the past and compels the living to participate in the hilarity and comradeship of a communal happening.

Drama, Ritual and Myth If, therefore, the festival is a celebration, drama is a reenactment of life. Drama is to the society what ritual is to religion: a public affirmation of an idea; a translation into action of a *mythos* or plot just as ritual is the translation of a faith into external action.[9] A divination scene, for example, is not in itself drama, though it may be dramatic. It is ritualistic or liturgical. That is to say, it is a representation in action of a faith or a dream, like communion or baptism. The pattern of action does not tell a story; it reasserts the essence of the faith in *symbolic* terms. Drama, on the other hand, allows for the reinterpretation of life through a pattern of ordered events, through that fragment of history we usually call plot.[10] Hence it is that myth gives substance to narrative just as faith gives substance to ritual. It is myth—i.e., plot—that gives mass and duration to ritual (and thence to faith), and leads it ultimately to drama.

Anthropologists have not been very helpful in sorting out these interrelationships. The so-called Cambridge School which argues that "myth arises out of rite rather than the reverse," that myth is "the spoken correlative of the acted rite" has misled many investigators by encouraging them to assume that rituals, especially among the so-called primitive peoples, have yet to evolve a conceptual embodiment in myth. Accordingly, they see ritual action simply as unorganized and perhaps spontaneous reaction of primitive peoples to the mystery of life. Other investigators, however, have tended to deny the relevance of any distinction between ritual and myth and identify them fully with the idea of the festival. They thereby, quite unjustifiably, give the impression that there are no special and important limits to the interpenetration of drama into the festival. A

New Yam Festival, for example, is a great ritual and festive event. Behind the ritual activities of the festival is almost certainly a *mythos* of a returning and beneficent god who is both welcomed and propitiated. But the festival itself, together with its associated ritual acts, is *not* drama which only emerges from the selective elaboration, reenactment and reinterpretation of significant aspects of the festival myth.

We need, therefore, to distinguish between drama and festival, not on the basis of their external "dramatic" characteristics (including dance, song and costume) but of their elaboration of action, whether or not this action is supported with dialogue (as distinct from speech). The masquerade, for example, which has strong roots in Igbo land[11] is drama only to the extent that its mime element carries with it a narrative or plot content. But, basically, the force of action of the masquerade is ritual or symbolic. Behind the masquerade is a dream or faith.[12]

Greek and Ancient Sumerian Analogies   Analogies with Greek tradition are common in discussions of the nature and origins of drama. Some of these analogies can be misleading. Arthur Koestler argues that dramatic art has its origins in ceremonial rites—dances, songs, and mime—which enacted important past or desired future events: rain, a successful hunt, an abundant harvest. The gods, demons, ancestors and animals participating in the event were impersonated with the aid of masks, costumes, tattooings and make-up. The shaman who danced the part of the rain-god *was* the rain-god, and yet remained the shaman at the same time.[13]

Speaking of the origins of Nigerian drama, J. P. Clark says "they lie where they have been found among other peoples of the earth, deep in the past of the race. We believe that as the roots of European drama go back to the Egyptian Osiris and the Greek Dionysius, so are the origins of the Nigerian drama likely to be found in the early religious and magical ceremonies and festivals of the peoples of the country."[14] It is true enough that there are close analogies between, say, the Nigerian New Year (February) Festivals and early Greek Dionysian festivals which usually preceded the planting season and lasted 5–6 days. (J. P. Clark says "seven is the magic number!"). But there the comparison ends, because early Greek dramas were, in fact, *one* item in the program of the festivals. In their dramas, the Greeks provided for a special presentation or enactment of a *mythos* within the framework of the larger (and generally ritualistic) festive event. In other words, the early Greek play was a dramatization of a myth undertaken as part of a festival. The play was never synonymous with the festival itself. As Cornelius Loew has put it, the dramatists resurrected the rich tradition of myth that all the people held in common and through a free manipulation of familiar themes they contributed more than any other group to the Greek Awakening.[15]

The difference being emphasized here becomes even clearer in the case of the ancient Sumerian New Year Festival which lasted some twelve days between March and April and again between September and October each year. This festival never led to drama, as was the case in Greece, in spite of the presence of ritual, dance and song. In the Sumerian Festival, the first four days are devoted to the purification of the entire community in readiness for the general atonement or cleansing which takes place on the fifth day of the Festival. The next five days are taken up with the arrival of the gods, the liberation and subsequent coronation of their Supreme God, Marduk, his triumphal entry to the city and the consummation of his return in a sacred ritual sexual orgy. The last two days of the festival are devoted to the blessing of the community by the gods who return on the twelfth day to the other world.[16]

There is, thus, no lack of event, even of dramatic event, in the Sumerian Festival. But unlike the Greek Festival, the enactment, for example, of the arrival of Marduk is embodied in the Festival itself as a ritual incident. That is to say, the drama is absorbed in ritual action and the *mythos* is subsumed in ritual. Hence, though the Festival has a great deal of dialogue, action, music, dance and decor, it does not crystallize in drama.[17]

The Igbo Festival The Igbo Festival, it seems to me, is at present structured on Sumerian rather than Greek lines. If this is so, then the emergence of Igbo drama based on our indigenous traditions will depend on how effectively it can be moved beyond the rich but ritual character of the festivals themselves.

(a) The "Mbom Ama" Festival

I take my first illustration from the *Mbom Ama* Festival in my own town, Umunumo. The festival is held between the first and second weeks of October each year and lasts about eight days. There is the usual feasting, dancing, and drinking; the invocations, propitiations and sacrifice. But the heart of the festival is the clearing of *all* footpaths leading from every homestead to the shrine of *Ebu*, the ancestral god of the town. In general, the festival has the following features:

   (i) All paths in the town are weeded and swept clean in anticipation

79

of the sixth moon and the departure of *Ebu* from the town;

(ii) The chief-priest of *Ebu* announces the sixth moon and fixes a day for the celebration.

(iii) Led by the chief-priest and his assistants, the town makes communal offerings at the *Ebu* shrine; families specially favoured by Him also make their offerings.

(iv) On the appointed *Afo* market day, which is also the eighth day of the festival, the town gathers at the market square for dances, wrestling competitions and various masquerades. There is general merriment and out-of-town guests are particularly well-catered for.

(v) The merriment becomes ecstatic and unruly as evening approaches. The day ends with a bitter verbal contest of insults. This takes place by the river separating the two sections of the town and is said to represent one way of accusing and chastising each section of the town for its crimes of the previous year.

(vi) *Ebu* leaves town with his consort, *Lolo*, during the thunderstorm which is expected to follow the end of the festival.

The overall structure of the *Mbom Ama* Festival is thus essentially ritual in character. Behind this ritual action is a suppressed (or at least, an unexpressed) *mythos*. When one unscrambles the rites, one finds that the Festival, in fact, celebrates the departure from the town of the ancestral god with his mate, *Lolo*. *Ebu* is the bringer of good fortune, not only of wealth but also of offspring. The special gifts presented to him are tokens of appreciation from those whose children born in the preceding year were divined to be reincarnations of one of *Ebu*'s two principal subordinates *Oparannu* and *Oparaocha*. It becomes evident, then, that the preliminary clearing of the paths is an anticipatory rite to make the path ready should the god and his queen choose to dwell with any of the suppliants in their several homes.

Implied or suppressed in the *Mbom Ama* Festival is the entire mythology of the town: the ancestry of *Ebu*, of his consort, *Lolo*; the circumstances of their domestication in the town; the crises of the past; the circumstances surrounding their annual departure from the town; the reason for propitiatory and thanksgiving sacrifices. Each detail is a plot or the germ of drama; each is liable to a thousand varying interpretations and reinterpretations, depending on the choice of fact and detail. Without this elaboration of the hidden myth, there can be no drama; only ritual and spectacle.

80

(b) *The Odo Festival*

A more elaborate festival is the Odo Festival in Aku, a small farming and trading community some fourteen miles from Nsukka. The festival is held between February and July every two years. In a sense, this festival is not unique to the Aku community but it is to be found all over Udi and Nsukka Divisions where it is sometimes called the *Omabe* Festival and is then held every four years. Nevertheless, there is no ritual link between the Aku *Odo* and other *Odo* in the Nsukka area, perhaps because for each community, the *Odo* (in spite of the common name) is a local phenomenon.

This is all the more important because the *Odo* is not a god, but the spirit of the departed returning for a six-month stay of communion with the living. Hence, there is no reverence and no worship of the *Odo*, but instead a kind of respectful familiarity. There is good explanation, perhaps, for this. The Aku people, though a very republican community, accept a common ancestral god, *Diewa*, who is quite clearly distinguished from that supreme Igbo deity *Chukwu* whom the Aku people (like most other Nsukka people) call *Ezechitoke*. But even so, *Diewa* is only a supervisory god in Aku. Most of the active gods are located in the thirteen village units of the town, and the only one for whom there is an Aku-wide festival is *Ojiyi*, the local or paternal god of Use, one of the six villages in the Eka-Ibute complex. Even the professional gods of Aku (war-god, *Nshi*; god of justice, *Egwu*; god of agriculture, *Fejoku*; goddess of the hearth, *Usere*, and of water, *Ujere*) belong, in the first instance, to one of the village units. The *Odo* festival is thus not even a festival of worship or even of propitiation of a god even though the ceremonies take place just after the planting season. It is, nevertheless, of sufficient importance for the community to bestow on the non-god, *Odo*, the second most respected festival in the town.

(c) *The Ojiyi Fertility Festival*

The next thing to notice is that the *Odo* festival is not a fertility rite. By a fertility rite I mean a ceremony designed primarily to ask the gods for children and good harvests. A fertility festival is usually associated with some actual or symbolic consummation of a union between male and female, earth and sky, benefactor-god and consecrated suppliant. Such ceremonies are accordingly Bacchanalian in character and feature orgies of one kind or another. There is a period of apparent sexual licence in the ritual pattern of these ceremonies deliberately meant to anticipate the hoped-for abundance of Nature and the gods.[18] Such a festival is the *Ojiyi*

81

festival in Aku, held during the "eighth month" of the Aku year.[19] The *Ojiyi* festival begins with a long procession of children, women, young men (with guns), priests, sword-bearers who receive the *Ojiyi* and move with him along the dried-up valleys to the accompaniment of heroic *Ikpa* music through every village unit of Aku. But the crucial act of the festival is the offering and dedication to the god of several young women. Through these women *Ojiyi* bears children the next year in confirmation of His continued interest in the community. These children are fully respected as *Ojiyi's* offspring, and though they are not regarded as sacred, they are admitted to all assemblies as freeborn.[20] This sexual consummation (or marriage) ritualizes the meaning of the festival and is followed by general merriment.

The Odo as an Apollonian Festival   In the *Odo* festival, then, the emphasis is not on consummation but on *communion*. This communion is, in the first place, between two levels of existence: between this and the "other" world; between the living and their departed kinsmen. There is thus a spiritual quality to the festival which is why it may be described, even if a little inaccurately, as an Apollonian event in order to distinguish it from a Dionysiac festival which usually commemorates the death of a hero, a god or a kinsman (Prometheus, Orpheus, Christ). The *Odo* festival celebrates the return of a lost or wandering hero, god or kinsman (Easter Sunday). The mood is that of rejoicing though, inevitably, this is associated with holy fear. It is important to appreciate this because it explains why every village unit of the Aku community has its own *Odo*, one of its own sons returning from the spirit world.

Broadly speaking, there are five distinct structural divisions in the festival: (i) Preparation, (ii) Welcome and Return, (iii) Communion, (iv) Dedication, and (v) Departure and Blessing.

(i) *Preparation*:
This actually begins early in January with the preliminary celebrations known in Aku as the *Egorigo* festival. The *Egorigo* is a light-hearted festival which ushers in the first *Odo*, called the *Ovuruzo*, a scout spirit whose arrival on the last but one *Afo* day in the "eleventh month" marks the beginning of festivities.

(ii) *Welcome and Return*:
Following the successful return of the *Ovuruzo*, the other twelve *Odo* begin to return. They are welcomed on successive *Afo* days

with drumming, feasting and dancing. At this stage, though the people speak of the *Odo* in the singular, there are in fact as many *Odo* as there are village units and each village organizes its own additional reception festivities at the local level.

(iii) *Communion*:

The *Odo* now withdraw to the sacred groves said to be under the protection of a kind of conservative but vigilant and well-meaning god, called *Uhamu*. From here the *Odo* maintain contact with the living. First some chosen young people take specially prepared food from the women and rarest palmwine from the men to the *Odo* in their several forest or hillside shirnes. Secondly, in return, the *Odo* visit each household very early each morning in a gesture of reciprocation and communion. The *Odo* do threaten violence but this is generally understood to be playfully meant and to be their way of reestablishing communion without too much familiarity. During these visits, the womenfolk again prepare very delicious meals for the *Odo* and their escorts.

(iv) *Dedication*:

The dedication precedes the return of the *Odo* to the spirit world. The ceremony takes place this time before a massed gathering of all the village units of Aku. One *Odo* now represents all the others. The main shrine at Umudiku is specially decorated and the entire community, including women and children this time, are allowed to take part or witness. The official *Odo* drummers and trumpeters are on hand and there is most impressive singing of *Odo* praise chants by the womenfolk. The climactic event is the *Odo*'s first race: a part playful, part deadly-serious contest between the spirit and a representative group of able-bodied males (between the ages of 14 and 30) from all the thirteen village units. It is a gesture of solidarity, the *Odo*'s last act of identification with the community.

(v) *Departure and Blessing*.

The departure of the *Odo* begins on another *Afo* market day. Its significance is to be seen quite clearly in the ritual character of the events. First comes the *Odo*'s meeting with the oldest woman of the town. This meeting takes place about midnight under a bridge across a very deep gully at a village called Legelege (Lelege). This old woman presents the *Odo*, now fully naked and stripped of his heavy six-foot-high headpiece, with a symbolic gift of fish (the *Odo's* favorite) and a piece of white cloth. After this, the *Odo* makes his round of visits to all thirteen units in Aku. At each stop, the host village provides a young man to replace the previous "spirit." The new *Odo* then stages a competition with youthful runners from the next village. This is a highly stylized event designed to generate a lot of bad blood but also structured to end in a free-for-all race of both *Odo* and people to the next village. At the end of these visits, the *Odo* retires again to the grove, waiting for the final all-night drumming and vigil which will precede his being escorted out of the town by a choice group of youths on his way back to the other world. It is at this point that the *Odo* gives his final blessing which usually materializes in a propitious July thunderstorm.

Conclusion   This structure is the vehicle for the meaning of the festival. It will be noticed that the narrative line is that of the festivity, not of the events provoking or sustaining it. Behind the ritual meeting of the *Odo* with the oldest woman of Lelege, for example, there is a story. But that story is not dramatized, and one can only derive the meaning of that action through older men or kind interpreters. The dramatic content is, in other words, buried in the ritual purity of the festival. What is needed then, it seems to me, is to force that ritual to yield its story; to cut through the overlay of ceremony to the primary events of the *mythos*. Ritual is, and has always been, a dead end: it cannot grow. It only shrinks steadily into inevitably inaccesible (though powerful) symbolism. The Igbo should do what the Greeks did: expand ritual into life and give that life a secular base. That way, we may be able to interpret and reinterpret that serious view of life which is now only so dimly manifested in our festivals.

FOOTNOTES

[1] Friedrich Nietzsche, *Philosophy in the Tragic Age of the Greeks*, tr. Marianne Cowan (Chicago, 1962), passim.

[2] J. P. Clark, "Some Aspects of Nigerian Drama," *Nigeria Magazine*, No. 89 (1966); Robin Horton, "The Kalabari *Ekine* Society," *Africa*, 2 (1963); Ulli Beier, "Yoruba Folk Operas," *African Music*, 1 (1954); "The Oba's Festival at Ondo," *Nigeria Magazine*, No. 50 (1956); "The *Egungun* Cult," *Nigeria Magazine*, No. 51 (1956); "The Oshun Festival," *Nigeria Magazine*, No. 53 (1957); S. A. Babalola, *The Content and Form of Yoruba Ijala* (Oxford, 1966); O. Ogunba, "Ritual Drama of the Ijebu people: a study of indigenous festivals," Ph.D. Thesis, Ibadan, 1967.

[3] Margaret Laurence, *Long Drums and Cannons* (London, 1968), p. 79. See also, pp. 12, 18, 78–80.

[4] G. I. Jones, "Masked Plays of South-Eastern Nigeria," *Geographical Magazine*, 18 (1945); J. S. Boston, "Some Northern Ibo Masquerades," *Journal of the Royal African Institute*, 90 (1960); J. P. Clark, op. cit.; Ruth Finnegan, *Oral Literature in Africa* (Oxford, 1970).

[5] Finnegan, pp. 500, 501.

[6] Horton, p. 98.

[7] Northrop Frye, *Anatomy of Criticism* (Princeton, 1957), p. 249.

[8] Cf. Arthur Koestler, *The Act of Creation: A Study of the Conscious and Unconscious in Science and Art* (New York, 1967), p. 309: ". . . though modern theatre hardly betrays its religious ancestry, the magic illusion still serves essentially the same emotional needs: it enables the spectator to transcend the narrow confines of his personal identity, and to participate in other forms of existence."

[9] Frye, p. 107.

[10] Cf. Melville J. and Frances S. Herskovits, *Dahomean Narrative: A Cross-Cultural Analysis* (Evanston, Illinois, 1958), p. 106: "A rite is—it must never be forgotten—an action *redone* (commemorative) or *predone* (anticipatory and magical)."

[11] Finnegan, p. 510: G. I. Jones, p. 191; J. S. Boston, passim.

[12] In my view, the masquerader is a performer; he requires only a plot-based role to become a character-in-drama.

[13] Koestler, pp. 308–309.

[14] Clark, op. cit.

[15] Cornelius Loew, *Myth, Sacred History and Philosophy: The Pre-Christian Religious Heritage of the West* (New York, 1967), pp. 239–240.

[16] Ibid., pp. 33–34.

[17] The reenactment of the coming of the god, *Ulu*, in Achebe's *Arrow of God* would be drama, in my sense of the word.

[18] As one Ebenezer Ozo, an Aku student formerly at Ahmadu Bello University, says of Aku morals during the *Ojiyi* festival: "Among the elders, even women and children for that matter, there is a proclivity to become drunk. Women and children are no longer hindered from drinking wine. This freedom, together with many other shelved restrictions, augurs well for a happier celebration."

[19] Another fertility festival is the *Alu* (or *Ani*) festival which is held in the "third month," within the period of the *Odo* ceremonies.

[20] In recent years, this practice has been held responsible for the unusually high incidence of prostitution among some of Ojiyi's wives who can thrive, as one source put it, "without molestation or discrimination" because they are sacred to the god and are "unable to secure alternative husbands."

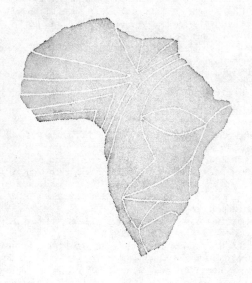

EARLY FICTION IN IGBO

Ernest Emenyonu

The first Igbo to publish fiction in Igbo was Peter Nwana. His novel *Omenuko*[1] was published in 1933 after it had won an all African literary contest in indigenous African languages organized by the International Institute of African Languages and Culture. It is a biographical novel based on actual events in the life of the hero Omenuko, whose home was a favorite spot for students and tourists in Eastern Nigeria in the fifties.[2] The novel has been reprinted several times in various Igbo orthographies and is still a classic in Igbo literature. It is today the most widely read novel in the Igbo language. Generations of Igbo children begin their reading[3] in Igbo with *Omenuko*, and children who do not have the opportunity to go to school still read *Omenuko* in their homes or at adult education centers. Omenuko's "sayings" have become part of the Igbo speech repertoire which the young adult is expected to acquire. Very little is known of the author of *Omenuko*. Nothing ever flowed from his pen again after the publication of *Omenuko*. His role seems, therefore, to have been that of the reporter of the pioneer generation of Igbo literature and not its creative genius.

Omenuko is set in Okigwi, one of the densely populated provinces of the East Central State. The action takes place in the rural communities, around busy marketplaces, where commercial activities go on side by side with serious matters, such as settling disputes and planning community projects. The market is more than a meeting place for local affairs. People drink palmwine, pour libations, as haggling and bargaining go on over their agricultural products. Families live within walled compounds where the head of the family supervises his immediate and extended families from his *obi*. Loyalty to the family often gives way to a larger cause— allegiance to the village, which in turn gives way to the clan. Villages are joined to each other by a tight pattern of intersecting paths which converge at major markets where the entire clan meets to consider affairs of primary concern to all the clan's people. Forests separate one clan from the other, constituting not just physical boundaries, but also symbolic cultural and economic boundaries. Justice at the clan level rests with the elders, who are believed to perform the will of the ancestors. This setting is relevant to the action in the novel and helps to bring out the conflict in which the hero is trapped. It is characteristic of the people, knit together as they are by natural and human factors, to stick together, see things as a group, and act as a group. To exist is to live with the group. Ostracism, whether voluntary or compulsory, is a result of an individual alienating himself from the group or consciously going against the tenets of communal life. The theme of the novel, offense and expiation, emerges from this communal attitude to life. Omenuko, the hero, openly commits a criminal act against his society.

When the novel opens, Omenuko, a merchant by profession, has lost all his goods on his way to the market following the collapse of a rickety bridge. With amazing rapidity, he sells most of his companions (neighbors' sons and relatives who were apprenticed to him) into slavery for his own economic survival. He refuses to take responsibility for this act, which is an abomination to the gods of the land, especially the earth and sky gods. Obstinate and very strong-willed, Omenuko waits too long before coming to terms with his people. Because of the enormity of his crime and his recalcitrant behavior, Omenuko is required to offer a sacrifice of atonement in the highest terms ever prescribed by the chief priests of the two angered deities. In the process, he learns self-discipline and comes to appreciate the true values of his society, their concept of right and wrong, true success and failure. For instance, after he has offered the sacrifice of reunion, Omenuko confesses to his brothers, "I am happier and more at ease now than I have ever been since the day I fled from our town. If death comes to me now, I shall not be afraid."

Towards the end of the nineteenth century, which is when the novel is set, the colonial system had been firmly established in the areas occupied by the Igbo in Nigeria. Many people had taken to the new Christian religion, which was one of the organs of the imperialist regime; Christianity was advertised as holding the key to the white man's "knowledge" and good jobs. But there were still many people who remained loyal to the old religion. They would not give up the rituals which honor the dead, nor would they cease to pour libations to the ancestors and make obligatory sacrifices to placate angered deities and restore harmony in nature. However, the author avoids a confrontation between the two religions; although some of the tensions capable of leading to inevitable collision of the two (as was the case in Chinua Achebe's *Things Fall Apart* set in the same time period) are present in the novel. Nwana manages to confine the falling apart of things to his hero alone, although he is sufficiently ambivalent, if not critical, about some of the traditions of his society. For instance, while Omenuko is at the shrine of the sky-god offering his sacrifice as conscientiously as possible, Nwana is able to interpose some conflicting thoughts: "It is true that the vultures approached Iyiukwa's house at the sound of the small bell, but you must realize that even the most stupid animal would respond to the name you call it, if you make it go through a period of training . . . The vultures had come to know that whenever Iyiukwa jingled the bells, he was summoning them." (Of course to the adherents of the traditional religion the vultures came as a result of the god accepting the sacrifice, and also through the supernatural power of the chief priest of the god).

The concentration on the hero allows Nwana to fully explore the fate of the alienated individual in a situation where identification with the group seems the only way to keep alive. The Christian religion was known to welcome apostates of the old religion as well as outcasts who were taboo in the Igbo culture. This trespassing is what spells disaster for the Igbo communities in Chinua Achebe's *Things Fall Apart* and *Arrow of God*, which like Nwana's are novels of Igbo tradition. But Omenuko does not embrace these easy alternatives which the new religion offers. When he commits an abomination against the traditional religion, he can seek refuge in the Christian camp, as Okonkwo's son does in *Things Fall Apart*, and Oduche does in *Arrow of God*. But Omenuko does not. Instead he goes into voluntary exile, where he lives his own life, often even remaining courteous to his natal home. He testifies to this when he appears before his people several years later to pledge loyalty to the laws of the land and seek reconciliation. He informs them that "although I was in another land, and even a chief there, I was still observing the laws and customs of my homeland. There are no laws of our land which I do not remember." The author clearly intends the fate of the hero to be linked with his personality and individual shortcomings.

Omenuko is intelligent and resourceful, but he is also cunning and capricious. He has an overpowering tendency to use to personal advantage anyone who comes his way. His first attempt at this—the selling of his apprentices to make up for his lost goods—is the source of all the conflicts in the novel. But after this first act, Omenuko's subsequent reactions show a series of progressions in evil and selfish aggrandisement. He knows that among his people, "no man however great can win judgment against a clan." He would be fighting a losing battle from the start if he tries to fight his people alone. So Omenuko uses his brothers for moral support, necessary in his fight with his people. When he initially solicits the support of his brothers, they respond with a serious reproach. "His brothers told him that it [the selling of his apprentices] is a thing un-heard of and can never please the ear that hears it . . . They blamed him for his rash act, because it is an event which can never be forgotten in life. They wondered how he could summon up courage to sell the children of his fellow men merely because his goods fell into a river. 'Was it the fault of your fellow men that you lost your goods?' " But Omenuko is able to coerce them into submission with a threat to their own existence. He threatens suicide and asks them to prepare to fend for themselves in life. He knows fully well the effect of this on his young, helpless brothers. Thus, they not only forgive him, but acquiesce in his plans to go into exile as a group. Omenuko recognizes the weak points of his brothers and fully capitalizes on them. He knows that they will offer little or no resistance once they realize how seriously any action of his could affect all of their individual destinies, especially since he threatened not only to kill himself but also the leading members of the community as well. "He told them that he had invited the chiefs of the land and the parents of the young men whom he sold to meet with him early in the morning. His plan was that all the chiefs and parents of the young men would die at the same time with him. When they had all assembled, he would set fire to two barrels of gun powder which he had stored in his bedroom. In that way, everybody within the building would be burnt to death. That was why he was warning them early enough to plan for their safety." The alternative he offers his brothers is in itself worse than death. His brothers realizing, as the Igbo say, that "it is not the bad dancer who is embarrassed but his relations who are watching in the crowd," choose to team up with Omenuko.

They had correctly assessed the situation as "what our ancestors de-scribe as the legacy that passes from generation to generation! Our chil-dren will have to suffer for it and our children's children likewise will suffer for it." Omenuko had made the suffering local, and his brothers had been personally touched; as they switched their sentiments, the author removed them from their role of impartial commentators and chorus to that of active participators and accomplices. They could no longer be the rationale that governed Omenuko's decisions, because they had themselves become one with Omenuko. As part of Omenuko, they no longer asked, "Is that not enough, must you but contemplate a crime worse than you had already committed?" They merely did things and ran errands for his interests.

But they had lost something else of a greater significance. They were no longer in a position to mediate between Omenuko and the people, nor could they ascertain the wishes of the deities on his behalf. It was an office which Igwe had to be called in to fulfill later in the story. Assured of their support, Omenuko becomes bold enough to challenge his townspeople more successfully, balancing his conflicts and estrangement in the town with the privileges of his brothers' firm support and cooperation. It was this togetherness that solidified their decision to flee the town. Although it would seem here that the original theme of the alienation of the individual from his community has been broadened into the alienation of a family unit from society at large, the author does manage to keep the focus of the action on Omenuko as a character. On the night of their flight, his younger brother Nwabueze was dispatched to go down the major road to see whether he would hear any sounds or observe anyone coming in the direction in which they proposed to escape. It is significant that Nwabueze never heard any sound except the ranting of a lunatic, one who had lost his senses. The cries of the lunatic were shattering to the peace and quiet of the night, in the same way that the turmoil inside Omenuko was affecting the peace of mind of his family and the immediate world around him. Omenuko was himself no less than a lunatic. Like Ibe Ofo (the lunatic) he had been chained (symbolically, but no less significantly) and confined to a cell. Ibe Ofo suffered physical pain and responded with cacophonous groanings; Omenuko's suffering was in his inside and he bore his torturing grief in silence. He owes this to his cocky character, and in any event we know he will take care of himself.

When they had left the town behind them, rain fell in torrents and there were clashes of thunder. The heavens and the natural elements seemed to have broken out in turmoil and rebellion. So the entire universe was not at ease, and this is a symbol that the harmony, the natural harmony, has been upset by the hero's cruel actions. This is the crux of the action of the novel. There is much in the novel to suggest (as was the case with Okonkwo in *Things Fall Apart*) that there is a general feeling by Omenuko's peers and contemporaries that he has upset the balance through his own actions and their ramifications both internally and externally.

Omenuko's overweening ambition to rise above his humble beginnings seems to have produced an extreme reaction in his character: he always puts profit above humaneness. This becomes his guide in most of his major actions in the novel; humaneness becomes a consideration only later when he can afford it. Consequently, he is always on top of things, scheming and grasping, the cool man and the easy-talking operator. Few of the people he meets recognize him truly for what he is—not even the white District Commissioner (who is as gullible as Omenuko's brothers and friends)—but each is skeptical in some way about his motives and intentions. Chief Ike hints at this when he equivocates about facing Omenuko in a public trial. "Sir, Omenuko is a great orator. Perhaps he would use this to my disadvantage when he comes here. He may falsely deny me and still appear to be saying the truth before your eyes." Indeed, Omenuko knows what to say and when to say it to disarm an opponent in any situation. He also knows when to create fear in the minds of people and then take full advantage of the situation he has created and manipulated, as he does with the Mgborogwu chieftaincy while in exile. It is these elements, destructive yet ingenious, that make Omenuko an effective and fascinating character.

He is admirable as a character, but not because he is a St. Francis. He is a grasping, smooth, cool operator, making his fortune even in the face of disaster, a never-say-die type, wholly wound up in himself, generous to a fault when he can afford it, grasping when necessary, cruel and inhuman when his own fate is in the balance. But for all that, he is still a lovable type.

It is significant that in his exile at Mgborogwu, it is these same factors —an overweening ambition and his grasping and indifferent nature— that bring him into conflict with his hosts. By Igbo custom,[4] when Omenuko fled his hometown, he could have sought refuge among the kinsmen of his mother's maiden family. Instead, he fled to Mgborogwu where he was without a patrilineage (Umunna) and therefore without citizenship either in the world of men or in the domain of the ancestors. The people seized upon this when they rose against him for seeking to hold their highest office in the land. They protested to the white District Commissioner, "We can never allow this to happen in this our own land, that one who is, after all, a stranger should be our head and chief executive." Although Omenuko views every opposing action from his hosts as due to their jealousy of his increasing prosperity, and therefore asks the District Commissioner to exonerate him but punish them severely, he is unable to adduce any strong case to prove that he is entitled to any rights of citizenship in Mgborogwu. The District Commissioner seems to have taken a simplistic view in this matter of citizenship for he only sees the threat on Omenuko's life and advises him to return to his original homeland to avoid being assassinated by his angry hosts.

For Omenuko, it is an episode that clearly goes beyond the rivalry over a vacant chieftaincy. It brings out to him the full implications of his sin against his people and his escapist method of severing connections with his heritage rather than facing the consequences of his rash conduct. This action, which leads to Omenuko's eventual return to his native land, is very important because it provides the plot with a very neat resolution in the end. It provides a circular structure for the novel as it shows a point of departure and return. (This has become a common characteristic of many later Igbo novels. Cf. Achebe's *Things Fall Apart*; Ekwensi's *Jagua Nana*; Agunwa's *More Than Once*, etc.) It ties in with the author's viewpoint in the preface of the novel that, "no matter how successful a man may be in a foreign land, he cannot fail to realize eventually that indeed there is no place like home." The bridge episode is an important landmark in the novel for it marks the point of Omenuko's departure from the right path of life. From then onwards, he wanders aimlessly like the prodigal son, pruning here and piling there to make a living, but never really achieving an organic whole in his existence until he returns at the end of the novel to that point from which he deviated several years before.

The novel thus lends justification to Austin Shelton's remarks that:

> The African writer sees social change in part as change from cultural wholeness to fragmentation and disorientation of the individual, who can regain "wholeness" of self and proper orientation to behavior as well as obtain the deserved rewards only through his maintenance of traditions or a return to the traditionally sanctioned behavior.[5]

Omenuko tries various devices to avoid his return. He tries exaggerated acts of charity, as well as his other diplomatic maneuvers, but to no avail. They only serve as a temporary bridge to reconciliation and continued tolerance of the offender by the offended hosts. Omenuko then realizes more than ever that his original sin against his people has left inerasable scars and though he may be tolerated wherever he goes, he would never win full acceptance anywhere but among his own people. This moral evolution in the hero prepares the way for the final and most

important action in the novel. Omenuko was later to inform his relatives and household in exile, "I am not a citizen of Mgborogwu and I have
also been rejected by my original homeland . . . The primary thing I
should do now is to seek a reconciliation with both human beings and
gods whom I have greatly offended and sinned against, and re-establish
links with them." Thus, Omenuko, true to his character, shows his sense
of insecurity and disillusionment only when desperately necessary. So
long as his exile did not seriously threaten his ambition to be wealthy and
prosperous, Omenuko could tolerate it. There were times when he considered it lucky that he had reason to flee his town, as, "Whenever he
thought about his past and reflected upon his present position (as Chief),
he thanked God and his brothers that he stayed alive." But, as at home,
Omenuko places material concerns above human life and interests in his
place of exile. He is able to grow rich on the Mgborogwu people, but has
little regard for the people themselves. He feels no compunction in plotting their destruction, and at a stage he wages a full scale war against them
to satisfy his selfish designs. No human life is worth preserving whenever
Omenuko's egocentricism is challenged.

He virtually seizes the Mgborogwu throne at the death of the ruling
king, and when the people press charges against him, he completely out-
wits them, so that instead of being stripped of the chieftaincy, Omenuko
wins for himself a separate kingdom. The bringing of Omenuko back
into harmony with man and the gods is accomplished through a ritual
sacrifice, in the process of which Igwe, a close friend of Omenuko, plays
a palliative role in the impasse between Omenuko and his family on the
one hand, and the people and their deities on the other.

This sacrifice offers the reader another opportunity to examine the
character of Omenuko himself, and his relationship to religious ritual, to
the priests, to the chiefs, to his cousins, and to everyone he meets. The
author examines sin and forgiveness within Omenuko, and projects a
kind of Islamic atmosphere in the later part of the novel. He portrays in
his hero a Moslem air of acceptance—an unquestioning acceptance of
one's fate, which seems to explain some of Omenuko's reactions to life
and its hard knocks. Consequently, he tackles the rituals of the sacrifice in
his characteristically carefree manner, doing the things that the priests
expect of him, saying the correct things, ransoming the men just as easily
and goodnaturedly as he once sold them into bondage.

Now, as in the other major actions in the novel, Omenuko is able to
dominate at the same time that he is asking for favor, and he tries to move

fate at the same time that he seems to seek expiation of his sins. Early in the novel, when he lost his goods in the river, he agonized and bemoaned his fate but at the same time he was plotting his way beyond the tragedy. When he accepted the fact that he would have to surrender the Mgboro-gwu chieftaincy to its rightful prince, Obiefula, he nonetheless went behind the scenes to work out (almost by swindling) a new crown for himself, outwitting the District Commissioner while appearing to be a humble servant who only took and carried out orders faithfully. He goes home at a time he can well afford it, having secured his future materially abroad. He swiftly placates the gods as a way of putting them (and their menaces) out of the way and also as a way of putting his past life behind him in a decisive act of finality.

He had gone the full cycle exploiting gods as easily as he exploited the white men and the local people. This fact may explain his voluntary retirement at the end of the novel. He has lived a full life with a chequer-ed history which in itself carries many moral overtones. This is why Nwana ends the narrative with, "I have written this book about the life of Mazi [Mr.] Omenuko so that anyone who reads it may have something to learn from Omenuko's life. The way in which this world is a perfect mixture of joy and sorrow, hardship and reward, laughter and tears, is in itself, enough lesson for anyone who seeks to learn."

If this appears an unsatisfactory ending for a rather complex story,[6] it must be remembered that Peter Nwana was writing for a definite audience —the Igbo. Like the traditional oral performer before him, it was incum-bent on him not to disguise his didactic intention or moral purpose for his narrative when the tale was done. It was a commitment the artist owed at least to the young members of his audience to whom the ethical formu-las of the story may not be clearly discernible in the course of the nar-rative.

Peter Nwana's concept of the hero makes an interesting comparison with Chinua Achebe's in *Things Fall Apart*. Both novels have historical perspectives, are set at approximately the same time in the past, and deal with the same ethnic group. Both provide vital information about the society of their heroes, but each novelist seems to be preoccupied with the hero who, as a character, seems more important than the universal things that his character and actions might have pointed to had he been treated and created differently. In both novels the society informs the character rather than vice-versa. And, in the embrace of both novels, we learn far more about Omenuko and Okonkwo than we learn of Igbo society. In both novels success is the aspiration of every member of the society and achievement is greatly applauded and honored. Both novelists show how the pursuit of success and achievement can lead to a lopsided development of the individual which, in turn, affects his society. In both novels popular expectations produce tragic consequences in the lives of the heroes.

Omenuko, like Okonkwo, has very humble beginnings. He strives according to popular expectations to overcome the handicaps of his birth by aspiring by all means (as Okonkwo does) to achieve status, wealth and fame. Both Omenuko and Okonkwo pursue this relentlessly to the point of obsession. At a time when they seem to have realized their dreams, the scales turn against both. Okonkwo kills a neighbor's son, Omenuko sells neighbors' sons into slavery. Both go into exile for several years, and while in exile, both are wealthy at the expense of their peace of mind. Omenuko, as Chief, exists in "a state of living death" in which he is dogged by a continuous trail of misfortunes. Okonkwo takes his exile in bad faith and names a son born there "Nwofia" (child of the wilderness), and suffers the humiliation of being abandoned by his heir. Both come back eventually to a changed society in which the powers and innovations of the white man have been firmly entrenched. Both achieve serenity at the end of the novel, but the fate of Achebe's hero is charged with bitter irony. Omenuko retires from public life, Okonkwo retires from life itself.

Nwana's hero is a man who is versed in the traditions and customs of his people. He is aware of the impact of change on these traditions and customs, but he responds only to those changes that will benefit him personally in a material way. For the rest, he is either indifferent or pretends to be ignorant of their existence. There is nothing in the old religion for which he is willing to die, but at the same time he is happier inside than outside it. He is very shrewd and can live a long time with the white man; he practices his own traditional customs but pays lip service to the laws and regulations of the white man's administration, appeasing the white man with kola nuts and fowls as he does his ancestral deities whenever he wants to ask for a favor or atone for a misdeed. He is ready to come to terms with the white man at any time except where his material ambitions are involved.

Achebe's hero, on the other hand, is more presumptuous and less tactful. He is strong-willed, inflexible to a fault, and a clog to the wheels of change and progress. He is dogmatically committed to his personal beliefs and so intolerant that he alienates himself from both the world of the old and that of the new. It is his wrong judgment as much as the pressures of the new order that destroy him in the end.

Both Omenuko and Okonkwo are self-centered, but Okonkwo is more fearless and given to bravado. He is the more towering figure, more self-made and therefore more disposed to order his own life regardless of the opinions of others, regardless of whom he cuts down in the process. The cross-cultural conflicts and the disintegration of Igbo life (i.e., the cultural life) muted in Nwana's novel are more intricately portrayed by Chinua Achebe and by later Igbo novelists, who also conceive the dissenting hero in more clear-cut, if not sympathetic terms. If Nwana's novel does not explore the full ramifications of this theme, it is probably because the events that created it were only just unfolding at the time he was writing. These similarities only prove the Igbo writer's historic sensitivity to the problems of his society. They show, too, that no matter his age, audience, form or the language of his work of art, the Igbo writer will reflect the same moral preoccupations that exist in his society.

The strong influence of *Omenuko* on later Igbo writers is most apparent in *Ije Odumodu Jere* (Odumodu's Travels),[7] a novel published in Igbo in 1963. The novel is set in the latter part of the nineteenth century. The hero, Odumodu, is born in a poor family but works his way to the top by dint of hard labor. His adventures carry him into foreign lands (Europe, North America, Cuba) where he is antagonized by many of his hosts. He survives, eventually returns to his original home a wealthy man, and then immediately sets about to modernize his community.

Like Omenuko, Odumodu is involved in a succession conflict (to a foreign throne) and a timely intervention of an outsider saves him from assassination. Omenuko loses his goods when he and his companions fall into a river. Odumodu also loses his possessions in a shipwreck in which he is the sole survivor. There is a very close similarity in tone and content between chapter ten of *Odumodu's Travels* and chapter four of *Omenuko*. The dying king of Finda wills his throne to Odumodu, a foreigner, in the same way that Chief Mgborogwu bequeaths his throne to Omenuko, an alien and fugitive from justice. In both cases, the people conspire to work against the dead king's wishes. The heir-apparent of Finda tries to have Odumodu assassinated while in Mgborogwu; the chiefs rise in rebellion against Omenuko and make attempts on his life. Odumodu flees from Finda, goes to Mimba, and finally escapes to his hometown, Ahaba, where he is received with great celebrations and festivities. He settles down, builds modern houses, and is appointed chief of his people. In the same way, Omenuko flees from Mgborogwu to Ikpa Oyi and then to his hometown in Okigwi. He settles down, builds modern houses, declines to be the chief of his people, but accepts the honorary position of peacemaker and "overseer." Thus both novels describe a departure and a return.

But *Odumodu's Travels* may have also been influenced by other sources. The preoccupation with European history and wars, the author's knowledge of navigation and oceanography, the sensitive reactions to life in Europe, and the theme of slave trade, have parallels in *Equiano's Travels*.[8] Odumodu is nearly as versatile as Equiano. He was a teacher, a carpenter, a cook, a sailor, an administrator, a counselor, and a preacher. Whereas *Odumodu's Travels* has many things in common with *Robinson Crusoe* and *Gulliver's Travels*, its account of the shipwreck of the hero and his subsequent captivity by a gang of dwarfish creatures "who crawled in and out of holes," reads like an account of Gulliver's experience with the Lilliputians.[9]

Perhaps the strongest influence on *Odumodu's Travels* is that of Christian missionaries. Apart from verbatim quotations[10] which the author makes from the missionary *Primer* (1927), there are more pervasive influences in plot and characterization. The hero is caught between two worlds. He tries to be Igbo but is caught up in Western ways. The author strives to build his theme into a race issue but succeeds only in making a case for his hero as a Christian. He succeeds in showing some differences in behavior which result from belonging to another culture. He does not succeed in portraying the deep-rooted racial conflicts that he seems to be striving for. However hard he stresses his hero's blackness, the question of race remains only on the surface of the novel. The narrative wavers between racial prejudice and a conflict in codes of values. Bell-Gam settles for the more manageable theme. Odumodu triumphs over the oppressive white race not because he is black but mostly because he is a Christian who practices the teachings of the Bible as well as the Christian doctrines. The opposition of the citizens of Finda to his marriage with their princess does not deter Odumodu from working to improve the standards of living, methods of government and moral values of the people of Finda. The author invests Odumodu with uncommon qualities of humility and selfless service. He wants to devote his time to serving fellow human beings, and when Finda does not give him the chance, his missionary zeal to spread the word moves him to migrate to Mimba, where he builds schools, trains teachers, and instills in the masses an appreciation of the dignity of labor. He admonishes them with, "whoever is not ashamed to work with his hands will never die of starvation. No work is too mean or inferior for a man in need." The image that the author projects of his hero throughout the novel is one of a suffering but undeterred missionary. He is rejected by the very people he seeks to "save." He loses everything in his possession, including his wife and children, but Odumodu is neither discouraged nor dissuaded from his mission to "go forth and teach all nations." He advises all the people he meets and converts to "live your lives according to the ten commandents."

His sterling qualities notwithstanding, Odumodu remains at the end of the novel a self-advertising redeemer for the heathen peoples of Finda and Mimba, one who has his smug patronage to show for all his troubles. *Odumodu's Travels* may have been intended as a bitter irony on the presumptions and ethnocentricism of the early missionaries in Africa. As a story of an African on a "civilizing mission" to the savages and cannibals of Europe and America (Finda and Mimba), the designed satirical effect of the novel may have been well calculated. The use of missionary vocabulary, often quoting or paraphrasing the missionary *Primer* used previously to "educate and Christianize" the Igbo, is an appropriate weapon to launch a counterattack based on reversed racism.

In the course of Igbo literature from its earliest beginnings to the 1940s, the influence of the missionaries and of Peter Nwana's *Omenuko* have been far-reaching. Because it is read and known only in the Igbo language, the impact of *Omenuko* on later Igbo writers who write in English may not be so apparent to the non-Igbo. But even without any literary influence on later Igbo writers, *Omenuko*, by virtue of its pioneer status, is still the foundation of modern Igbo creative writing, and its author is truly the father of Igbo written literature. As for the missionaries, their impact can be felt in the language, culture, attitudes and values of the present Igbo, and therefore a modern Igbo writer who reflects Igbo life (as most do) cannot help but reflect something of the Europeanized Igbo approach to life. This is most evident in those writers who formed a point of transition from writing in Igbo to writing in the English language:

FOOTNOTES

[1] Peter Nwana, *Omenuko* (London: Longmans, 1933). Published in Igbo. Recently translated into English by Ernest Emenyonu. Remarks and analysis based on the original

99

text.

[2] This author had the privilege of one such visit organized by the Cultural Society of Bishop Lasbrey College, Irete, Owerri, in 1956.

[3] Many also read the Igbo Bible, but the Bible does not have as much readership as *Omenuko* since the latter appeals to people of all Christian denominations as well as non-Christians, unlike the Igbo Bible which is read essentially by Protestants.

[4] Cf. Okonkwo's exile in Chinua Achebe's *Things Fall Apart* (London: Heinemann, 1958).

[5] "Behavior and Cultural Value in West African Stories," *Africa*, 34 (1964), 357.

[6] Cf. O. R. Dathorne, "Ibo Literature: The Novel as Allegory," *African Quarterly*, 7 (1968), 365–68.

[7] Leopold Bell-Gam, *Ije Odumodu Jere* (London: Longmans, 1963). Published in Igbo.

[8] Paul Edwards, ed., *Equiano's Travels* (London: Heinemann, 1967). First published in 1789 as *The Interesting Narrative of the Life of Olaudah Equiano, or Gustavus Vassa the African, Written by Himself,* this is one of the first creative works to be published by an African. It has now been established that its author, Olaudah Equiano, was an Igbo: see Philip D. Curtin, ed., *Africa Remembered* (Madison: University of Wisconsin Press, 1968), p. 61.

[9] Cf. *Gulliver's Travels* (Boston: Ginn and Co., 1914), pp. 7–12, and Bell-Gam, pp. 12–13.

[10] Cf. *Akwukwo Ogugu Ibo* (London: James Townsend and Sons, 1927), pp. 33, 28, and Bell-Gam, p. 41.

LITERATURES IN ENGLISH

THE NARRATIVE AND INTENSIVE CONTINUITY: *THE PALM-WINE DRINKARD*

Robert P. Armstrong

INTRODUCTORY NOTE The following is the greatest part of a chapter from my book *The Affecting Presence: An Essay in Humanistic Anthropology*, to be published by the University of Illinois Press. In this book I am concerned to establish feeling as a separate, coeval, and considerable part of human culture, a part whose expressed existence is in large part to be found in works of art, which I call affecting presences. I use the word "presence" because the work of art has as its critical and definitive features many of the same characteristics as a person. I assert what is patently true, that the existence of the affecting presence is to be perceived in terms of time and space *emotionally* executed through the media proper to them (thus, for example, volume for space and movement for time) and that these media are exploited to create discrete works in *forms,* and the forms are music, sculpture, narrative, and so forth.

The universe of time is to be conceived of as being asserted by means of either continuity or discontinuity, and that of space through either extension or intension. I develop the point that the traditional mode of affecting *being* for the Yoruba is by means of a space-time universe that is intensive and continuous. After showing how intension and continuity characterize a spatial art, sculpture, I proceed to the following discussion of narrative as a time art.

All the affecting forms in my view constitute a system in that they are related one to the other in the relationship of identity, since they all bring into concrete existence forms actualizing an affecting life common to the culture. The means by which physical works incarnate feeling I call metaphor, and the respects in which the identical affecting view of time

A slightly different version of this essay appears in Armstrong's *The Affecting Presence: An Essay in Humanistic Anthropology* (Urbana, 1971), pp. 137-73.

and space are incorporated into works I view equivalents of one another. Thus the means Tutuola uses to achieve intensive continuity in his work are similetically equivalent to the means by which a carver achieves the incarnation of the same mode in his figures. The following is a detailed study of these means in Tutuola.

I have elected to work with *The Palm-Wine Drinkard*-kind of folk-fantasy by Amos Tutuola[1] rather than with the novels of Wole Soyinka or T. M. Aluko for the simple reason that the novel is an imported phenomenon. Its mere exercise interposes a certain distance between practitioner and tradition, such that it becomes the more difficult to see the traditional affecting principle at work in an alien form because that form is exotic and learned, and its very exercise implies a further degree of acculturation. At the very least one cannot perceive the principle's effects with the same sharpness of focus one can have in the case of the more traditional sub-forms (if narrative is the form, then "novel" and "short story" are to be seen as sub-forms).

Prior to analysis, however, it is necessary for us to consider the media which comprise narrative, discussing them in general, and indicating the respects in which we should expect continuity and discontinuity, intension and extension to be expressed in these media. The reader will recall that these media are situationality, language, relationality, and experience. Each of these media is to be seen as having both synchronic and diachronic dimensions existing both in instantaneity and in sequentiality.

Situationality

Situationality is the dimension of human activity which most readily comes to one's mind when he thinks of narrative, for when one is asked what a given narrative is "about" and proceeds to recount the plot he is giving a synopsis of that narrative medium. Situation is composed of actor, action, motivation, sense detail, and psychological detail, and it exists as readily in the internal world of the individual actor as it does interpersonally. The properties of situation are inextricably related one to the other in specific times and places and for specific reasons by virtue of the simple fact that there must be a logic—an entailment, a follow-through—about human action if it is not to be chaotic. There is a decreasing entropy of action with every action committed. Granting a situation where actor and action have no predictable or reasonable relationship one to the other, where motivation is irrelevant to action and to actor, and where sense and psychological details are either not significant or counter-significant to each of the other properties, it is doubtful whether meaningful narrative could exist. I am bearing in mind here the fact that disjunctions among the properties may be used for special effect, and indeed that surrealistic works may exist in which other logics prevail, such as the hidden logic of relationships among dream symbols. But in the first instance, such disjuncture does not characterize the total work, and in the second *a* logic does prevail, even if it is not the daily logic of fully disclosed cause and effect.

Situation is divisible into *acts,* which are identifiable, synchronic units constituting in their totality the medium of situationality in a given work. More specifically, an act is defined in terms of all the properties of situation, insofar as they are to be found in the span of situation under consideration, which conspire together to constitute an identifiable phase in the diachronic progression of the narrative, An act is that bit about which it can be asserted that at a given time and in a given place such and such an event of dramatic import occurred.

Concerning the properties of situation, it is clear that there are, in narrative, instances in which the distinction between sense detail and psychological detail would appear to be less than clear. It is readily apparent that sense detail can be used for the purposes of providing psychological information, as when it is used to create mood or when it comes to have significant or symbolic value representing or conveying something of the state of mind of one of the actors. For the purposes of analysis, however, it would seem best to take such details as they are given rather than as they are intended. Sense and psychological details may be used to give extension to a synchronic act, or indeed to restrict it, thus making the act intensive, much as the variously voiced instruments of a symphony orchestra may be used in wide or narrow range in order to extend or to restrict the synchronic structures of a given musical composition. Sense detail and psychological detail also contribute to the establishment of the durational existence of a work by maintaining continuity of scene and mood.

The psychological detail which is used to create the emotional milieu of a work, as sense detail creates its physical world, is to be distinguished from the psychological elements of a character adduced to give depth— or not adduced, thus producing shallowness—and believability to the motivation which links together actor and action in any given act and indeed in any given sequence of acts. Motivation may be explicit or implicit, simple or complex, obvious or subtle, resident in present situation or in situations past or yet to come, and it may be rooted in one's self, in another, or in the interests of some event quite removed from either. Motivation is the seed of action, expressed or repressed, and as it constitutes the license for action, so, when it is believable, does it establish action's historicity and authenticity. Finally, for the properties of situation, there is little that need be said of actor and action since these properties would appear to be self-explanatory.

Language

Language is the second medium of narrative, and it has several properties —denotation, connotation, images, irony, wit, paradox, ambiguity, rhythm, contrast, alliteration, sound, and the whole range of rhetorical devices which may be used to give fabric, metre, balance, and affect to the narrative—all these, of course, in addition to the common properties of language: tense, mood, voice, and case. Primarily the affecting properties of language are useful in creating range of act, and thus they are chiefly of concern in the consideration of the problem of intensionality/extensionality. But it is obvious that in their duration and frequency they are of relevance also in the consideration of continuity/discontinuity, such that any property or indeed any group of properties consistently employed constitutes an added stratum of durationality.

Relationality

By relationality I mean to designate synchronic relationships among components of acts as well as the durational ones among acts in sequence. In both cases one is concerned with the consideration of either integration, by which one means that the properties of situation and of language are functionally or causally—in any event, meaningfully—related one to the other, or disintegration. It is characteristic of the continuous work that consequentiality characterizes the relationships among acts and larger patterns of acts, but such dependency does not characterize such relationships although, obviously, it must at the very least govern the relationships among the constituent elements comprising an act.

Experience

With respect to the medium of experience, one expects that it will tend to be more or less implicit and centripital in the intensive work and the opposite in the extensive one; that a constant state of evolving experience will characterize the continuous while a succession of estates of experience, doubtless unrelated, will characterize the discontinuous. Experience, one will recall, is that flush of pertinence that characterizes an affecting presence and makes it valuable, intimate, and believed.

Modelling

Modelling, which is not of course an affecting medium but is nonetheless a critical factor in considering the style of a people, will be either high or low, with the former leading to fully individuated characters and situations developed with marked credibility, and the latter leading to the characters' being portrayed as types, with their actions lacking something of both credibility and distinctiveness. Diachronically, in the case of high modelling, one sees characters develop and believes their change. This is less notably the case in low modelling. High synchronic modeling we would expect to characterize extensionality, and high diachronic modelling continuity. Conversely, low synchronic modelling would be equivalent to intensionality and low diachronic modelling to discontinuity.

It will be useful to present in schematic survey the characteristics of each of the media in intensionality and extensionality, in continuity and discontinuity. (*See Table, pages 14 and 15.*)

There is, it must be noted, a difference between competence and lack of it, so that there is in effect excellence or failure in the practice of narrative, satisfaction or defect in the use of the media and their properties. Thus when best executed the intensional character is subtle, but when less well realized he is shallow and unbelievable. Similarly the extensional character at his best is complex and exciting, while at his worst he is disorganized, bombastic, hollow. The complexity of action or of language that characterizes the extensional is at best rich, and at worst rococo. The outward-tending, the reaching, in defect becomes mere disorganization; the intending, cramped; the subtle, shallow; the continuous, tiresome; and the discontinuous, chaotic.

As is sometimes true of models, they can reflect more entities than can in reality be readily found to exist. This is particularly the case with the question of continuity and discontinuity as it relates to narrative. This is to say that in point of actual fact, narrative existing in language and language being characterized by certain demands of consecutivity, absolute discontinuity would not be possible. Taken at the level of the smallest meaningful isolable unit—the act—it is inconceivable that either one of the only two possibilities of discontinuity would exist; namely, either that each act would be so explicitly defined and executed in such a way as to focus affective attention upon those acts themselves, at the expense of

SYNCHRONIC

	Intensionality	Extensionality
1. SITUATIONALITY *Sense detail*	There is an economy and close relevance to such sense detail as is included.	There is a richness to sense detail and it may or may not be tightly integrated into the structure of act.
Psychological detail	There is an economy and close relevance to such psychological detail as is included.	There is a richness to psychological detail and such detail may or may not be tightly integrated into the structure of act.
Motivation	Motivation is spare, pertinent, and closely integrated.	Motivation is elaborately conceived and intricately extended to the periphery of the act.
Action	Action is characterized by a strong focus, is definite and clear.	Action is complex, ranging, implicative.
Actor	The actor is well defined, executed with strong, clearly drawn lines.	The actor is richly drawn with a wealth of evocation, variety of motivation, complexity of personality (or simple personality completely, complexly shown).
2. RELATIONALITY	A narrow range of kinds of relationships among components of situation and other affecting media.	A wide range of kinds of relationships among components of situation and other affecting media.
3. LANGUAGE	Economical and rigorously pertinent use of images and other affecting properties of language so that the act is a tightly integrated synchronic event. Images tend to restrain the attention and focus the feeling.	Wide, indeed even lavish, use of images and other affecting properties of language so that act is a ranging affecting structure. Images are richly connotative and suggestive. Indefiniteness rules and implication and suggestion are vastly important.

DIACHRONIC

*Continuity**	*Discontinuity*
Sense detail is closely controlled diachronically with attention to warp, and woof being either lavish (extensive) or restrained (intensive).	Sense detail shows little evidence of supporting any notion of through-development.
Psychological detail is closely controlled and the development of the psychological dimensions of the work (mood) are evolutionary.	Psychological detail is loosely controlled. There is no sense of careful, evolutionary development of successive psychological details.
Motivation is rigorously consequential and evolutionary.	Motivation is loosely consequential, or perhaps not consequential at all.
Action is carefully consequential and evolutionary.	Action is sequential and tends to interrupt forward movement.
The actor is developed in a carefully evolutionary fashion, such that all acts are logically derivable from previous conditions or referrable to future ones.	The actor is loosely evolutionary or not evolutionary at all. He is seen stroboscopically rather than realistically through causal time.
Temporal integration is tight and the principle of diachronic development is consequentiality. In the event of an episodic work, where sequentiality is apt to characterize the work, overall evidences of integrative relationality will occur.	There is a sense of disjuncture among the parts such that sequentiality characterizes the work. The discontinuous episodic is not clearly overridden by larger, integrative plans.
Carefully integrative patterns of use of images and other affecting properties of language.	A disregard for the temporal *patterning* of images and other affecting properties of language.

* Continuity by means of a dense frequency of discrete "atoms" poses different considerations. See text.

before and *after,* or that sequentiality would be handled in such a way that no act would follow from any other act. As we shall see when we come to consider *The Palm-Wine Drinkard*, this argument has special relevance to the episodic work, the existence of which would be made problematic under the mode of continuity. It is probably the case that there is an *intention* toward continuity and an *intention* toward discontinuity which are made manifest in the work. If this is true then it is in this area that we must search for continuity and for discontinuity. Once again, the discussion of Tutuola's work will make clear the evidences of such intentions in the case of a work which is episodic yet continuous, if not in terms of action, at least in other affecting media and their properties.

Amos Tutuola's *The Palm-Wine Drinkard* is one of those marvellous works of the human imagination which, rich with fancy, goes simply and directly to the heart of a perennial and profound human concern, that about the nature of the estate of being dead. It is therefore, although inevitably and inextricably involved with Tutuola's being Yoruba, equally inevitably and inextricably bound to the fact pure and simple of his being a man. Thus it is necessarily the case that the impact of much of what he writes is supracultural. It is, in a word, of the nature of that special and very basic level of pertinence which one calls Myth. I capitalize the term in order to distinuish it from that "myth" which the anthropologist sees culturally, a belief whose function is to "validate" action.

In *The Palm-Wine Drinkard* Tutuola relates the adventures of a first-person narrator whose palm-wine tapster has fallen from a tree while tapping palm-wine and been killed. The victim of a prodigious appetite for palm-wine and a generous host who is deserted by his friends once he can no longer supply them with the hospitality to which they have become accustomed from him, he sets off to find his palm-wine tapster.

> When I saw that there was no palm-wine for me again, and nobody could tap it for me, then I thought within myself that old people were saying that the whole people who had died in this world, did not go to heaven directly, but they were living in one place somewhere in this world. So that I said that I would find out where my palm-wine tapster who had died was. (p. 9)

This is not a "descent to the underworld" only because there is no underworld. The Town of the Deads is in the same world as the towns of the living. But in spirit, the mythic formula obtains, for the way to the town of the deads is fraught with harrowing escapes from monsters who would destroy the narrator and, eventually, the wife whom he acquires in one of his earliest experiences, that with the "incomplete gentleman." There is no river Styx for him to cross, although it must be noted that at the end of his odyssey the narrator encounters the last monsters in a mountain just across a river, but seven miles from his own village. The bush in which the Deads' Town is located (years away from his own village) is, there can be little doubt, raised to the power of Myth. But this radically generalizing action comes perhaps more easily to the Yoruba than to the urban European, and more readily to the Yoruba of Tutuola's generation (Tutuola was born in 1920), perhaps, than to the "enlightened" young of today. For the fact of the matter is that to the Yoruba the bush has traditionally been a place of mystery and often of fear. One encounters again and again in the fiction from the region accounts of experiences and of beliefs which would indicate a certain awe toward the bush. Because of the Mythization of the bush, therefore, one expects to encounter a functional equivalent of "crossing the Styx," and he is not disappointed. From the narrator's introduction—recounting his situation, the death of his tapster, and his determination to set forth in search—to the first adventures there is a perceptible boundary. The world of the introduction is a real world, save for the gargantuan appetites of the palm-wine drinkard, but the world of the first adventure is a world of the marvellous and the highly generalized—thus his first experience takes him on a labor whose objective is the capture of Death.

Not unlike some other accounts of the world of the dead, the deads of Tutuola's bush do not care for the living. In fact, the living are not allowed in the Deads' Town, though the drinkard and his wife succeed in visiting there. The deads behave differently from the living also— notably, they walk backwards, which we are to read as a primitive form of behavior, the evidence for which is to be found elsewhere in the story, notably in the section about the red people where we learn that at one time people had their eyes on their knees and walked backwards. In the long run the narrator learns that his trip was in vain. His tapster, once found, no longer wishes to return to the towns of the living. The tapster's transfiguration has been completed. He has visited some of the very towns the narrator himself has visited along the way, but having at last reached Deads' Town his transformation into a dead is both complete and irreversible.

The narrator himself is by no stretch of the imagination an ordinary mortal. A person of enormous appetites, the palm-wine drinkard is not only somewhat gargantuan. When he begins his journey he is careful to take along with him both his own and his father's juju, or power-containing substances. But the merit of this juju is not only to ward off evil; it is also used to effect basic physical transformations of himself, his wife, and their possessions. The juju is more that of the magician than of the ordinary man protecting himself against witchcraft. Unlike the ordinary mortal, furthermore, he can "sell" his death and "lease" his fear. And the first characterization he gives of himself, once he has launched himself into the bush of adventure, is as "father of the gods." One does not necessarily believe that this is in fact who he is, nor indeed that he himself takes this self-description fully seriously, although at one point at least he does appear to do so. He is in a fair sense very much like the hero in Greek myths. He is as generic as they, and like them he can—as generic—engage in those highly generalized experiences which have within them the conditions essential to becoming Myth. We shall see something more of this subsequently when we have the occasion to discuss his lack of individuation.

So a hero he is, and though his task may lack something of the dignity of purpose of Prometheus', his ultimate objective is nonetheless of social worth and is to be viewed as heroic. For after having spent years in the search of his tapster, when he reaches Deads' Town and locates his tapster, he takes back with him not the tapster but a gift—a miraculous egg which will upon address fulfill all that is asked of it. He returns home to find that a famine has settled upon the earth, and whereas he had undertaken his journey in order that he might supply both himself and the men of his village with palm-wine, he uses the magical powers of the egg to become the universal provider, defeating the famine and alleviating the hunger of all who come to his compound.

It is obvious that *The Palm-Wine Drinkard,* because it is of a given type, is reminiscent of other works in world literature. Gerald Moore is particularly aware of these similarities, for he specifically cites—in his discussion of Tutuola in *Seven African Writers*—Bunyan and Dante, and likens the search of the palm-wine drinkard to Orpheus'. But what distinguishes Tutuola's work from that of Bunyan and Dante is perhaps more significant than the similarities they share. Notably, *The Palm-Wine Drinkard* lacks anything of the sense of explicit moral purpose to which *Pilgrim's Progress* and *The Divine Comedy* are dedicated. Especially in contrast with the latter work, Tutuola's masterpiece is not dedicated to the purpose of summing up, as it were, a body of theological doctrine.

The two works with which *The Palm-Wine Drinkard* has most in common, though in very different ways, are the *Odyssey* and the *Canterbury Tales*. The *Drinkard* shares with the *Odyssey* many of its tale properties, notably the "descent" to the "underworld," wherein that special sense of the marvellous which characterizes the episodes of both Odysseus and the drinkard prevails. There are other points in common as well, chiefly a similarity of character which is to say that both Odysseus and the palm-wine drinkard live by the exercise of their cunning. But there is about the *Odyssey* a greater sense of the particular, and thus to some extent the mythic quality (which is always the more powerful the more nearly it approaches the general) of the *Odyssey* is less marked than that of *The Palm-Wine Drinkard*. Both these two works, and the *Canterbury Tales* as well, are similarly episodic, and they share in common the fact that each of them was written in a "popular" language, Chaucer in English rather than in the French of the Court, Dante in Italian rather than in Latin, and Tutuola in a marked English dialect rather than in Yoruba or in the standard "literary" English his contemporaries learned in their colleges and universities. Further, Tutuola's work has an added feature in common with Chaucer's—an immediacy, a forthrightness, a freshness, and a keen sense of delight, a delight particularly to be seen in the common determination to undertell the touching, the outrageous, the amusing.

Chinua Achebe notes that:

> The English language will be able to carry the weight of my African experience. But it will have to be a new English, still in full communion with its ancestral home but altered to suit its new African surroundings.[2]

This is clearly also how Tutuola has felt about and used the English language. Yet his diction, which is that of the proletariat rather than that of the university graduate, has undoubtedly caused some among his contemporaries to deny him the great esteem he deserves as a major literary artist. Such persons have perhaps been "embarrassed" by his "illiteracies." In this respect, his publishers were kinder and more honest than his African critics. It was the personal decision of Sir Geoffrey Faber[3] that Tutuola's English should not be "normalized," thus permitting a work of major significance to reach the public in all the striking and often breathtaking originality of its prose.

In the long run, however, comparisons of one work with others, particularly when those works are from different cultures, are of limited utility. In the final analysis, any work must stand naked in its own terms before those who come face to face with it in affecting interaction. The greater its universal features—as contrasted with those which are appreciable only by those who are co-cultural with the work—the greater the extent to which the work will win international acceptance. This has been the case with Tutuola's book.

This impressive fact notwithstanding, as well of course as its manifest and numerous other qualities, *The Palm-Wine Drinkard* has been rejected and maligned by those who should have been first to accept it—numerous of Tutuola's contemporaries, notably younger writers. Not only have they slighted the work on the mean basis of the normative considerations of grammar as indicated above, but they have also suggested that *The Palm-Wine Drinkard* is derivative. By such an observation, I suppose the intent has been somehow or other to demean the stature of the work. The sophisticated reader, however, jealously defends those works he values, and he is not to be put off by such observations. He knows there is much to be encountered in world literature that is borrowed. Embarrassment of his contemporaries or mean envy cannot hide the fact that Tutuola's work is rich with imagination (and if that imagination is the imagination of a people, to be encountered elsewhere in their works, it is then surely no less Tutuola's than anybody else's), incredibly inventive, superbly well told, touched with dignity and humor, with the poetic as well as the prosaic, with naiveté and with sophistication, with joy, with pathos, and with a strong appreciation of what is universal in the human condition.

At the other extreme of criticism, I have heard informed people criticize Tutuola because he has gone too far astray from the traditions of the oral tale as told by the Yoruba. Such people, typically Europeans and Americans, feel that Tutuola has not done the traditional tale well because he has not done it "properly." It appears to be the case that Tutuola is to be damned if he does and damned if he doesn't.

In any case, such evaluations, negative or positive, have as little to do with the grounds on which *The Palm-Wine Drinkard* is relevant to our present purposes as they do with the work itself. They constitute merely an interesting added dimension of context to the work's existence. What is of relevance here is solely the fact that the work was created by a Yoruba, and that it is in the narrative tradition of the Yoruba, a fact attested to by Ulli Beier, who points out that typical of the tradition is the use of "bizarre imagery," and the avoidance of moralizing and sentimentalizing. He also points out that in this last respect, in addition to drawing more heavily upon traditional folklore, Tutuola is more Yoruba than Fagunwa, from whom it is asserted Tutuola has somewhat derived.[4] Tutuola further provides the student with a unique advantage— authentic Yoruba narrative "behavior" which is in many significant respects traditional and yet written in English! This English of Tutuola's is as authentic a presentation of the language uses of the Yoruba in the achievement of narrative as is a presentation in Yoruba. I assume that one's method of telling a story is the same whether he does it in one language or in a very different one; he will assert metaphors at the same kinds of places, similarly shape incidents, similarly proportion them and invoke their relationships, and will even tailor the second language somewhat—if he is not a master of its own idiom—along the stylistic lines of that mother tongue he more perfectly knows, much as he will shape the sounds of a second language to conform to the phonemes of his mother tongue.

Even so, the work reflects acculturation. Thus its relationship to the traditional narrative is more nearly the relationship of Lamidi Fakeye, a contemporary carver who works in the tradition but with marked innovations, to the history of Yoruba art than it is that of young sculptors trained at the university to work in the idioms of Europe to that same history, for these, while doubtless influenced by the Yoruba tradition, are consciously and more greatly influenced by Europe. It is more nearly the relationship of a village drummer to the mainstream of Yoruba music than it is that of the music of the modern, symphonic composer Fela Sowande to that same tradition. Tutuola's relationship to the tradition of narrative is thus that of Fakeye to his carving and the traditional drummer to his music; the counterparts of the modern sculptor and Sowande are "university" writers, preeminently exampled by Wole Soyinka.

The mere fact that one searches for Yoruba features in Tutuola's work indicates that what I have said is taken for granted by scholars in the field, that is to say that he is of the tradition but acculturated. Beier's writing of "more Yoruba" and "less Yoruba" as between Tutuola and Fagunwa is a case in point. So is the essay of Bernth Lindfors, a work of admirable scholarly imagination which shows the common presence in contemporary Yoruba rhetoric of certain traditional devices, notably of a "string of hyperboles, the concern with number and amount, the climactic contrast."[5] He also lists as a feature of the traditional rhetoric the use of long strings of appositives and the enumeration of many items, which he calls "inventories."

In gross examination, the most immediately notable feature of *The Palm-Wine Drinkard* is its linear structure comprised of segments of action which are more or less independent of one another. These segments may be said to constitute separate stories, so lacking is any sense of contingency or geneticity in their interrelationships. With respect to one another, then, these segments are more accurately to be characterized as sequential rather than consequential. They are however contingently related to the basic condition of the story, which is the search by the drinkard for his palm-wine tapster. There is little doubt therefore that the work is to be called episodic.

The episodes of the story are of three kinds: those which involve fantastic monsters who attempt to victimize the protagonist—always to be defeated; those which are almost pastoral; and those which constitute the frame of the narrative. The first class of episodes tends toward the bizarre, the second toward the idyllic, and the third toward what we must accept as the "real" world. "The Complete Gentleman" sequence provides an example of the first class, a sequence in which a woman (later the drinkard's wife) is captivated by a handsome man whom she follows home only to learn that he is naught but a skull who has borrowed the various parts of his body and must return them. The sequence in the white tree with the Faithful Mother is one of the two developed idyllic interludes, and it provides the drinkard and his wife with an opportunity for happiness and security—respite from the awful experiences they have already endured and are yet to undergo. Episodes of the frame, and frequent allusions to the chief dramatic purpose of the story which the frame represents, taken together constitute the dramatic center of gravity for the work, while the two other kinds of episodes are constellar, dramatic forces which play about that center of gravity, endowing the total structure with a rhythm of the three forces.

The action of the story is thus constituted of discrete segments, and, as far as concerns the protagonist, these segments furthermore are almost wholly comprised of reactions of the drinkard to situations which have not been brought about as a result of anything he himself has done, save insofar as he made the initial decision to seek and subsequently to persist in his search for his palm-wine tapster. This is to say that as the episodes are not genetically related one to the other, neither are they genetically derived from the actions, the personality, or the free will of the protagonist. This leads to a narrative in which the protagonist persists outside of a dramatic framework described by the exercise of self and free will, with the result that, subjected to the inevitable encounter with bizarre and primarily evil forces which dominate the land in which he finds his adventures, he is subjected to events which are structurally of radically limited kinds. One must note, however, that such limitation does not describe the substantive nature of the experiences he undergoes, for, by content, all that he endures is varied and richly inventive. The universe within which the palm-wine drinkard exists, then, is one characterized by acts which result not from his being but from his circumstance; by acts exerted upon him and to which he responds; by acts which are generically limited even though substantively varied. In a world where the protagonist cannot do as he will but as he must, the range of kinds of actions is limited and the cause of the protagonist's actions is external to himself.

Existence in a world of limited possibilities, most of which amount to a threat to the individual's well being, and where free will is irrelevant to all that happens to one, such existence entails a one-dimensionality of actor. Where reaction and not action is the rule, the scope of motivation is necessarily severely limited; and where what befalls one is universally physical, the development of character interiority is significantly restricted, if indeed it exists at all. The simultaneous operation of these two factors produces actors to match the world in which they find themselves —wooden beings subject to circumstance, victims rather than masters of their fate.

Perhaps it is not necessarily the case that characters who are primarily reactive lack something of believability, but in any case this is markedly true in *The Palm-Wine Drinkard*. Since there is no significant development of the interiority of characters, psychological detail is radically limited. Even where the narrator does acknowledge fear, that fear is asserted rather than created in prose. The actors are one-dimensional, stimulus-response creatures living in a story world whose apparatuses work neatly and inevitably, with precision, without ambiguity, in a world where clean action is all. It follows that the motivation which takes the actors from one action to the next is minimal, simple, and obvious, involving the preservation of one's self and the reduction of his needs. Further the actors exist and the story is enacted within a bizarre world which exists minimally in description and is not at all constituted in the work. Chiefly, this world may be said to exist only because we are presented with assertations to the effect that such and such a bizarre creature has come upon the scene, or that an exotic condition of climate or of scene prevails. Even such assertations are rare, and it is thus readily to be concluded that scene, to the notably limited extent to which it is evoked, is not made integral to the story, and that it does not in any meaningful or believable sense exist. In the first instance it is intension by default, and in the second, as we shall see, contributory as a stratum to the continuity of the work.

As for language, it is marked by assertion rather than by connotation, and by description rather than by enactment. This latter characteristic would seem almost inevitable in view of the absence of any development of interiority and of sense and psychological detail. Imagistic devices are seldom used, and there is little evidence of any exploitation of the connotative edges of words, those which suggest color, texture. What is most notable is the exploitation of speed—though this is more properly to be considered a function of the pacing of actions rather than of language— a keen sense for the bizarre invention, and a propensity toward incredibly and therefore very funny precision, particularly in matters of quantity, size, and price. Thus the drinkard asserts:

> So my father gave me a palm-tree farm which was nine miles square and it contained 560,000 palm-trees, and this palm-wine tapster was tapping one hundred and fifty kegs of palm-wine every morning, but before 2 o'clock p.m., I would have drunk all of it; after that he would go and tap another 75 kegs in the evening, which I would be drinking till morning. (p. 7)

Further, he asserts, his wife:

> . . . used the canoe as "ferry" to carry passengers across the river, the fare for adults was 3d (three pence) and half fare for children. In the evening time, then I changed to a man as before and when we checked the money that my wife had collected for that day, it was £7: 5: 3d. (p. 39)

The total they make for the month is £56: 11: 9d. As for the physical description, the following:

> As we were going further, we did not travel more than one third of a mile on this riverbank, before we saw a big tree which was about one thousand and fifty feet in length and about two hundred feet in diameter. This tree was almost white as if it was painted every day with white paint with all its leaves and also branches. As we were about forty yards away from it, there we noticed that somebody peeped out and was focusing us as if a photographer was focusing somebody. (p. 65)

This striking image of the photographer "focusing" the drinkard and his wife is one of the very few explicit imagistic devices in the entire narrative.

Yet this use of quantification to the point of spurious accuracy constitutes a kind of "metaphoric" (in the traditional, literary sense) device, and although the more traditional classes of such devices are rarely to be encountered, this one of spurious accuracy is rife and rich. There is an effective difference of metaphor function that must be noted in passing, however. Whereas images are traditionally used in Western literature to suggest something of the nature of the unusual by creating some of its parameters in metaphor and simile, here in contrast by means of spurious accuracy, the bizarre is made discrete and familiar in this strange world Tutuola has created for us. The image is therefore in fact a kind of anti-image.

This use of the precise hyperbole is to be seen as an expression of the drive toward concreteness, and it is, one suspects, a traditional Yoruba narrative device. Certainly it is used equally by Tutuola and Fagunwa, as Lindfors demonstrates with the following excerpt from *The Forest of a Thousand Daemons:*

> My name is Akara-ogun, Compound-of-Spells, one of the formidable hunters of a bygone age. My own father was a hunter, he was also a great one for medicines and spells. He had a thousand powder gourdlets, eight hundred *ato,* and his amulets numbered six hundred. Two hundred and sixty incubi lived in that house and the birds of divination were without number. It was the spirits who guarded the house when he was away, and no one dared enter that house when my father was absent—it was unthinkable.[6]

The precise hyperbole is not only quantitative, however. Tutuola (and Fagunwa as well) resorts to visual hyperbole as well, as indeed he must if he is to communicate the bizarre creatures which inhabit his forests.

But it is something more than the mere fact of necessity that one notes in Tutuola's writing—it is a positive delight in the astounding invention. Here is the famous description of the red fish from *The Palm-Wine Drinkard:*

> . . . its head was just like a tortoise's head, but it was as big as an elephant's head and it had over 30 horns and large eyes which surrounded the head. All these horns were spread out as an umbrella. It could not walk but was only gliding on the ground like a snake and its body was just like a bat's body and covered with long red hair like strings. It could only fly to a short distance, and if it shouted a person who was four miles away would hear. All the eyes which

surrounded its head were closing and opening at the same time as if a man was pressing a switch on and off. (pp. 79–80)

Such devices deliver us into a world of hard concreteness and sharp definition, one that is an intensive universe of discrete entities. But it is interesting to note that clarity of delineation and physical individuation do not have actional counterparts. The most bizarre monster yet acts *generically,* in much the same way that is expected of any monster. The monster is thus in no sense individuated in terms of his own, unique monster-ness. What is achieved by this drive toward precision and concreteness of the physical world is the evocation of the *category* of the specific rather than the specific itself. The affecting result of this process is that the unique is physically but not affectingly realized. On the contrary, it is the power of the general that is invoked. This amounts to a kind of paradox, and this paradox is a category of devices properly to be considered under the heading of the inhibition of range in the affecting medium of language in narrative.

The dramatic result of paradox is tension, and there is a system of such paradox-derived tensions in *The Palm-Wine Drinkard.* Take for example the situation near the end of the book where the drinkard is chased by the mountain-creatures. In order to escape, the drinkard:

... changed my wife into the wooden-doll as usual, then I put it into my pocket, and they saw her no more.

But when she had disappeared from their presence they told me to find her out at once and grew annoyed by that time, so I started to run away for my life because I could not face them to fight at all. As I was running away from them, I could not run more than 300 yards before the whole of them caught me and surrounded me there; of course, before they could do anything to me, I myself had changed into a flat pebble and was throwing myself along the way to my home town. (pp. 116–117)

The paradox involved in transforming one's wife and possessions into something one can carry and subsequently changing one's self into a pebble, then throwing one's self is that between the probable and the improbable, the possible and the impossible which typically occurs in the book. Further, there is the paradox which results when the discrete meets the universal, a situation which prevails when the drinkard encounters "Dance," "Drum," and "Song," who aid him in his troubles with his monstrous son.

When "Drum" started to beat himself it was just as if he was beaten

by fifty men, when "Song" started to sing, it was just as if a hundred
people were singing together ... (p. 38)

Subsequently he encounters "Band" and "Spirit of Prey." Further, although these are somewhat different phenomena, in that they are not
"Platonic" abstractions, yet they meet "images" of themselves and per-
sonifications of "Land" and "Heaven." The structure of these encounters
running through the story creates a rhythmic counterpoint to the total
structure which provides a dynamic factor of some importance.

Involved in these paradoxes is the affecting medium of relationship,
for paradox implies contradiction and contradiction cannot exist without
parts in interrelationship. Paradox is to be conceived of as a relationship
in range, rather than in duration, and I have already said that its intent
is to establish dynamics of tension. But because the terms of the paradoxes
exist within the boundaries of a wildly improbable and circumstantial
universe where the extraordinary is ordinary, their impact is by no means
as great as it would be were they to appear in a more orderly, more
"logical" context.

This is true also of the relationships which cement the work into a
durational whole. Facts are not always related only in terms of simple
cause-effect relationships. The Faithful Mother in the white tree is a sister
of the Red King, but the Red King asserts that his whole family, indeed
all his people, were turned red and sent to the place where they now
reside. Now there is no mention of the Faithful Mother's being red, and
so we assume she is not, for such an extraordinary fact would have been
mentioned by Tutuola, who never fails to note the outlandish whenever
it is possible to do so. On the other hand, neither are we given the circumstances under which she became other than red. Those numerous
instances in which the drinkard is threatened with death also fall under
this a-causal relationship, for he knows, as well as do his readers, that it
is—as he often reminds himself—impossible for him to die since he has
sold his death, and thus the threat of death is meaningless to him. The
situation is not wholly reduced by the fact that he did not sell his fear,
and thus is yet able to be afraid, for the fact of the matter is that he yet
seems to entertain the prospect of death as a reasonable one. There are
numerous instances in which actions are joined one to the other by means
of relationships which defy the ordinary logic of the orderly procedure
of human action.

Intension/Extension

We are here concerned with the question of range in *The Palm-Wine Drinkard,* such that if there may be said to be noticeable range in the situationality, language, relationality, and experience of the work we may say of it that it is extensive, whereas if the opposite is true we may say only that it is intensive.

With respect to the question of range as an inventory of classes of situations and of kinds of action-actor patterns, we have already noted that there are but three classes of actions which occur in the narrative, those which constitute the frame of the work, those which are idyllic, and those predominating ones which involve experiences with monsters. Even if we remove some of the generalization involved in this last and most numerous category, removing the consideration from so structural a level and glimpsing something of the particularities of experience, we see that there is little significant differentiation among the episodes with the monsters. The monster is always physically remarkable, always threatening to the welfare of the narrator, always outwitted by the narrator. The pattern of action-actor relationships is such that preponderantly the protagonist responds to actions initiated by agents other than himself.

The actors themselves also exhibit markedly limited variety. There are the good characters and the evil ones, and there is no significant moral shading, with the result that none of them is morally problematic. Their motivations are of limited variety as well, involving primarily action from the monsters and reaction from the narrator and his wife. The use of details of sense and psychology in scene and character creation are so minimally used that there is little point even to mentioning them here.

The situation is not markedly different for language. Only one kind of "imagistic" device is typically used, that of the precise hyperbole which we have described as an anti-image. As for diachronic relationships, it may be said that these tend to display greater variety than is characteristic of the other media, for in durational terms not only does cause beget adequate and predictable effect in many instances, but in others it does not. Examples of the first sort are commonplace, and even those of the second are numerous. But perhaps these latter ones require an example or two since they are far and away less common in narrative. The fact that the narrator and his wife produce a monster for a child, one who grows to maturity within days and who outstrips his parents, relegating them to the role of servants, is such an a-causally related eventuation. So also are the relationships among the various episodes a-causal. These relationships contrast with even the most remarkable of the other kinds of events in the narrative, for as bizarre as they might be, they yet are rooted in causality, either in the power of the narrator's juju (such as the magical transformations) or in the nature of the peculiar laws of the spiritual world of the bush (the strange habits of the deads).

The synchronic dimension of relationality lacks careful definition and integration. There is thus no necessary relationship between the kinds of monstrosity of character, of which there is great variety if not great range, and the kinds of actions those monsters commit. Neither is particularity of place related to the kind of action which occurs, nor even the general place (i.e., the bush of monsters and the Town of the Deads), for the prodigious, the strange, and the magical happen as readily in the "real" world of the protagonist's village as they do in the bush of monsters and the Town of the Deads. In short, there is no close exploitation of relational integration such as one would expect of the intensional work, but on the other hand, neither is there the complexity or richness of relationality one would expect to find in the extensive work.

Finally, as for the medium of experience, which we have defined in terms of its relevance to man and his human condition, one can assert only that it is limited, for there is little of universality in the affairs of the drinkard. Raised to the level of Myth, however, the search takes on rich significance for every man.

Range is also to be understood in terms of the "spread" of given instances of the above items, as opposed to their taxonomy. In this connection, one can say only that range is inhibited in nearly every case,[7] the sole exceptions being in two areas: the first of these is in terms of the richness of invention applied to the devising of the physical and behavioral characteristics of the monsters and the deads on the one hand, and the prolific use of the images of discreteness on the other. There is thus a certain amount of extensiveness—of spread—to the medium of language, though as we have suggested, since it is in the direction of concreteness its net effect is intensive. The second area is to be found in the use of language, which since it tends to create a world of the particulate and is used toward the ends of invention rather than of imagination—of artifice rather than of constituting experience—has its focus on the discrete, the specific, the quantified and the evaluated. There is in the work a drive toward precision and clarity, despite the substantive fantasy of the work. The inhibition of imagination, connotation and evocation is an exercise in the direction of the reduction of ambiguity, and is thus an exercise in intension. There is, in short, range in invention if not in imagination—as we here define the term.

Otherwise the draft of the media is shallow. For situation, actions reach but feebly and without marked penetration into the depths of possibility of subtlety, variety, richness of experience and of the exercise of the human fancy. Motivation is neither profound nor revealing and the actors, in large measure because of these factors, are one-dimensional, even though lively, and there is hardly any development at all of the physical world within which actions occur, let alone the careful elaboration of its properties. There is present in the work a radical inhibition of the complexity of causality, with the result that there cannot be said to be any significant range to relationality either. Language, as we have said, denotes rather than connotes.

The philosophical framework within which the work exists is one characterized by the proscription of the exercise of free will. The narrator persists in a world in which he has no choice over what happens to him. But since he endures by his own free will at least, even though in a world where freedom of will is abrogated, he submits to a moral order that is one of imposed and unpredictable outrage. In this world in which free will does not exist, only limited evil can happen—the protagonist cannot die, for example. It is a world in which planned, logical, and genetic action is severely limited if not impossible. The revocation of free will must be seen as the sufficient cause of the action-reaction pattern described earlier as well as of the absence of the meaningful development of motivation. The inhibition of the possibility of doing as one will restricts the volitional world, shrinking the world of will almost to the point of nonexistence. The fact that actions happen to the protagonist does not alter the situation, both by reason of the limited variety of those actions and by reason of the fact that no matter how varied they might conceivably be such variety would not change this fact about the moral universe of the work.

The philosophical nature of *The Palm-Wine Drinkard*, the restriction of range in situation and its properties of scene, actor, action, motivation, in language, and in relationality—all bespeak the influence of a strong drive toward intension in the execution of narrative. All elements which would tend to make acts extensive are avoided—the connotative values of words, the use of imagination as opposed to invention, full-dimensioned characters rather than types, and a full spectrum of human motivations and actions.

Continuity/Discontinuity

The absence of geneticity of relationality characterizes the durational dimension of *The Palm-Wine Drinkard,* which is thus episodic, and, in effect, discontinuous. If this is true, then narrative in this respect negates the mode of continuity we have hypothesized for it, as indeed it negates the argument of the essay, for we have maintained the existence of an affecting system of similetic equivalents as a condition of a homogeneous culture. We have assumed late, traditional Yoruba culture to have such homogeneity, at least as far as concerns the affecting presence in it.

But the relevant question now is whether it is the discontinuity between episodes which is affectingly important, or whether it is that episodicism itself. The former is suggested to be false by the test of system (which is the case in the other forms), while the latter would appear to be affirmed by the same test, for in the other forms we have seen continuity asserted not in the way Europeans and Americans should have chosen—which is to say by means of long lines of through-development—but rather atomistically, for in the temporal works of the Yoruba, continuity is to be seen as a function of the density of multiple, discrete parts. Continuity as a function of a high frequency of discrete integers can be achieved in narrative only by means of the episodic, and in order to come into being the episodic requires a certain amount of disjuncture with respect to the relationships among its components and their immediate contexts.

Looked at somewhat differently, the situation amounts to this: we cannot regard the discontinuity of episodicism as an important feature in its own terms, since discontinuity defines the conditions under which episodicism may be said to exist. Were we to stress the fact of discontinuity as of critical import, we should have to deny to those peoples, who in their affecting works assert the mode of continuity, the possibility of creating an episodic work. We should therefore have to run the risk of denying the possibility of much of oral literature, for it is obvious that the conditions of oral tale telling are such as to be favorable to the generation of the episodic. *The Palm-Wine Drinkard,* then, is to be seen as achieving continuity through density, in much the same way, which is to say as a similetic equivalent to the way in which the discrete beats of drumming occur with such dense frequency as to create a temporal "solid," or continuity.

This, I think, is our most important evidence in support of the continuity of Tutuola's work, and it thus defends the integrity and ultimately the reality of the system we have described. There is other evidence, how-ever. There are in the work certain constants which clearly indicate a drive toward continuity. At least five of these constants can be readily identi-fied, and doubtless the researches of others would reveal even more.

    1. The constancy of the improbable. The total, durational fabric of the work is to be characterized by a markedly high frequency of appearance of the remarkable, the wondrous, the unlikely—the im-probable, in short.

    2. The constancy of the permanence of the narrator. One means by this not only the constancy of point of view as a technical device of executing the narrative, but also—and indeed primarily—the constancy of the dramatic value of knowing that the protagonist, having sold his death, is bound to endure.

    3. The constancy of the generalized character of the event. We have adequately discussed this point elsewhere in connection with the absence of individuation.

    4. The constancy of the contrast between the real world of the reader and the fanciful one of the narrative. This is perhaps best regarded as the equivalent in scene of the improbability of event discussed under the first entry above.

    5. The constancy of the frame. It is above all the unity of protag-onist and of purpose which demonstrates the narrative's drive toward continuity.

But continuity through density is achieved not only by means of the episodic characteristics of the work. There is a noticeable drive toward the proliferation of entities that gives further support to the view that with respect to duration the esthetic of the Yoruba is expressive of the atomistic approach to continuity. Doubtless this is conditioned by the predominance of percussive instruments in music, which (save for the pressure drum) cannot sustain sound, and by the basically oral nature of the narrative, including *The Palm-Wine Drinkard* of which it may justifiably be main-tained that the fact that it is written is purely accidental to its nature.

How else does one explain the frequency of the precise hyperbole? Does one maintain that it is only a nonfunctional, decorative element found as a characteristic of the execution of the language of Yoruba narrative, or does one assume on the contrary that there is some reason for having opted for this out of all possible kinds of images—indeed out of all kinds of hyperbole? Reason would seem to me to argue in support of the latter alternative, and when one says that one drinks seventy-five barrels of palm-wine of an evening rather than "some," or "a great quantity," or even "barrels," one is stressing the atomistic aspect of the situation—he is searching for the proliferation of entities, composing the situation of its bits and pieces and calling attention to them..

It is doubtful, given the nature of the content of the narrative, whether one can maintain that the invention of the story, essential as it is to create the bizarre with which the story is concerned, reflects in any direct way the imperative toward atomistic density. Yet one cannot help but note that there seems to be a kind of special interest in the particulateness of the monsters' enormities, so inventively are they made, so lovingly are they noted. In order to demonstrate this, I merely invite the reader's attentions to the description of the Red Fish quoted earlier above.

An excellent instance of the interest in the particulate is to be seen in the following:

> My wife had said of the woman we met: "She was not a human-being and she was not a spirit, but what was she?" She was the Red-smaller-tree who was at the front of the bigger Red-tree, and the bigger Red-tree was the Red-king of the Red-people of Red-town and the Red-bush and also the Red-leaves on the bigger Red-tree were the Red-people of the Red-town in the Red-bush. (p. 83, punctuated thus.)

It is difficult to doubt that in this passage, which is perhaps the most remarkable one (for the terms of our discussion) in the entire work, Tutuola takes delight in being as specific as he can, in maximizing every opportunity to give to his prose a density of discrete reference which indeed is contributory to *constituting* the mode of continuity in the work.

I am not the first to mention the "drumming" feature of the contemporary Yoruba popular prose style. Ulli Beier says of Fagunwa, "He is a master of rhetoric, who can make repetitions and variations swing in a mounting rhythm, like Yoruba drumming."[8] One notes this same characteristic in Tutuola—in the passage quoted immediately above, in the pace of his inventions, in the rhythm of his actions, and in his regulation of pace with the diminuendo effect brought about by the inclusion of idyllic interludes. But the work of Tutuola is like drumming in more respects than these, for the narrative exists in terms of its properties of situation and language, its system of tensions, its relationality, the contrasts between its world and the world of the reader, between the general and the specific, the probable and the improbable. These various voices, like the voices of different drums, assert their own drives toward continuity and one has an interwoven structure therefore, all contributing their strata of particulate reality to the general density by which the continuity of the narrative is constituted.

All that *The Palm-Wine Drinkard* esthetically *is* is to be accounted for by that network of synapses and interstices (which feeling ultimately fills in) comprised of the nerves of media and properties I have identified. The affecting reality of the work is this, and nothing more. Who wrote it, under what circumstances, his role in society, the identity and social placement of his readers, their opinions of the work as to its quality, originality, and impact—all such considerations, while of undoubted import in other considerations, are irrelevant here.

As one would expect, *The Palm-Wine Drinkard* actualizes the Yoruba esthetic as it has been described in this essay, owing its affecting existence to the discipline of those same principles of intensive continuity as characterize the other forms of the affecting presence. To be sure, intensive continuity has determined the nature of the narrative's media in ways proper to narrative.

Those conditions of the affecting media which express or execute intension, as well as those which express or execute continuity, are esthemes. The contributions these esthemes make toward the systemic whole are such that, even more surely than was the case after we concluded our examinations of sculpture, dance, and music, we may speak of intension and continuity as para-esthemes of the part and of intensive-continuity as the para-estheme of the whole. The estheme of the whole in *The Palm-Wine Drinkard* is obviously that confluence of the expression of intension and continuity such that the work may be demonstrated to exhibit intensive continuity.

There can be no doubt that Amos Tutuola is closer to the traditional esthetic of the Yoruba than are those of his contemporaries who have turned to the novel. This is a relative estate at best, to be sure, for the traditional culture has been heavily acculturated. One would expect therefore, upon further study, to perceive a continuum of "Yorubaness," extending from Tutuola at the deeply Yoruba end to Wole Soyinka at the more Europeanized, modernized end, with T. M. Aluko standing somewhere in between.

Raised to the level of the culture area, at least as far as concerns those writers publishing in English, one would expect to explain in terms of the suasion of the traditional esthetic many of the characteristic "flaws" or "shortcomings" Europeans often appear to see in the West African practice of narrative. Thus episodicism is to be seen as the affecting desire to achieve continuity by means of a density of discrete elements rather than by the attenuation of long lines of dramatic—actional, psychological—development. "Shallowness" of draft, lowness of modelling in the delineation of characters and of scene development, is to be seen as the exercise of the imperative to achieve intensity—that on the one hand, and on the other hand as the drive toward the generalized presentation of character, the concern with the type, the role.

All West African, English-speaking writers show these characteristics to one degree or another, and that critic who fails to take into account the operation of the imperatives of an esthetic *system* at the unconscious, cultural level practices the art of criticism irresponsibly. One can only wonder what innovations might have been wrought in the perpetration of narrative if the writers of West Africa had pursued and developed their craft in accordance with the dictates of their traditional esthetic.

FOOTNOTES

[1] Amos Tutuola, *The Palm-Wine Drinkard* (London: Faber and Faber, paper, 1962).

[2] Chinua Achebe, "English and the African Writer," *Transition* 18 (1965), p. 30.

[3] Told to me through personal communication.

[4] Ulli Beier, "Fagunwa: A Yoruba Novelist," *Black Orpheus* 17 (1965), pp. 52, 54.

[5] Bernth Lindfors, "Characteristics of Yoruba and Igbo Prose Styles in English," (Paper given at seminar on Contemporary African Literatures held at the annual meeting of the Modern Language Association of America, New York, December 27, 1968), p. 5.

[6] Daniel O. Fagunwa, *The Forest of a Thousand Daemons: A Hunter's Saga*, trans. Wole Soyinka (London: Nelson, 1968), p. 9.

[7] See the outline of the features of range of these various respects in the preceding table.

[8] Beier, "Fagunwa," p. 53.

CULTURAL NORMS AND MODES OF PERCEPTION IN ACHEBE'S FICTION

Lloyd W. Brown

As Frantz Fanon has reminded us, the colonial experience has invested definitions of culture with a special significance. Generally, the exploitation of language "means above all to assume a culture, to support the weight of a civilization." And whenever any colonized people faces the language of the "civilizing nation" it is confronted with the "culture of the mother country." The colonized man is "elevated above his jungle status in proportion to his adoption of the mother country's cultural standards."[1] More recently, the West Indian novelist George Lamming has examined the cultural significance of language within the context of Shakespeare's well-known colonial archetypes: Caliban is Prospero's convert to "civilization," after having been "colonized by language, and excluded by language." Language is only Caliban's way of serving Prospero, and the latter's instruction in a "civilized" tongue is his way of measuring the distance which separates him from Caliban.[2]

Of course these findings are not really new. The European's ethnocentric definitions of "language" and "civilization" have always been fairly self-evident. In presenting Caliban as a brutish savage without a language (and civilization) of his own, *The Tempest* remains faithful to the philosophical assumptions of Shakespeare's culture. And Bernard Mandeville is a representative spokesman for that myth-making process which served the causes of eighteenth century slavery and colonization: on the one hand, the mindless savage in the "wild State of Nature" is defined by his lack of even rudimentary language skills; and on the other hand, "civilization" *par excellence* is embodied by the language of Europe's courtly *beau monde*.[3]

However, reminders like Fanon's or Lamming's are timely; for they do underline those cultural and emotional tensions which are inherent in the ex-colonial's use of the metropolitan language, but which are often obscured or ignored by a paternalistic preoccupation with the African's

131

European grammar. The syntax of the African who writes in English has been the object of exhaustive studies—with the usual ethnocentric caveats against the African's possible, or actual, liberties with the mother country's tongue.[4] And in a less perscriptive, more useful, vein both Western and African critics have repeatedly demonstrated the techniques whereby the African novelist has modified his English in order to "translate" the characteristic patterns of his native culture.[5] But European languages in African literature also function in a highly dramatic sense that results from their old colonizing roles. The ex-colonial writer is consistently ambivalent towards the metropolitan tongue. On the one hand, it is the historical tool with which his colonial status was shaped and the indigenous traditions of his "jungle" distorted. And, on the other hand, this alien tongue is the useful *lingua franca* through which he reaches his discrete readership in Europe and Africa.

But above all, English, French, or Portuguese is the old colonial badge which simultaneously recalls the exclusivism of Prospero the colonist, and gives voice to Caliban's cultural revolution. The ex-colonial transforms the cultural "burden" of the mother country's language into the means of expressing a sense of human identity, and of liberating his modes of self-perception. On the archetypal level, George Lamming's interpretation of Caliban's revolt in *The Tempest* projects Shakespeare's character as an unintended symbol of the ex-colonial. The gift of Prospero's language has made Caliban "aware of possibilities."[6] And in the day-to-day tactics of political revolution, the metropolitan language continues to enjoy this dramatic ambiguity. As Fanon has demonstrated, the Algerian rebels transmuted French from "a vehicle of the oppressing power" into "an instrument of liberation." In psychopathological terms, the Algerians exorcised the "automatic character of insult and malediction" from French: "Under these conditions, the French language, the language of the occupier, was given the role of *Logos,* with ontological implications within Algerian society."[7]

Finally, contemporary studies have generalized on the *literary* significance of the tensions created by the historical relationship between the ex-colonial and his European language. According to Mercer Cook, "Taking the white man's language, dislocating his syntax, recharging his words with new strength and sometimes with new meaning before hurling them back in his teeth, while upsetting his self-righteous complacency and clichés, our poets rehabilitate such terms as Africa and blackness, beauty and peace."[8] And in his preface to Frantz Fanon's *Wretched of the Earth,*

Jean-Paul Sartre notes the fundamental irony of the ex-colonial's literature: "An ex-native, French-speaking, bends that language to new re-
quirements, makes use of it, and speaks to the colonized only."[9]

However, useful as these generalizations are, they do not exhaust the
implications, for each writer, of the relationship between African literature and the psychopathology of language. It now remains to investigate
the precise effects of that relationship upon the characteristic themes and
individual development of specific authors. Chinua Achebe is an apt
choice in this regard, for the Nigerian's fiction demonstrates his preoccupation with language, not simply as a communicative device, but as a
total cultural experience. At this level, language is not merely technique.
It is the embodiment of its civilization and therefore represents or dramatizes modes of perception within its cultural grouping. Accordingly, the
white man's failure to understand African customs in *Things Fall Apart*
is bound up with his ignorance of the African's language.[10] In other
words, Achebe seizes upon the perceptual values represented by an alien
European culture and its language, then exploits these criteria to portray
external conflicts between the African and the white colonialist, or to
project the internal crises of African society.

On the whole, therefore, the familiar tensions generated by the African's use of his European language do not only dramatize the cultural
conflicts represented by Caliban's archetypal rebellion. They also emphasize the underlying problems of cultural perceptions (ethnocentric or
otherwise) which are inherent in the colonial functions of the metropolitan tongue, and which are a paradigm of the universal problems of human
insight and judgement. Or, as Jamaica's Andrew Salkey has pointed out,
the ex-colonial's heritage of language is bound up with his total perception of self and humanity. It embodies his *Weltanschauung*. Hence Catullus Kelly, the hero of Salkey's latest novel, has a "two-way *Weltanschauung*: his Kingston-dialect mood, and his Standard English mood."
The former allows Kelly to detach himself completely from Western
standards as he uses his Jamaican Negro dialect to ridicule the sterile
austerity of Euro-American "progress." And in the latter mood he dons
the serious-mindedness of the Westerner's scientific rationalism in order
to subvert this civilization from within.[11]

Achebe's interest in the relationship between cultural norms and per-
ceptual values is also comparable with yet another ex-colonial novelist—
Ferdinand Oyono of the French Cameroons. In *Houseboy*, for example,
Oyono's hero, Toundi Onduoa, embodies a fundamental irony. He grows

into self-awareness and human self-identification in direct proportion to his initiation into the colonial language—into cultural norms which do not recognize his humanity, and which are geared to stifle his self-consciousness. Thus the literacy which he acquires from the French missionaries provides Toundi with the literary and morphological keys to the white colonist's modes of perception and behavior. Father Gilbert's diary is a "grain-store for memories." It preserves and re-enacts the sadistic impulses of the colonist who is incapable of apprehending his victims as human beings: "These white men can preserve everything. In Father Gilbert's diary I found the kick he gave me when he caught me mimicking him in the sacristy. I felt by bottom burning all over again."[12] And when Toundi demonstrates his mastery of European customs by keeping his own diary (in the Ewondo dialect), he has, in effect, transformed the self-serving literacy of the egocentric colonist into a legitimate tool for the expression of his maturing personality. For Toundi's fictional diary serves as the narrative of *Houseboy* itself. In transferring the literary norms of the colonist's language to his own writing, in using this medium to subvert white ethnocentrism in favor of the African's self-perception, Oyono's Toundi symbolizes the creative imagination of the ex-colonial writer.

Neither is it difficult to trace the links between Achebe and Oyono's literary archetype. Like Toundi, the Nigerian novelist consciously expropriates the European's literary techniques, and related perceptual values, in order to postulate an African, or even anti-European, point of view. Hence he consistently borrows European historiography in order to explode the notorious Western myth that Africans have no history. The title of the first novel, *Things Fall Apart*, announces Achebe's fairly obvious debt to Yeats's poem, "The Second Coming" (1921). In Yeats's work the vision of human history projects a succession of gyres, of epochal cycles in which the pre-Christian era gives way to the age ushered in by Christ's first coming, and the Christian phase must be followed in turn by a new and terrifyingly unknown cycle—by the new "cradle" and the new "Bethlehem" of another era or "coming." Achebe's nineteenth century Africa witnesses the end of an era and the beginning of twentieth century Europeanization, with all its implied consequences for yet another stage—the future history of postcolonial Africa.

But these very parallels between Yeats and Achebe are a source of irony, for they touch upon those characteristic tensions which govern the relationship between the ex-colonial writer and the metropolitan culture. Yeats's subject, history, and the rich associations of past events which the poet evokes through the Judaeo-Christian symbols of the "first" coming—all these belong to that area of human experience and understanding from which the myths of Christian Europe have always excluded the African. Namely, in evoking Yeats's themes, Achebe implies that the sense of history and tradition, the burdens of cultural continuity, decay, and rebirth, have all been the African's lot as well as the Westerner's. And in the process the novelist has exploited the European's cultural criteria—his literature and historiography—in order to reverse the white man's exclusivist definitions of history and culture.

In his second novel, *No Longer At Ease*, Achebe establishes an equally ironic relationship with T. S. Eliot's "The Journey of the Magi." The poem is among several (including *The Waste Land*) in which Eliot bases his themes and structure on what he called the "historical sense"—"the sense of the timeless as well as the temporal and of the timeless and of the temporal together." This involves "a perception, not only of the pastness of the past, but of its presence."[13] Accordingly, "The Journey of the Magi" dramatizes the successive epochs of Christian history which seem to coalesce in the Wise Men's recollection of the Nativity. The birth of the Christ-child is the death of the pagan, pre-Christian order. Moreover, His crucifixion heralds the birth of a new morality. And the personal conversion of the magi implies that the transitions and conflicts represented by this Birth and Death will be repeated in future confrontations between the new faith and the old dispensation:

> this Birth was
> Hard and bitter agony for us, like Death, our death.
> We returned to our places, these Kingdoms,
> But no longer at ease here, in the old dispensation,
> With an alien people clutching their gods.
> I should be glad of another death.

Obi Okonkwo, the hero of *No Longer At Ease*, is a twentieth century magus. As the graduate of a British university he has been sufficiently Westernized to feel alienated from the old dispensation of his Nigerian background. But Obi's self-conflicts are not an isolated individual experience. Achebe requires us to view his hero through the sense of simultaneity which Eliot attributes to historical perception. Hence Obi's story reincarnates the tragedy of his grandfather Okonkwo. Obi's individualism has alienated him from family and tribe, just as Okonkwo's fierce pride frequently brought him into conflict with his fellow villagers in Umuofia.

Obi is destroyed by simultaneous pressures from two incompatible worlds —the old Africa of his Umuofia village and the Westernized milieu of urban Africa. And before him, Okonkwo had succumbed to both the internal tensions of his own society and the external impact of the growing British presence.

The parallels between Obi and Okonkwo are implied by Nwoye (Obi's father) in his story of the old Umuofia warrior. But these implications go beyond the immediate context of *No Longer At Ease*; for in recalling Okonkwo's life, Nwoye has really recapitulated the narrative of the preceding novel, *Things Fall Apart*. On the whole, therefore, the themes of *No Longer At Ease* exploit that sense of simultaneity which Eliot derives from historical perception in "The Journey of the Magi": the historical cycles of Christendom's own history are evoked by the titular reference to Eliot's magi; they are linked to, and made contemporaneous with, successive conflicts between Christianity and paganism in *Things Fall Apart* and *No Longer At Ease*; and finally, these recurrent cycles coalesce and are internalized in Obi's personal conflicts as an African magus.

But in exploiting Eliot's poetic archetypes and philosophy, Achebe subjects these European models to the same kind of ironic manipulation which marks his relationship with Yeats's work in *Things Fall Apart*. For he uses the perceptual implications of Eliot's "historical sense" in order to invest paganism with a sympathetic identity. Whereas Eliot, the orthodox Christian, sees the conflict between the old paganism and the new Christianity in clear moral terms, Achebe the African insists that the "old dispensation," as well as Christianity, had its own beauty and human dignity. Consequently, traditionalist Africans in Obi's world are the victims of cultural unease and disintegration, just as much as the African magus himself. They are unable to make the communal ideals of African humanism effective in what is now an alien society based on the divisive individualism of Western modernity. In keeping with the old ways they expect to share the prestige and advantages of Obi's Civil Service post because they underwrote the cost of his education. But the very life-style which they have opened to him has destroyed this communal link with their protégé. And their failure with Obi demonstrates *their* unease with the "new" dispensation.

To sum up, Achebe accepts the historiographic principle which allows Eliot to telescope multiple cycles of history into one moment, to compress repetitive conflicts between Christendom and paganism, or between hostile cultures, into a single event or personal experience. But Achebe also exploits this material in order to assert the validity of pagan values which the Christian feels impelled to minimize or deny. And on an ethnological level, the operation of the historical sense in *No Longer At Ease* is invested with the same irony that influences the handling of Yeats's "Second Coming" in *Things Fall Apart*. Once again, European historiography has been used to articulate that sense of tradition and history which, according to Western myths, is alien to the "dark" continent. And, particularly in his second novel, the irony with which Achebe manipulates the Westerner's historical perception is intensified by the dynamics of African society itself. For when we have cleared away the cobwebs with which Western "experts" have obscured the very existence of African history, it is clear that the kind of historical sense which Eliot applies to Western culture and literature has a special appeal to the African.

The structure and functions of African society define the individual's identity within a cosmic context which approximates Eliot's synthesis of the "timeless" and the "temporal," the past and the present. Hence the simultaneous existence which Eliot imparts to different eras through the historical sense is comparable with that "logic of love" which Léopold Senghor attributes to the old traditions of African society: "The feeling of communion in the family and the community is projected backwards into time, and also into the transcendental world, to the ancestors, to the spirits and, unconsciously, to God." The supernatural and the temporal, the past and the present, all unite in the African's self-awareness. He is "held in a tight network of vertical and horizontal communities, which bind and at the same time support him."[14] Generally, therefore, whenever Achebe draws upon English literature for his titles and themes, he adheres to the familiar strategy of the ex-colonial's cultural revolution: he uses the literary traditions of the English tongue to liberate the African's identity and history from the ethnocentric images that have been enshrined in the psychopathology of the colonizer's language. The ironic manipulation of Prospero's culture has reversed the colonist's modes of perception.

Apart from Achebe's titles, this ironic relationship with his English medium is seldom obtrusive in the first two novels. But, especially in *Things Fall Apart*, there are occasional episodes which leave no doubt about the ambivalence with which the novelist regards the cultural standards and literary traditions embodied by the English language. The most notable of these incidents is the concluding scene of the novel when the white District Commissioner plans a book about his colonial experience—*The Pacification of the Primitive Tribes of the Lower Niger*. Okonkwo's suicide has attracted the Commissioner's literary genius. "Every day brought him some new material. The story of this man who had killed a messenger and hanged himself would make interesting reading. One could almost write a whole chapter on him. Perhaps not a whole chapter but a reasonable paragraph, at any rate. There was so much to include, and one must be firm in cutting out details" (p. 187).

The District Commissioner is an archetype of those numerous Europeans, particularly missionaries and administrators, whose instant expertise on Africa has contributed to the Westerner's profound ignorance of the continent. And the ethnocentric bias of the Commissioner's imperial handbook underlines the historical inability of the Western scholar to emancipate himself from the usual perspectives on African "primitives."

But here, too, Achebe's handling of the colonizer's viewpoint is influenced by the ironic ambiguity with which the African novelist invests his European tools. The white colonist lacks the capacity to perceive the human dimensions of Okonkwo's tragedy. Thus the anthropological machinery of the Commissioner's book will reduce the Ibo warrior to a sensational paragraph on the irrational violence of the "savage." But Achebe's historical novel has used this same machinery to present the "primitive" as a complex human being who reflects, and is a part of, Africa's history.

Thus the anthropological framework of Achebe's narrative clarifies the moral and cultural significance of Okonkwo's suicide: "It is an offence against the Earth, and a man who commits it will not be buried by his clansmen. His body is evil, and only strangers may touch it" (p. 186). Okonkwo's death dramatizes the dominant impulses of his life: it is the culmination of a self-destructive pride, but it is also the inevitable outcome of the demoralizing effects of the new order. In effect, the anthropological background of Okonkwo's death projects the tragedy as an apocalypse: the old Africa with all its beauty and power is crumbling under the simultaneous pressures of white imperialism from without, and self-destructive forces from within. But when these social data and cultural judgements are presented to the white anthropologist, he distorts them because of his narrow perspectives. The tragedy and the taboos surrounding the dead Okonkwo can therefore be seen only on the basis of some self-serving point of colonial etiquette: "a District Commissioner must never attend to such undignified details as cutting down a hanged man from the tree. Such attention would give the natives a poor opinion of him. In the book he planned to write he would stress that point" (p. 187).

Altogether then, the episode of Okonkwo's death dramatizes the degree to which Achebe heightens our awareness of perceptual conflicts between two civilizations by exploiting the literary and cultural media of one group. The ethnocentric criteria of the European and the complex humanity of the African's past are both illuminated through the once self-serving methods of Western historiography and anthropology. Furthermore, Achebe's religious themes emphasize this relationship between conflicting viewpoints and cultural standards, especially when the latter are embodied by differences in language. Hence, in *Things Fall Apart*, the hostile judgements of an alien Christianity are brought to Umuofia through African interpreters whose strange dialect becomes symbolic of their role. Like the French missionaries in Oyono's *Houseboy*, Achebe's African Christians are embarrassed by unintended vulgarities or obscenities whenever they use the dialect of the pagan and the unconverted: "Many people laughed at his dialect and the way he used words strangely. Instead of saying 'myself' he always said 'my buttocks'. . . . He told them that they worshipped false gods of wood and stone" (p. 131). And when the white missionary debates religion with Umuofia's Akunna the absurdities of the interpreter's earlier malapropisms merge into a tragicomic impasse—into an exercise in non-communication over which the suggestive figure of the interpreter presides:

"You say that there is one supreme God who made heaven and earth," said Akunna on one of Mr. Brown's visits. "We also believe in Him and call Him Chukwu. He made all the world and the other gods."

"There are no other gods," said Mr. Brown. "Chukwu is the only God and all others are false. You carve a piece of wood—like that one" (he pointed at the rafters from which Akunna's carved *Ikenga* hung), "and you call it a god. But it is still a piece of wood."

"Yes," said Akunna. "It is indeed a piece of wood. The tree from which it came was made by Chukwu, as indeed all minor gods were. But He made them for His messengers so that we could approach Him through them. It is like yourself. You are the head of your church."

"No," protested Mr. Brown. "The head of my church is God Himself."

". . . We appear to pay greater attention to the little gods but that is not so. We worry them more because we are afraid to worry their

Master. Our fathers knew that Chukwu was the Overlord and that is why many of them gave their children the name Chukwuka—'Chukwu is Supreme.' "

"You said one interesting thing," said Mr. Brown. "You are afraid of Chukwu. In my religion Chukwu is a loving Father and need not be feared by those who do His will."

"But we must fear Him when we are not doing His will," said Akunna. "And who is to tell His will? It is too great to be known."

In this way Mr. Brown learnt a good deal about the religion of the clan (pp. 162–163).

Achebe's footnote to the discussion is ironic, for Mr. Brown's grasp of the Ibo religion does not include real understanding or a sympathetic recognition of the African's morality. The missionary's "lesson" is merely an intellectual insight into the dynamics of a culture that he is determined to destroy. The European's ignorance of African languages (and culture) therefore complements the ethnocentric bias of his Christianity. And this connection between white religion and cultural perception is demonstrated by the pathological implications of the *European's* language. Mr. Brown's successor, the Rev. James Smith, "saw things as black and white. And black was evil. He saw the world as a battlefield in which the children of light were locked in mortal conflict with the sons of darkness" (p. 166).

The description of the Rev. Smith is crucial to an understanding of Achebe's ironic strategy. The deliberate emphasis on "black" and "white" as the familiar cornerstones of white religion demonstrates that the maladictive patterns of the English language are integrated with the European's racial bias and cultural perceptions. The Rev. Smith therefore conforms with the perceptual values which the French scholar Mannoni has ascribed to the colonial traditions embodied by the Prospero-Caliban myth: "What the colonial in common with Prospero lacks, is awareness of the world of others, a world in which Others have to be respected."[15] Thus Europeans like Smith really reverse the perspectives which Senghor attributes to the African's apprehension of reality: "Subjectively, at the end of his antennae, like an insect, he discovers the *Other*. He is *moved* to his bowels, going out in a centrifugal movement from the subject to the object on the waves sent out from the *Other*."[16]

On the whole, therefore, Achebe links the ethnological implications of language to the perceptual conflicts between African and Western cultures. Smith's maledictive English illuminates the colonizer's white exclusivism. And the ironic manipulation of historiographic and literary traditions in the colonial language reverses the European's ethnocentrism: the African's "reason-by-embrace" (as Senghor describes it), his inclusive view of society and history, is articulated through media and cultural definitions which were once used to limit his humanity. At the same time, the external confrontation that is inherent in the cultural significance of language is analogous to the internal conflicts of Achebe's fiction. In *Things Fall Apart* the ethnocentric European is a paradigm of the ego-centricity which initiates a moral crisis within the African community. For, in addition to his power and integrity which reflect the beauty and strength of the old Africa, Okonkwo is fiercely, and destructively, proud. In his own society he lapses into that unawareness of "the world of others" which marks the colonizer's cultural perception. The impending disintegration of the old ways is attributable to an egocentric strain in African heroism as well as to the European's exclusivism. And this parallel between two limited modes of perception is illustrated by Okonkwo's relationship with his son Nwoye.

The heavy hand with which Okonkwo rules his family is due to fear, the fear of resembling his father in "failure and weakness." But in shunning Unoka's vice, idleness, Okonkwo's pride rejects the old man's virtue —gentleness (pp. 12–13). This fearful preoccupation with a certain image of manhood distorts Okonkwo's view of his son's real personality. The self-made man confuses Nwoye's diffidence with "incipient laziness" (p. 13). Nwoye is repelled by his father's equation of masculinity with violence and bloodshed. But he displays his own kind of courage when he elects to join the strange religion of the white Christians, for his conversion is partly in response to the shortcomings of his own society: "It was not the mad logic of the Trinity that captivated him. He did not understand it. It was the poetry of the new religion, something felt in the marrow. The hymn about brothers who sat in darkness and in fear seemed to answer a vague and persistent question that haunted his young soul— the question of the twins crying in the bush and the question of Ikemefuna who was killed" (p. 134).

The "question of Ikemefuna" is crucial, for Ikemefuna's death, at Okonkwo's hands, is the crucial example of the destructive pride, the fearful egocentricity, which compels Okonkwo to prove his "courage" even at the cost of sacrificing a war hostage who had become a member of his own household. The corrosive effects of this sacrilegious act on the relationship between Nwoye and his father is comparable with the impact of other forms of Ibo morality—including the superstitious exposure of newborn twins. In effect, Okonkwo's egocentric failure to recognize or respect the humanity of Ikemefuna and Nwoye, is symptomatic of those weaknesses which have made his society vulnerable to the promises of Christianity. The problems of human perception which are dramatized by the colonial functions of language have been repeated, on an internal level, within African society itself.

Altogether then, Achebe exploits the English language and its cultural norms in order to explore differences in modes of perception. The European's ethnocentric perceptions are exposed and ironically reversed in order to accommodate the African's self-awareness. Or they are compared with the perceptual norms of divisive individualism in the African community. And even in *A Man of the People* (1966) where there is less emphasis on the literary and pathological traditions of English, Achebe's basic objective remains the same: cultural norms embody modes of perception which are intrinsic to the emotional and moral experiences in the novel. Indeed, in his fourth novel Achebe rejects European judgements even more explicitly than he does in the ironic manipulations of the earlier novels. The European's ignorance of African customs has led to shallow and misleading generalizations. Some foreigners, for example, think "we are funny with figures." Hence Odili's father astonishes a British visitor because the former seems to be unaware of the size of his own family: "My father grinned and talked about other things. Of course he knew how many children he had but people don't go counting their children as they do animals or yams" (p. 125).[17]

Neither does Odili trust the foreigner's critical interpretation of African art. According to an Englishman, the old African, "quite an illiterate pagan," who shakes her fist at the modern sculpture of a god is expressing annoyance at the "un-African" art of the European-trained sculptor. But as Odili points out, the gesture with the fist "is a sign of great honour and respect; it means that you attribute power to the person or object." Moreover, this blunder is comparable with the *faux pas* by a French reviewer of an African religious mask. The divine "detachment and disdain" depicted by the mask had been missed by the critic's infatuation with the figure's "half-closed eyes, sharply drawn and tense eyebrows, the ecstatic and passionate mouth." The problem arises from differences in cultural perception: the critic has "transferred to an alien culture the same meanings and interpretation that his own people attach to certain gestures and facial expressions" (p. 56).

The art of dancing is also pertinent, for the "foreign enthusiast of African rhythm" who tends to "overdo the waist wiggle" is simply responding to stereotyped perceptions of the African: "It all goes back to what others have come to associate us with. And let it be said that we are not entirely blameless in this. I remember how we were outraged at the University to see a film of breast-throwing, hip-jerking, young women which a neighbouring African state had made and was showing abroad as an African ballet" (pp. 57–58). Altogether, the perceptual problems created by the foreigner's cultural norms have been compounded by those Africans who accept or pander to the European's irrelevant judgements.

But above all, these problems are not limited to the relationship between African and Western cultures. As in *Things Fall Apart* or *No Longer At Ease*, the kinds of perception which underlie the external conflict are pertinent to the internal crises of the African community. When Odili resents an American for criticizing his country he implies a parallel between the incompetence of alien judgements on African art and the irrelevance of the outsider's insights into African politics: "Who the hell did she think she was to laugh so self-righteously? Wasn't there more than enough in her own country to keep her laughing all her days? Or crying if she preferred it?" (p. 61). And, as in the case of the pseudo-African ballet, Odili's anger is also directed inwards—at those Africans who have glibly accepted, or prostituted themselves to shallow imitations of Western politics. Chief Nanga's "democratic" politics, like his colorful English, are fraudulent externals which are unrelated to the socio-economic complexities of African culture and nationhood. But Nanga's charlatanism only partially accounts for the emptiness of his claim to be a man of the people. For the fact is that Achebe is not being chauvinistic in either the matter of art criticism or political systems. He is acutely aware of all those intransigent facts of modernity which compel the contemporary African to come to terms with, or accommodate, non-African values.

Yet, at the same time, he is conscious that the outsider's nonperception of the African's culture and identity is counterbalanced by the fact that the majority of Africans do not always perceive of themselves within the context into which the twentieth century has inevitably thrust them. Hence, quite apart from his chicanery, Nanga fails to be a "man of the people" because the "people" do not exist—at least, not on the level of that democratic nationhood which has been handed down by the Western colonialists. The "nation" over which Nanga presides is nonexistent because most of the individuals within its boundaries do not *perceive* themselves as components of an organized, national whole, but as members of specific communities described by the limits of village or tribe. This has nothing to do with the African's allegedly *inherent* incapacity to view or verbalize his condition in Western terms. It results from the colonial experience in which the African acquired dual perspectives on government and politics. The central authority was formerly an alien white power, operating on principles and within physical boundaries that conformed with the Westerner's spatial and sociopolitical concepts of nationhood. But the social and political unit which related most directly to the African's everyday experience and to his sense of tradition was defined by the village.

This duality is dramatized by the public's contrasting reactions to dishonesty. Having been accustomed to think of a central authority in terms of powerful, alien exploiters, the people suspend moral judgements on those African leaders who have succeeded the white colonists: " 'Let them eat,' was the people's opinion, 'after all when white men used to do all the eating did we commit suicide?' " (pp. 161–162). On the other hand, when the shopkeeper in the village of Anata is caught cheating his customers, he is promptly and effectively ostracized, for the continuing traditions of village life make the people both able and willing to exercise their moral authority on this level. And the effectiveness of traditional African morality in this sphere is contrasted with the "people's" impotence in the ghostly milieu of nationhood: "The owner [of morality and goods] was the village, and the village had a mind; it could say no to sacrilege. But in the affairs of the nation there was no owner; the laws of the village became powerless" (p. 167). Hence, the "collective will" of a people was not involved in Nanga's eventual defeat, because the perceptual values which could have created such a will are absent or underdeveloped: "No, the people had nothing to do with the fall of our Government. What happened was simply that unruly mobs and private armies having tasted blood and power during the election had got out of hand" (p. 162).

Having exposed the narrowness or irrelevance of Western perceptions of African traditions, Achebe now underscores the limitations of traditional African values vis-à-vis the Western criteria of twentieth century modernity. The external confrontations of the colonial era have given way to the internal conflicts of an independent, and hybrid, nationhood. And in the process, the familiar cultural differences have persisted, in a new internal setting, together with the related conflict between modes of perception.

FOOTNOTES

1 *Black Skin White Masks*, trans. Charles Lam Markmann (New York, 1967), pp. 17–18. Originally published as *Peau Noire Masques Blancs* (1952).

2 *The Pleasures of Exile* (London, 1960), pp. 15, 110.

3 Bernard Mandeville, *The Fable of the Bees: Or Private Vices, Publick Benefits*, ed. F. B. Kaye (Oxford, 1924), II, 285–92. Originally published 1729.

4 Paul Edwards and David R. Carroll, "An Approach to the Novel in West Africa," *Phylon* XXIII (1962), 319–31; Alan Warner, "A New English in Africa?" *Review of English Literature* IV (April 1963), 45–54.

5 Ezekiel Mphahlele, "The Language of African Literature," *Harvard Education Review* XXXIV (1964), 298–305; Bernth Lindfors, "African Vernacular Styles in Nigerian Fiction," *College Language Association Journal*, IX (1965–66), 265–73.

6 *The Pleasures of Exile*, p. 109.

7 *A Dying Colonialism*, trans. Haakon Chevalier, Evergreen ed. (New York, 1967), pp. 89–91. Originally published as *L' An Cinq de la Révolution Algérienne* (1959).

8 "African Voices of Protest," in *The Militant Black Writer in Africa and the United States* by Mercer Cook and Stephen E. Henderson (Madison, Wis., 1969), p. 52.

9 *Wretched of the Earth*, trans. Constance Farrington, Evergreen ed. (New York, 1968), p. 10. Originally published as *Les damnés de la terre* (1961).

10 *Things Fall Apart*, African Writers Series (London, 1962), p. 160. References to the other two novels examined here, *No Longer At Ease* (1963) and *A Man of the People* (1966), are based on the African Writers Series editions.

11 *The Adventures of Catullus Kelly* (London, 1969), pp. 2–3.

12 *Houseboy*, trans. John Reed, African Writers Series (London, 1966), p. 11. Originally published as *Un Vie de Boy* (1960).

13 "Tradition and the Individual Talent" (1917), in *Selected Essays 1917–1932* (London, 1932), p. 14. References to "The Journey of the Magi" are based on Eliot's *Later Poems 1925–1935* (London, 1941), pp. 29–31.

14 Léopold Sédar Senghor, *Prose and Poetry*, trans. John Reed (London, 1965), pp. 39, 43.

15 O. Mannoni, *Prospero and Caliban: The Psychology of Colonization*, trans. Pamela Powesland (London, 1956), p. 108. Originally published as *Psychologie de la Colonisation* (1950).

16 Senghor, p. 30.

17 Achebe's Britisher is comparable with Canada's contemporary Marshall McLuhan: "The most primitive tribes of Australia and Africa . . . have not yet reached finger-counting," *Understanding Media: The Extensions of Man*, McGraw-Hill paper ed. (New York, 1966), pp. 110–11.

FROM HAUSA TO ENGLISH: A STUDY IN PARAPHRASE

Neil Skinner

In 1950 Cyprian Ekwensi wrote:
> While I was writing *Ikolo The Wrestler*, I was lucky enough to meet an aged Hausa Mallam who told me a single folktale of book length. Amused by the short tales which I was collecting, he asked me if I would care for one which would keep my readers awake all night. Thus was born my *African Night's Entertainment*, which is still to be published. But such chances are rare, and one cannot bank on them.[1]

In 1962 *An African Night's Entertainment* was published by African Universities Press, and has been reprinted several times since.

Eighteen years before, in 1934, a Hausa booklet entitled *Jiki Magayi* had been published for the Literature Bureau, Zaria by West African Publicity, Lagos. Its authors were Rupert East, Superintendent of the Literature Bureau and Malam J. Tafida Zaria. The circumstances of its birth as told by Dr. East[2] are as follows. An attempt was made to encourage the writing of fictional prose by Hausas for publication and Dr. East travelled to various cities to encourage the Hausa intelligentsia to participate in the effort. The result was, as likely in the circumstances described by Dr. East, meagre. "It wasn't a question of selection; the ones printed were the only ones we received." At that time Tafida worked in the Literature Bureau and Dr. East suggested to him that he try his hand. He did so, but Dr. East felt that the first draft lacked a "consistent story in the Western sense," so most of it had to be scrapped and he and his junior colleague rewrote it together. "The final result was such a long way from the original manuscript that I didn't feel it was quite honest to publish it over his name as sole author."

The plot of both these works, henceforth referred to as AN and JM, is as follows. Malam Shehu is a rich man who lives in a town called Galma and lacks nothing but a child. He prays to God to give him a child–of any sort. He has a dream, in which he sees a horse [AN] (mare [JM]), which he greatly desires. He outbids another buyer, buys it and takes it home. There it—according to AN still a horse!—produces a foal. The foal is much admired and when it is old enough he has it saddled and mounts it. He gallops it, it stumbles and he falls and breaks a leg [AN]. (It is unmanageable, throws him and gallops away, leaving him in great pain [JM]). He summons a malam [JM] (Malam Sambo [AN]) to interpret his dream, which is explained to him as a warning to him of a marriage which would produce a son, but to his great shame. The malam goes on to admonish him to eschew any idea of this marriage. But he falls deeply in love with Zainobe [AN] (Zainabu [JM], the Hausa spelling) daughter of Malam Audu. However, Zainabu has been pledged to Abu Bakir [AN] (Abubakar [JM]) since childhood. They love each other and Zainabu's parents are committed to the match. Shehu tries to win her away from Abubakar, but she will have nothing to do with him. So Shehu sends for a much-feared Malam Sambo [JM] (the above mentioned Malam Sambo [AN]) and gets from him a "medicine" which he is told to mix with musk (AN adds "from a deer") and have Zainabu use on her body. She does put a little of it on, and later her mother agrees that she shall marry Shehu rather than Abubakar.

In desperation Abubakar goes off into the world, his one idea to seek vengeance. Shehu marries Zainabu who a year later bears a son, who is given the name Abdullahi [JM] and the sobriquet Kyauta (AN makes this his name). Meanwhile Abubakar falls in with some thieves, who take him to their town, Zauna-da-Shirinka "Remain ever-ready." There he meets their chief, Tausayinka-da-Sauk'i "You-Have-Little-Mercy." Abubakar tells him his tale (which, Tausayi, through his magic, already knows) and is promised assistance in getting vengeance. As a first step, Tausayinka-da-Sauk'i sends him on to the town where he was born, Kobonka-Naka "Your-Penny-is-Yours" [AN] (Yale [JM]), to seek guidance from his father in getting hold of the sap of a certain tree [AN] (the gum of a *kalgo*[3] [JM]). He gives him a charm, by which his father will recognize that he comes from his son.

Abubakar's mission proceeds. Tausayi's father, having failed to dissuade him from his vengeance, tells him the tree with the magic sap is to be found in the Ruk'uk'i Bush [JM] (Kurmin Rukiki—Hausa for "Rukiki Forest" [AN]). After a day or two's rest, the old man sends Abubakar on his way with horse, food, and money, and directions on getting to Ruk'uk'i. Travelling through a vast bush Abubakar is stripped of what he has by two robbers, who also beat him and cut off his left ear [AN] (half an ear [JM]). He is rescued by some travellers coming along with their donkeys and taken to another town. Later, sleeping in the marketplace [AN] (of another town called Rimi [JM]), he finds himself in the middle of a hue and cry and is arrested for a thief. He is taken before the king who sentences him to three months [AN] (judge who sentences him to fifty lashes and three months [JM]).

After this there are two or three episodes as Abubakar presses on with his quest, with JM and AN diverging slightly. They converge again, when Abubakar falls in with a hunter, who takes him as far as he dares and points out the way to the magic forest. Here he spends many days; he gets occasional glimpses of a glittering object; he is struck by lightning; his teeth are knocked out [JM] (his mouth is battered and swollen [AN]); climaxing in an encounter with a python and a very old woman [AN] (the king of the jinns [JM]), who gives him the object of his quest, saying [JM] that he does so because he helps all evil (that she does so because she pities his wrongs and sufferings [AN]). He makes his way back to Tausayi's father, who at first does not recognize him, so changed is he from all his sufferings. But, when he is convinced, he gives him food and rest and eventually sends him on his way with his son, Tausayi's younger brother.

Tausayi also at first fails to recognize his visitors, but when he knows who they are, welcomes his brother and proceeds to use the magic sap to mix into a "medicine," which is to be rubbed on Kyauta's body. He also gives Abubakar an invisibility charm to help him. Abubakar returns home to be not recognized, but later warmly welcomed by mother and brother. The latter tells him of Kyauta, points the boy out to him and (when asked by Abubakar [AN]) describes where he sleeps. At night Abubakar makes himself invisible, goes to Kyauta's room and anoints him with the "medicine." Then he passes on to Zainabu's room, where he wakes her and tells her that the child of her marriage, for the sake of which she did him wrong, will become a curse to her. Zainabu is terrified, but after she has got up and inspected Kyauta, who is sleeping soundly, she is somewhat reassured and keeps what she thinks is her dream to herself.

Next morning Kyauta steals two shillings from his father and plays truant from school. On his return, questioned by Malam Shehu, he lies about the money. Malam Shehu mentions to Zainabu how the boy seems to have changed. She says she will inquire whether he has something on his mind. She prepares a nice meal for him and calls him to come and eat. He ignores her for some time, but, when he does come and finds the food cold, kicks it over and insults her. Kyauta rapidly goes from bad to worse. Here JM and AN diverge slightly in the episodes of the boy's downward path. Zainabu's fellow wives mock her for the way the longed-for child has proved a bane. Kyauta takes to stealing and steals a bag of money containing three pounds, ten shillings [JM] (fifty pounds [AN]—postwar inflation!) from a trader in a neighboring market. Taken before the judge, he at first lies, but later admits the theft. His father comes and pays the money, and is given Kyauta to take home and discipline. Malam Shehu tries both discipline and excessive kindness—in vain. The boy finally runs away to Kano, taking some of his father's money with him.

At Kano he continues to steal and gets caught and given [JM] two years for stealing cloth from a house (eighteen months for raiding the white man's shops as part of a gang [AN]). Word reaches Malam Shehu, which makes him think his son may be a prisoner in Kano and he sends to find out. His emissary finds Kyauta and manages to speak with him, when on a working party, but the boy deceives him about his date of release, and so, when he gets out of prison, again vanishes. The order of some episodes varies in JM and AN at this point (see below), but eventually Kyauta goes by train to Lagos where he falls in with a "dreaded robber" called Dogo [AN] (accompanies a thief called Dogon Yaro by train to Lagos [JM]). Meanwhile, heartbroken and humiliated at his public shame, Malam Shehu persuades Zainabu to leave Galma with him and go somewhere they are not known. She agrees, he makes provision for his other wives and they set off with a donkey and a camel [JM] (with two horses [AN]). They travel a long way and eventually settle in a town, where there is no contact with Galma. There Shehu announces himself as Malam Usuman and after a while begins again to prosper.

One day, however, Kyauta and his evil friend move into the area. Seeing a fine house—which, of course, is Malam Shehu's—they case it. Later, they return at night and climb in over the wall. They are disturbed at work by Malam Shehu and Kyauta kills him. As they run out to get away, they bump into Zainabu, who recognizes Kyauta. They talk, while Dogo runs away. They go in and see the body and Kyauta realizes that he has killed his father. Zainabu helps him to escape, but Dogo is caught in the hue and cry. His captors refuse to believe his story of a confederate who had done the murder, and he is jailed while the investigation goes on. There he dies, falling into a well while drawing water.

At this point JM and AN again diverge slightly in the order of episodes, but both agree in having Zainabu tell Kyauta of her "dream" and how Abubakar is to blame for his tragedy; in having Kyauta recognized as Malam Usuman's heir and escort his mother back to Galma; and in Kyauta's going to Abubakar's house to exact vengeance. They differ in the way that the mission ends (see below). After this [AN] Kyauta and Zainabu live sadly ever after (Kyauta settles his mother and goes off a repentant wanderer for the rest of his life [JM]).

I have given in some detail the common plot of these two works, so that a reader who does not understand Hausa can be convinced that they are, to an overwhelming extent, the same. Further evidence, if it is needed, can be found in the following short passages:

JM translated (1971 reprint)	AN
p. 4–5 *Abubakar* ". . . a horse, a river and a woman, one doesn't trust them . . . because, if you like a horse, you will go to every trouble for it, but one day it will kick you. A river, too, one moment you will cross it safely, dry shod; but when you return, it will be in flood, impossible to cross. And a woman—they say her promise is for forty days only. . . ."	p. 16 *Abu Bakir* "Women are like water and horses. . . . Women are like water, because you'll cross a stream in the dry season and when you return in the rains the same stream will drown you. If you love a horse very much and you feed her [sic], when you come to ride her, she'll throw you down and break your backbone. So is a woman's love. . . .
p. 15 *Abubakar* "But because of my lack of judgment, when I was leaving, I forgot to ask him the name of his father."	p. 39 *Abu Bakir* "I was so foolish as not to ask my informer the name of his father. . . ."
p. 18 His father built him a fine house in his own stable-area, and there he would sleep with his age mates.	p. 31 His father built him a separate house within his own compound and there all his friends came to visit him. . . .
p. 21 They put him on a donkey.	p. 44 They . . . put him on a donkey.

151

p. 27 *Tausayi* "cut off hair from his head . . . go and find a new grave, dig it up and hide it there. Your wish will then be fulfilled."

p. 29 *Abubakar* "The son that you have born . . . shall be a curse to you. . . ."

p. 30 *Kyauta* . . . went out and into his father's room. He found some money lying on the sheepskin. He took two shillings and went off.

p. 31 *Malam Shehu* ". . . but I am missing two shillings. Do you know who would take them?"
Kyauta "What business of mine is it? Did you make me their watchman?"

p. 32 *Kyauta* "Is this the food—cold, as if I were a dog?"

p. 40 The servant said to him, "How many more months do you have to serve?" He answered, "Six more"—when, in fact, he had only one more to go.

p. 42–43 He collected his wives and said to them "I intend going on the Pilgrimage. . . ." He called his chief servant and handed over to him all the affairs of his home.

p. 47 In the prison there was a very deep well . . . and one day he went out in the afternoon to draw water, and—*tsundum* he fell into the well!

p. 60 *Tausayi* ". . . cut some hair from his head and bury it in a newly dug grave. This is all you need to do."

p. 65 *Abu Bakir* "That son shall be a curse to you."

p. 65 *Kyauta* . . . went into his father's house and took two shillings from the sheepskin. With this he went towards the main gate. (No inflation here!)

p. 67 *Malam Shehu* "Do you know who took two shillings I placed on my sheepskin?"

Kyauta "Do you keep me in the house as a watchman?"

p. 68 *Kyauta* "This cold food for me? Am I a dog?"

p. 79 "He wants to know how long you have to serve. . . ."
"I have three months more" Kyauta lied, knowing well that he had only one more month.

p. 86 . . . he went to the king and told him he was going on a pilgrimage to Mecca. His other wives he left in the care of his chief servant. . . .

p. 91 One afternoon Dogo went to draw water from the well. He slipped and falling down a hundred and eighty feet crashed into the water below.

While there can be little doubt that we have in AN an English version of the 1934 Hausa JM, and that this latter must be the ultimate source of the tale told by the "aged Hausa Mallam," it is equally clear, even from the twelve pairs of passages quoted above, which have been chosen for their closeness to each other, that AN is not a word-for-word translation of JM, though it is close to an episode-for-episode version. It is slightly shorter, about 17,000 as against 20,000 words, omitting several minor episodes, merging others and usually paraphrasing rather than expanding the individual episodes. It is, of course, not possible to judge to what extent these changes are the work of Ekwensi himself or were already inherent in the version told him. His informant must have had a fine memory for detail and must have read or heard the story many times. Could it perhaps have been Tafida himself? One wonders too at what point the tale went into English. Presumably this is Ekwensi's major contribution, for he speaks Hausa.[4]

Turning now to the minor changes made to the plot. The following list is not exhaustive, but deals with most of the obvious ones:

Omissions
1. The episode of Malam Shehu's winning Zainabu away from Abubakar has beeen reduced and some subtlety lost. JM makes it combined pressure from relatives that Zainabu's father yields to before allowing her to switch from Malam Shehu to Abubakar. AN makes Malam Shehu send a present to the king who brings pressure to bear on Zainabu's father.
2. Minor episodes between Abubakar's suffering attack by robbers and being arrested as a thief have been omitted. The towns of Sanga and Rimi have become anonymous.
3. Similarly the narrative of sufferings in the magic forest has been shortened. In JM, there is much greater passage of time. "He lost count of the years," "At night he would seek out a cave or a hollow tree and sleep there," etc., are missing from AN.
4. AN omits to specify that Abubakar carried out the second part of the charm to bewitch K — the burying in a newly dug grave.
5. When Kyauta discovers that it is his own father that he has killed, JM says "he lost his senses and became like a madman, drawing a knife to kill himself." Zainabu, his mother, stops him. AN completely omits this.

6. In JM, at the same climax, Kyauta's mother tells him how Abubakar has bewitched him, and how all his degeneration is not his fault but God's will, and they must wait and see how God will bring vengeance. In AN, his mother tells Kyauta—later, when they are on their way back to Galma—simply of Abubakar's night visit to her and how he must have done something terrible to Kyauta.

Additions

Given that AN is shorter than JM, we should expect there to be fewer of these. In fact, there are a considerable number, but none of any length:

1. Abubakar is given the title "Malam" (title of respect) throughout, whereas in JM, the only one of the three main male characters to be accorded the title is Shehu. In Hausa culture, for Abubakar to have earned the title as a young man, he would have had either to be very learned indeed or of royal blood.
2. In JM, before Tausayi agrees to help Abubakar get his vengeance, he asks him whether he accepts full responsibility before God for all the evil that will result. AN adds that he makes him swear on the Koran to that effect.
3. A somewhat implausible addition by AN is where Tausayi's father begins to suspect that Abubakar may have come from his son, whom he has not seen for twenty-eight years. Abubakar describes Tausayi as "tall and black, a big strong man with a pointed nose and a big head . . . ," and later the old man remarks "your description of the man fits my son." Twenty-eight years is a long time. More neatly —shades of *Great Expectations*!—JM allows Abubakar to produce a particular charm that Tausayi always wore. AN's addition is redundant as, in AN too, the charm is produced, but at a later point in the narrative, merely to confirm identification.
4. There are one or two brief anthropologicalisms, as when AN describes the betrothal of Zainabu and Abubakar as children; or where Tausayi gives Abubakar an invisibility charm, "what we call *layan zana*." It would be interesting to learn to whom Ekwensi was referring with the pronoun.
5. When Abubakar is in prison, AN introduces the character of a sympathetic warder, who later gives him a home and helps him. He fills the role of an anonymous benefactor in JM, who plays an even smaller part.

6. In the magic forest AN introduces a metamorphosis, where the aged crone turns into a leopard who pursues Abubakar out of the forest, after he has got the magic sap. Leopard-men are more significant in the traditional beliefs of southeast Nigeria than those of the Hausa.

7. AN has a paragraph describing how Tausayi mixed the "medicine" he gave Abubakar, including telling how he used a "little antimony that women use for their eyes"—more anthropology—"and a few other ingredients known only to him." In contrast, JM states simply "he mixed the medicine, he gave it to him."

8. When Abubakar returns to his home determined to bewitch Kyauta, AN makes him—somewhat gratuitously—threaten his mother and brother with death, if "anyone in this town knows that I am back."

9. Lastly, interesting from the point of view of the development of written as opposed to oral style—for though JM can hardly be described as "oral," one imagines that Tafida's style would be closer to oral than Ekwensi's—are a number of places where AN adds descriptive detail. Such are: "his eyes blazing," "she whispered," "stamped her foot angrily," "trying to control his rising temper," and many others. Some are somewhat cliché, but all attempt to substitute for the dramatic accompaniments inherent in oral style.

Alterations

1. JM allows Malam Shehu, being a rich man, to have his full Islamic complement of wives at the start of the book, four. When, like David and Bathsheba, he seeks someone else's one ewe lamb, and gets it, he—correctly—divorces one of them, so as not to exceed the prescribed number. AN introduces this last detail, *after* telling of his marriage to Zainabu and the birth of Kyauta, with more anthropology—"In keeping with the custom, he sent away one of his wives. . . ."—apparently failing to realize exactly what the custom was, for on page 1, AN tells us that Malam Shehu had three wives! Having reduced the number from four to three in the first place, it was redundant to include an incident whose *raison d'être* was to reduce four wives to three in order to let Malam Shehu marry Zainabu. Especially when, apparently, he had already married her and had a son by her, in any case!

2. The celebration of Zainabu's marriage to Malam Shehu and the birth of Kyauta a year later is in JM an episode that occurs as flashback after Abubakar has been on his quest for some time. AN uses it to round off the initial episode of Malam Shehu's grabbing of Abuba-

kar's bride. In this case AN is closer to the oral tradition where—at least in Hausa tales—flashbacks are rare, while JM—one of East's touches?—again uses a technique which adds an element of duration to Abubakar's travels and sufferings.

3. AN expands the role of Tausayi's younger brother. In JM he is casually introduced when Abubakar is finally saying goodbye to Tausayi's father, who sends him with Abubakar to see where Tausayi is. But in AN, on Abubakar's first meeting with Tausayi's father, he tells him Tausayi would like him to send his brother to him with news of home. There is no obvious structural reason for this.

4. As already said, AN and JM diverge in their accounts of Kyauta's degeneration from the time he is charmed to the time he finds himself in jail in Kano. In particular the following episodes get transposed: [JM has the order]—(A) Kyauta steals in market–(B) Malam Shehu bails him out–(C) Malam Shehu gives him to Malam Sambo to lock up and discipline–(D) Kyauta escapes, works for and cheats clerk–(E) Malam Shehu bails him out again and locks him up–(F) Kyauta escapes and flees to Kano; [while AN has] C (but the teacher is anonymous)–A–B–F–, while D and E occur after Kyauta leaves prison in Kano, E ending instead with his flight to Lagos.

5. When Malam Shehu's emissary spots Kyauta among the work party of prisoners in Kano, JM makes him request the warder for speech with Kyauta. Then afterwards, he slips the warder money. In AN, more mistrustingly, the bribe has to occur at night, before the emissary can have speech with Kyauta.

6. Perhaps a crucial difference between JM and AN is the end of the three surviving protagonists. In JM when Kyauta confronts Abubakar with his guilt, intending to kill him, the shock is too much for Abubakar and he dies, exclaiming that God has exacted vengeance for Kyauta. Kyauta then goes out, exclaiming on the omnipotence of God. Later, when finally he has seen his mother safely back to Galma, he departs with nothing but stick, bag, and water-gourd— the humble student's equipment—to spend the rest of his life seeking to reduce the guilt he has incurred. AN simply allows Kyauta to cut Abubakar's head off "with one sweep of his razor-edged sword"—echoes of Onitsha market—makes him "run amok" for one year (in a single sentence) and then return to his mother to finish his days in Galma.

Summing Up

On Ekwensi's own admission AN is simply a record of a tale told him by a Hausa. In fact, we have seen that it is a translated paraphrase, and one moreover in which a number of important elements of JM are missing. One such is the exact nature of Malam Shehu's *hubris*. In JM he prays "Oh God, but give me a child—of *any* sort!" In the event, his reckless prayer is answered, and nemesis pursues him until it kills him. In weakening Malam Shehu's words to "He did not ask Allah to give him a son or daughter of any particular talent, but any child . . ." AN misses the essence of the *hubris*. Note, incidentally "Allah" for "God." More anthropologicalism? Same fellow?

On several occasions too, AN lacks minor elements of *k'addara* "predestination," which were part of the essentially Muslim background of JM. So when Abubakar returns to Galma to take his revenge on Kyauta, JM has Abubakar and his brother sitting chatting in the afternoon, when—as predestined—along comes Kyauta. In AN, on the other hand, Abubakar has to ask, "Will you show the boy to me when he passes here?" But it is particularly in the character of Kyauta that AN gravely weakens the story. In JM, Kyauta is guiltless. He is bewitched and so acts evilly. But when he understands that he has killed his own father his remorse is unbearable. However, he still pursues thoughts of vengeance against Abubakar. But here again *k'addara* steps in and God does not allow him—when no longer under the spell—to further soil his hands with blood. Finally he goes off into the world again expressly to expiate what he feels is his guilt. All of this is gone from AN. No remorse for killing his father. No *k'addara* steps in to prevent Kyauta's acquiring bloodguilt. No word of Kyauta's conscience at the end.

AN has then, on the whole, weakened the tale through its omissions, while its anthropological additions have hardly added to the art. As for the extra items of descriptive detail (see above) where they are not cliché, these are probably improvements. This is the natural line of development that a writer should follow to turn oral into written art. But paraphrase is a retrograde step, justifiable only where the original is exceptionally difficult and it is desired to simplify its content for young students. However, whether we are to reproach the "old Hausa mallam" or Ekwensi himself with failing to come up to the standard of JM, God —as JM would say—alone knows.

FOOTNOTES

[1] *West African Review* (January 1950), p. 19. I am indebted to Bernth Lindfors for drawing my attention to this article by Ekwensi.

[2] See R. M. East, "A First Essay in Imaginative African Literature," *Africa*, 9 (1936), 350–357; also private communication from Dr. East; also Neil Skinner, "Realism and Fantasy in Hausa Literature," *Review of National Literatures*, 2,2 (1971), 167–187.

[3] *Kalgo "bauhinia reticulata"* is a very common shrub in Hausa country, but it does not normally produce gum. I suspect that a botanical impossibility is here used to indicate the hopelessness of the quest. Cf. "the land where the rainbow ends," etc.

[4] Ernest N. Emenyonu, "The Development of Modern Igbo Fiction: 1857–1966," (Ph.D. dissertation, U. of Wisconsin, 1972), p. 130.

PLAGIARISM AND AUTHENTIC CREATIVITY IN WEST AFRICA

Donatus I. Nwoga

In the course of doing my annual bibliographies of West African literature for the *Journal of Commonwealth Literature*, I find that much energy has been devoted to the case of plagiarism made against Yambo Ouologuem with regard to his novel *Le Devoir de Violence*. It is really Professor Sellin's reply to Paul Flamand[1] that provokes my contribution, especially the statement that "no number of legal releases will render authentic the alleged Africanness of Ouologuem's book." This is apparently based on two issues—the structural similarities to *Le Dernier des Justes* and the passages adapted, (alright plagiarized!), from Graham Greene's *It's a Battlefield*.

Perhaps I should start in the matter of "plagiarism" with our authentic poet, Christopher Okigbo. Sunday Anozie, in his book, *Christopher Okigbo : Creative Rhetoric*, writing of Okigbo's earliest poems, the "Four Canzones," talks of the four-movement division in each of the Canzones, which continues in the 4th Canzone, "each movement introducing a new variation upon the central theme, and all rounding off in that last ritual exorcism inspired by Miguel Hernandez, the Spanish author of "El amor ascendia entre nosotros . . ."[2] "Inspired," writes Anozie, but look at the similarities:

"Lament of the Lavender mist"

Okigbo	*Hernandez*[3]
"Lament of the Lavender mist"	"El amor ascendia entre nosotros"
The moon has ascended between us—	Love ascended between us like the
Between two pines	moon between two palms
That bow to each other;	that have never embraced;
Love with the moon has ascended,	Love passed like a moon between
Has fed on our solitary stem;	us and ate our solitary bodies.

159

And we are now shadows	And we are two ghosts who seek
That cling to each other	one another
But kiss the air only.	And meet afar off.

Anozie comments later, in summary, of these early poems: "Okigbo's poetic language at the same period is both unoriginal and diffident, vacillating between different, often conflicting traditions, and adapting whichever poetic forms and diction may have appealed to his curious and impressionable mind. It is evidence of Okigbo's genius and labour that he practically overcame in his later poetry most of these difficulties and succeeded in creating a poetic technique and an idiom purely his own."[4]

Yet, Okigbo's last set of poems ends with:

Okigbo	*Alberto Quintero Alvarez*[5]
An old star departs, leaves us here on the shore	What departs leaves on the shore
Gazing heavenward for a new star approaching;	Gazing seawards at the star fore-seen;
The new star appears, foreshadows its going	What arrives announces its fare-well
Before a going and coming that goes on forever . . .[6]	Before a coming-and-going that goes on for ever.

Various sections of Okigbo's poetry are traced by Anozie to various authors and poets. Here is one that he did not trace. The two later versions of "Lament of the Drums" (*Black Orpheus*, 17, [1965], 13, and *Labyrinths*, p. 45) start with invocations. The *Labyrinths* version starts:

> LION-HEARTED cedar forest, gonads for our thunder,
> Even if you are very far away, we invoke you:
>
> Give us our hollow heads of long-drums . . .
>
> Antelopes for the cedar forest, swifter messengers
> Than flash-of-beacon-flame, we invoke you:
>
> Hide us; deliver us from our nakedness . . .
>
> Many-fingered canebrake, exile for our laughter,
> Even if you are very far away, we invoke you:
>
> Come; limber our raw hides of antelopes . . .

This is clearly an adaptation of the drum invocations of the Ashanti drummers recorded in 1926 by Rattray:

Kon, kon, kon, kon,
Kun, kun, kun, kun,
Spirit of Funtumia Akore,
Spirit of Cedar tree Akore,
Of Cedar tree, Kodia,
Of Kodia, the Cedar tree;
The divine Drummer announces that,
Had he gone else where
He now has made himself to arise . . .
We are addressing you,
And you will understand;
We are addressing you
And you will understand.

Much of the material of this stanza is repeated in following stanzas in which the Earth, the Elephant which supplies the hides for the drums, the fibre with which the hides are tied to the drums, the pegs that tense the fibres, and the kokokyinaka bird, the totem of drummers, are invoked. These drum incantations are the first things played in the morning before the formal drumming of the Drum-History of Mampon.[7] Kwabena Nketia gives the title of this drum piece as "The Awakening" and gives another version of the invocation of the elephant.[8]

Obviously the forms of words differ greatly, and Okigbo makes explicit request for the functioning of the various invoked elements which the original drum piece takes for granted, and it is antelopes, not elephants, that Okigbo asks for hides. But there can be no doubt that he was inspired by the traditional "The Awakening," followed its pattern starting from the invocation of the cedar tree, and abbreviated some of its ideas.

Now, I doubt very much that Dr. Anozie, if he had known this, would have desisted from his comment which gives stylistic and thematic validity to the introduction of this invocation into the poem. What he does say is: "that the new versions of Movement I of 'Lament of the Drums' should start in each case with an invocation and a prayer is a clear sign of greater visionary consistency and an improvement upon the original version. For example, by invoking their own proper elements . . . and also by drawing attention to their own traditional roles of communication . . . the Drums assert themselves as the principal actors in the present drama."[9] It would appear that Sunday Anozie was not disturbed by the sources of Okigbo's material, only that the material should stylistically and thematically conform with the total poem in which it appears.

Another source of borrowing in Okigbo from traditional literature is represented by his poem for Yeats. The *Centenary Essays for W. B. Yeats* edited by D. E. S. Maxwell and S. B. Bushrui and published in Ibadan in 1965, contains his "Lament of the Masks: For W. B. Yeats: 1865–1939."[10] This is a long poem in four sections. From Section II one begins to hear echos. The lines:

How many beacon flames
Can ever challenge the sun? . . .
Ten thousand rivers
Can never challenge the sea.

echo Ewe religious poems that I have seen but I cannot immediately recall their place of publication. However, the parallel to the Yoruba *Oriki* of the King of Ikerre is quite close:

Two hundred needles do not make a hoe
Two hundred stars do not make a moon[11]

The next lines:

Thunder above the earth,
Sacrifice too huge for the vulture

take the second line from the Yoruba *Oriki* to Shango, which, in Ulli Beier's translation starts

Huge sacrifice,
too heavy for the vulture
it trembles under your weight[12]

In Section III, the following lines form the second stanza:

They put you into the eaves thatch
You split the thatch
They poured you into an iron mould
You burst the mould.

These remind one of a section of the Yoruba *Oriki* to Eshu, again translated by Ulli Beier:

Eshu slept in the house—
But the house was too small for him.
Eshu slept in the verandah—

but the verandah was too small for him.
It is worth noting here that the Yoruba poem continues
> Eshu slept in the net—
> at last he could stretch himself.[13]

which introduces an element of paradox, consistent with the trickster nature of Eshu, but which Okigbo did not need and therefore did not use.

A definite "plagiarism" in this section is that from the Yoruba salutation poem to the Timi of Ede. The third stanza reads:

> For like the dog's mouth you were never at rest,
> Who, fighting a battle in front,
> Mapped out, with dust-of-combat ahead of you,
> The next battle-field at the rear—
> That generations unborn
> Might never taste the steel—.

Christopher Okigbo was the Cambridge University Press representative in Nigeria and was living in Ibadan in 1965. Ulli Beier's *African Poetry*, published in 1966 by Cambridge University Press, must have passed through his hands. Ulli Beier's translation of the *Oriki* of the Timi of Ede, published in this collection, contains the following lines:

> Fighting a battle in front
> You mark out the next battle-field behind.
> My Lord, please give the world some rest.[14]

Okigbo took the two lines and left the third, and concluded his stanza with words very reminiscent of J. P. Clark's line in "The Imprisonment of Obatala."

> And generations unborn spared the wrong.[15]

Incidentally, I did a study in another context which showed that quite a few of the images and lines in Okigbo's "Fragments from the Deluge" were derived from and paraphrased and reworked from J. P. Clark's little-known long poem "Ivbie" in his collection *Poems*, which was published by Mbari in Ibadan in 1962.

It is an interesting scholarly exercise tracing these borrowings and parallels. But I have yet to see any critic who is so bothered with them that he casts doubt on the creativity of Okigbo and his "authentic Africanness."

In a recently published article on Nkem Nwankwo's novel, *Danda*, Oladele Taiwo quotes the following prayer by Danda over *Oji* (cola, not "wine" as translated by Taiwo):

The world is bad nowadays . . . Let the world be good. Let this *Oji* cleanse the world. Let it make us friends. May each man have what is due to him. The hawk shall perch and the eagle shall perch. Whichever bird says to the other don't perch let its wings break.

Taiwo goes on to analyze the passage to indicate its implications for the understanding of the paradoxical role which Danda plays in the novel and concludes: "So this apparently frivolous speech refers by implication to matters which are of paramount importance to the listeners."[16] Now, a similar prayer over cola had been printed in Achebe's *Things Fall Apart*. Both Achbe and Nwankwo are Igbo and had lifted the prayer straight from speech made practically every day in Igboland over cola. Would Taiwo have changed his opinion on the implications of the passage if he knew this?

I have been trying to create the impression that African writers and critics have not bothered with the question of plagiarism. This is not quite true. One remembers Soyinka's vitriolic attack on Camara Laye's *Le Regard du roi*:

> . . . most intelligent readers like their Kafka straight, not geographically transposed . . . It is truly amazing that foreign critics have contented themselves with merely dropping an occasional "Kafkaesque"—a feeble sop to integrity—since they cannot altogether ignore the more obvious imitativeness of Camara Laye's technique. (I think we can tell when the line of mere "influence" has been crossed.) Even within the primeval pit of collective allegory-consciousness, it is self-delusive to imagine that the Progresses of these black and white pilgrims have sprung from independent creative stresses . . . the contemporary interpreters of African themes have not truly assimilated the new idioms. It is merely naive to transpose the castle to the hut.[17]

This is as strongly as a view opposite to that I am presenting can be put. And Soyinka's stature as an African writer and critic gives a heavy weight of conviction to his viewpoint. (I wonder what the implications are in the fact that it is two writers in French who have provoked this violent argument.) Since I am not dealing with particulars, I will not take up the issue of Camara Laye, but I think Soyinka's attack provides a useful expression with which to continue a discussion of the question of plagiarism, namely, "sprung from individual creative stresses."

I take it that a work of art proceeds from the interplay of three elements—vision, material and manner. The artist has an experience he wishes to communicate, an idea, a significance; he has to find material adequate for the expression of this vision; he adopts chosen techniques and stylistic devices with which to deploy his material to his purpose.

In different cultures, at various times, the individuality of the "creative stress" has been assigned with differing emphasis to the three elements. Somebody has said something before—to his own time or to his own contemporaries; another person wants to say the same thing again—to his own time and to his own contemporaries. Some materials have been used before for a certain purpose; another person wants to use the same materials to give expression to another significance. Certain devices that were used traditionally on some material are now again available for use on other materials. Some cultures, at some times, are satisfied to acknowledge, for any of these activities, that the work has "sprung from individual creative stresses."

In African traditional culture, for example, it was taken for granted that a storyteller would tell the same stories that others had told before him, that he would be using materials that were already there in the culture. Originality was a function of manner rather than of matter. Hearing a well-told story was a more satisfying esthetic experience than hearing a new story badly told. It was crucial that the storyteller, as he travelled from place to place, as his audience changed in terms of age or status, adapted his material for relevance, and his stylistic devices for pleasure and conviction, but it did not matter from where he derived his materials.

The basic critical questions then were, what did the storyteller have to say? Did he use material adequate for his theme? And did he say it well? The question of where he got his matter was legalistic rather than artistic since each performance was an independent exercise and experience.

I am not even sure that this situation in oral traditional cultures is completely restricted to that context. The number of books that scholars have written on sources and influences from Shakespeare down to the present would indicate that writers, even since plagiarism became despicable, have been shopping around for models and ideas of other writers to steal from. I refuse to quote T. S. Eliot on this issue. Let me be facetious and say that if European writers have stopped stealing, perhaps it is a sign of genuine African authenticity to continue the tradition of disregarding legal ownership of the products of the imagination and rifling the traditional and the modern for the materials for giving expression to one's vision.

I have not written this piece in order to defend Ouologuem. My purpose has been to defend Schwarz-Bart from the charge of "fatuous largesse" (that was unkind and wrong-headed). My approach has been purely theoretical. I have not read *Le Dernier des Justes* and cannot therefore determine to what extent Ouologuem created something new out of what he apparently borrowed. My consideration is that borrowing is not the issue. Originality, in African tradition, has not much to do with where the artist derived his material. The essence of originality is the use to which the artist put his material, both borrowed and invented. Swift's "The Spider and the Bee" allegory, which incidentally he borrowed from traditional folklore, should not still need retelling. There is no need for a new Battle of the Books.

FOOTNOTES

[1] *Research in African Literatures,* 4 (1973), 129–30.

[2] Sunday Anozie, *Christopher Okigbo: Creative Rhetoric* (London: Evans, 1972), p. 36.

[3] In J. M. Cohen, ed., *The Penguin Book of Spanish Verse* (Harmondsworth: Penguin, 1956), pp. 423–24.

[4] Anozie, pp. 36–37.

[5] Cohen, p. 431.

[6] "Elegy for Alto," *Labyrinths* (London: Heinemann, 1971), p. 72. Chinweizu, in an article, "Prodigals, Come Home!" in *Okike,* 4 (1973), 1–12, has pointed out some more of Okigbo's borrowings from traditional Yoruba poetry.

[7] R. S. Rattray, *Ashanti* (Oxford: Oxford University Press, 1929, reprinted 1969), pp. 278–80.

[8] J. H. Kwabena Nketia, *Our Drums and Drummers* (Accra: Ghana Publishing House, 1968), p. 42.

[9] Anozie, p. 140.

[10] D. E. S. Maxwell and S. B. Bushrui, eds., *W. B. Yeats, 1865–1965: Centenary Essays on the Art of W. B. Yeats* (Ibadan: Ibadan University Press, 1965), pp. xiii–xv.

[11] Ulli Beier, ed., *Yoruba Poetry* (Cambridge: Cambridge University Press, 1970), p. 38.

[12] Ibid., p. 31.

[13] Ibid., p. 28.

[14] Ulli Beier, ed., *African Poetry* (Cambridge: Cambridge University Press, 1966), p. 42.

15 Gerald Moore and Ulli Beier, eds., *Modern Poetry from Africa* (Harmondsworth: Penguin, 1963), p. 87.

16 *"Danda* Revisited: A Reassessment of Nwankwo's Jester," *World Literature Written in English,* 13, 1 (1974), 7–16.

17 "From a Common Back Cloth: A Reassessment of the African Literary Image," *American Scholar,* 32 (1963), 387–88.

The Early Writings
of Wole Soyinka

BERNTH LINDFORS

Wole Soyinka's first books appeared only twelve years ago, in 1963. Since that time he has earned an international reputation as one of Africa's most abundantly gifted writers. Prolific and versatile, he has published eleven plays, a collection of satirical dramatic sketches, two volumes of poetry, two novels, a translation of D. O. Fagunwa's first fictional narrative, an autobiographical work based on his experiences in prison during the Nigerian civil war, and numerous essays on literary, social and political matters. What is most impressive about this extraordinary output is not its gross quantity but its fine quality; Soyinka is one of the few highly productive African authors writing in English whose works are original, creative, imaginative and satisfying. He is neither an inveterate autobiographer like Ezekiel Mphahlele nor a reformed "Market" writer like Cyprian Ekwensi nor an incontinent iconoclast like Taban lo Liyong. His imagination, vision and craft distinguish him as a creative artist of the very first rank, as a writer of world stature. Some would say he is the only truly original literary genius that Africa has yet produced.

His prodigious talent has not gone unrecognized by scholars and critics. Three critical books and one study guide on his writings

Research for this essay was done in Nigeria in 1972–73 on a Younger Humanist Fellowship awarded by the National Endowment for the Humanities. I wish to thank NEH and the University Research Institute at the University of Texas at Austin for their support.

Reprinted from the *Journal of African Studies* 2 (1975), 64-86, with the permission of the Editor and the University of California Press.

have recently been published,[1] and he is featured prominently in nearly every serious appraisal of modern African drama, poetry and fiction. Indeed, no survey of contemporary African literature would be complete without at least one chapter devoted to Soyinka's writings. He is already a classic, already a monument in the pantheon of African letters.

But though his life and works have been subjected to careful academic scrutiny, no one has given much attention to his early formative period as a writer. Little is known about his literary activities prior to 1960, when he returned to Nigeria after completing a B.A. in English at the University of Leeds and working for three years in London as a bartender, bouncer, substitute high school English teacher, and script-reader at the Royal Court Theatre. Even less is known about the writing he did before leaving for England in 1954, and not much has been said about how he spent his year in Ibadan as a Rockefeller Research Fellow in 1960–61. This article attempts to fill in a few of these large lacunae in Soyinka's literary career by examining some of his unknown writings.

Soyinka's first published works probably appeared in annuals or literary magazines at Government College Ibadan, the elite secondary school he attended before enrolling in 1952 in a preliminary course necessary for entry into University College Ibadan. It is known that he contributed to "house" magazines at Government College,[2] but his contributions have never been exhumed and discussed, probably because copies of these publications are now extremely hard to find. In an interview recorded in August 1962, Soyinka said:

> I would say I began writing seriously, or rather taking myself seriously, taking my *writing* seriously about three, four years ago, but I can only presume that I have always been interested in writing. In school I wrote the usual little sketches for production, the occasional verse, you know,

---

[1] Gerald Moore, *Wole Soyinka* (London, 1971); Alain Ricard, *Théâtre et nationalisme. Wole Soyinka et LeRoi Jones* (Paris, 1972); Eldred Durosimi Jones, *The Writing of Wole Soyinka* (London, 1973); James Gibbs, *Study Aid to "Kongi's Harvest"* (London, 1973).

[2] Information supplied by Dapo Adelugba, Theatre Arts Department, University of Ibadan. See Soyinka's comment below.

the short story, etc., and I think about 1951 I had the great excitement, of having a short story of mine broadcast on the Nigerian Broadcasting Service and that was sort of my first public performance.[3]

One wonders if the story Soyinka remembers as his "first public performance" was "Keffi's Birthday Treat," a brief narrative broadcast on the Children's Programme of the Nigerian Broadcasting Service's National Programme and published in one of the earliest issues of the *Nigerian Radio Times* in July 1954.[4] Even if "Keffi's Birthday Treat" is a later radio contribution, it may be significant as Soyinka's first short story to be published in a national magazine. Earlier stories may have appeared in high school and university publications, but these would not have been available to the general public. "Keffi's Birthday Treat" was very likely Soyinka's first public performance in print, if not on the air.

The story is a charming vignette telling of a young boy's attempt to treat himself to a visit to the University College Zoo in Ibadan on his tenth birthday. Here is the entire 850-word text, which must have taken about five minutes to read on the Children's Programme:

"I'll be ten tomorrow," said Keffi to himself as he lay in bed, staring at the ceiling of his home in Yaba. Yes, Keffi would indeed become a ten-year-old boy the following day. He had received some presents already, he was sure he would receive some more the next day, and finally, there was going to be a birthday party for him at seven o'clock in the evening. But, of all the presents he had received, there was not one which attracted him more than the book which had been sent to him by his big brother in England. And of the treats which he had been promised, the most exciting was the one which he had promised *himself*. The book contained beautifully coloured pictures of the animals in the London Zoo, and the treat was a trip to Ibadan to see the animals in the University College Zoo.

As far as Keffi was concerned, Ibadan was merely a street in Lagos! So, after breakfast the following day, he went to the nearest bus stop,

---

[3] Cosmo Pieterse and Dennis Duerden, eds., *African Writers Talking: A Collection of Radio Interviews* (New York, 1972), pp. 171–72.

[4] *Nigerian Radio Times* (July 1954), pp. 15–16. Chinua Achebe, who was working for the Nigerian Broadcasting Service at this time, may have edited this story for publication.

taking with him his week's pocket money, leaving a note on his mother's bed telling her where he was going, and promising to be back before the party. Keffi had no idea that Ibadan was a huge town and was over a hundred miles from Lagos; he had read of the University College Zoo in the Children's Newspaper, and had determined that some day, he would go and see it for himself.

Luck seemed to be with Keffi: for, as he stood waiting for the bus, he saw a kit-car pull up outside a petrol station, and—was he dreaming? —on its doors was written, "UNIVERSITY COLLEGE, IBADAN." Keffi at once ran towards the driver, begging him for a lift. But when he got to the car, he saw the driver's back was turned, and—his heart began to beat very fast—the door at the back was open! How very exciting to climb *in,* remain very quiet, and surprise the driver by coming out of the car when they got to the college! And this was just what Keffi did. He lay flat on the floor of the car, and waited for the driver to start it. Very soon, he heard the driver's voice. There was also another man, and they seemed to be coming to the back of the car, carrying something rather heavy! Keffi dared not look up, for fear he would be caught. He heard the driver say,

"Just lift it up and throw it inside."

What would they throw inside? Was it a box, and would they throw it right on him? Suppose it was a very heavy object and it was thrown on him; would it break his bones? Or was it a new animal for the zoo? Suppose it was a tiger, fresh from the jungle. Poor Keffi's knees were knocking and he began to be sorry that he ever started on this adventure. Should he scream? But before he could make up his mind, the two men threw the object into the car. It was a motor car wheel, and luckily, only a little part of it caught Keffi on the back. The driver did not even look inside the car, but shut the door, went to his seat and drove off.

Half an hour later, the car pulled up inside a place which looked like a big plantation. Keffi watched the driver get out of the car and after a while, he too crept out. He saw cows grazing in the fields, and a lot of fowls in the special little houses which had been made for them. This amused him a great deal, for the houses even had steps leading from them to the ground! And then Keffi grew very much interested in some vehicles called tractors. These had large iron spades, large iron wheels, large iron teeth and claws, all of which were used in uprooting the ground and felling trees. But he had not yet seen any wild animals, and it was while looking for them that a kind-looking official saw him, enquired where he lived and what he wanted. When Keffi told him, he burst out laughing. After laughing very heartily for a long time, he told Keffi,

"You are a little unfortunate, my boy. The lions and leopards and gorillas have all been taken away for a holiday. They will return after a week.

172

Will you come back then?" Keffi promised to return after a week, and thereupon the kind gentleman took him home and put him right on his doorstep.

He had spent only two hours away, and when, feeling sure that he had been to the University College Zoo, he told his mother his adventures, he was surprised to see her burst out laughing. When he asked why she laughed, she replied,

"You were very lucky that the driver did not go straight to Ibadan. That was not the University College Zoo, it was Agege Agricultural Station!"

"Next time," Keffi promised himself, "I really shall go to the Zoo."

What is most appealing about this story is the delightful combination of gentle humor, suspense and drama Soyinka manages to achieve in less than a thousand words. He is essentially telling a joke or humorous anecdote but he never allows the comedy to get out of control. He deftly builds up an air of excitement around the boy's escapade, inserts a few good laughs toward the end, and finishes with a punch line which Lagos and Ibadan listeners would especially appreciate. The University College Zoo at Ibadan, which was opened in the early 1950s, has always been a favorite tourist attraction for Nigerians, so Soyinka's story about a young boy's curiosity to see wild animals would have appealed to a wide radio audience, not just to children. "Keffi's Birthday Treat" was topical and entertaining, a harbinger of the creative harvest to come.

Soyinka's first contribution to campus publications at University College Ibadan appears to have been a poem entitled "Thunder to Storm" published in the second issue of *The University Voice*, the official organ of the Students' Union, in January 1953.[5] (Soyinka would have been eighteen years old at this time.) Written in rather jerky iambic tetrameter couplets with occasional slant rhymes and awkward syntax, the poem describes the impact of a brief but devastating tropical storm on a seaside community somewhere in Africa. One could say that "Thunder to Storm" bears a vague resemblance in narrative strategy to eighteenth and nineteenth century English

---

[5] *The University Voice* 2 (January 1953): 21. The poem is the earliest I have been able to trace. It was published six years before the poem Moore cites as "the first of Soyinka's work to appear in Nigeria" (Moore, *Wole Soyinka*, p. 6).

meditative verse devoted to pondering man's relationship with his natural environment, but specific comparisons would be ludicrous because Soyinka's poem lacks art. Indeed, his craftsmanship is so crude and his tone so uncertain that one frequently cannot tell whether some of the comical side-effects are accidental or deliberate. One imagines Soyinka's puckish grin somewhere beneath the fractured surface, but it is conceivable that this ninety-eight-line jingle was actually intended as a serious poem. Certainly it is the most juvenile of his juvenilia. To prove the point, here is the whole catastrophic cloudburst, with every minor typographical disaster preserved:

A low, long rumble from the sky,
That dwindled off into a sigh.
Querying eyes looked up. The sky was clear.
And this of course soon quelled all fear.
No heavy cloud, the day was bright,
So thought they all. but none was right.
Said two young boys, "we'll go for wood,
When we return, we'll have some food."
"I'll hurry home," a woman said,
"I've got to put my babe to bed."
Boasted one man, "I'll win this game,
In chess I have a lot of fame."
The homeless tramp, he laughted and shrugged
He'd had no luck, and on he jogged.
The fishermen upon the sea,
They hauled their nets for all to see.
The rich old man watched them at work,
From his near home, he mused, "what luck!"
About their daily tasks they went
All were happy, all content.

Then hell broke loose; the bright clear sky
Was covered up, dense clouds rolled by.
Quite soon their heavy tears they'd shed
And down below the humans fled.
Huge streaks of lightning flashed about
As if the whole world they would rout.
And down to earth, a march with the wind
'Twas all-destroying, nowhere kind.

This tree was stubborn, down it went
Poles and cables, them it bent.
This house stood firm, it soon crashed in;
And with the wind went the dust-bin.
Some roofs were slack and off they went
To some far place by the wind sent
Electric wires soon were cut
They'd stood for years, their pride was hurt.
The dead alone were free from this,
But wait! They would not have this bliss.
Into the graveyard the wind marched
And for a mighty tree it searched.
It soon found one—its great shadow
Had sheltered graves—but no ado.
A deafening crash and down it fell.
The ghosts cried out, "This's worse than hell."
Its long stout roots all gave a tug
Up came the graves without a clog.
Its mighty trunk on others crashed
And round the wreckage the wind lashed.

Then came a lull—nerves were on edge
The wind seemed shamed of its sacrilege.
All things stood still, all places quiet;
Was that the end—none could say yet.
But when the people's hopes had soared,
The winds unfurled, the thunder roared.
"We do but rest and muster strength
You'll fell our mighty arm at length."
And so again the elements marched
The ground was sodden where once was parched.
Imams called 'Allah', Christians, 'Lord';
On blew the wind by their stouts bored,
Twisting, felling, crashing, breaking,
Tearing, smashing—all destroying.
"Forgive our sins," they cried with tears
They had not called on God for years.

Spent and weary the wind retired,
So did the rain; the clouds were tired.
Behold the sky—already bright
Could one believe it spelt such plight?
But look below—this is no fun,

But scene of sorrow, sight for mourn.
Dead bodies—torn and mangled
'Neath the cables bent and fangled.
The woman who some time before
Had hurried—making for her door;
The two chess-players who'd been so well
They reached home safe but their home fell;
Two little boys who went for wood
They too were in a happy mood:
The merry tramp for shelter fled
The friendly tree his body bled:
The fisherman who'd worked all day
He did not see the sun's next ray:
The rich old man who'd loved the sea
The sea grew rough and claimed him fee:
The quiet families at home
Thought they were safe; no more they, droam.
Some killed by lightning, some by walls
Some smashed by trees, none heard their falls
Electric wires by trees were cut
Some touched them and—that was their lot!
The homeless wept when morning broke
But what of those who never woke?
They little thought so soon they'd leave
Their loved ones for them to grieve.
The child no more his mum could call;
Why do they poke beneath the wall?
The wife no more her spouse would storm
He'd gone off in a thunderstorm.

It is a wonder that young Soyinka, after composing this uninspired undergraduate doggerel, managed to escape being struck down by one of Shango's thunderbolts!

In 1953–54, his second and last year at University College Ibadan before leaving for Leeds, Soyinka was involved in a number of campus activities which made demands on his literary abilities. As an enthusiastic member of the Progressive Party, a student political organization set up in opposition to the more powerful student Dynamic Party, he took over the editorship of *The Eagle,* an irregular cyclostyled newssheet of campus commentary and humor. Three issues edited by him can be found in the African collection of the

Ibadan University library.[6] Each begins with a half-page cartoon (drawn by a student named Bodede) and a column of quips and queries called "Sneezy Nosey Wants to Know." Some of the things Sneezy Nosey wanted to know in Soyinka's years as editor were:

—Why people say, "I'm on the level"—as if a level-crossing is not the same as a double-crossing.
—Why we no longer have poached eggs in the mornings. Or have the game-keepers grown too vigilant?
—If the average 'Dynamic' councillor was drunk when he stood elections. Or have students not heard of the Dynamite, who when reminded that a council meeting was in progress said, "Get away! Do you think I have time for nothing else?"—very illustrative of the 'Dynamic' sense of duty.
—Whether every student knows he is first a student before being a noise-maker and when we will save lecturers the energy expended in begging for silence.
—Whether the use of pyjamas on the Bar Beach was that its variegated colours attracted sea-anemones and agamemnones from their beds into the research nets.
—Whether students know it is hitting below the belt to refer disparagingly to a stewards's office when he is getting the better of you in an affably begun argument over the evil effects or otherwise of drinking ice-cold water after hot tea.
—Whether there is not a great gap between a "gentleman" and a gentle man.
—How many students make one Union and how many Unions make one University College.
—How much you enjoy reading the "Eagle."

Soyinka also wrote an editorial column on page two in which he commented on campus affairs. In his first issue he used some of this space to welcome incoming freshmen and to outline the editorial policy of *The Eagle,* which he called "the cleanest paper for reading in this college":

The policy of the paper differs from the others in this, that we believe more in attacking general faults than in putting individuals to ridicule. This does

---

6 I wish to thank the librarians at the University of Ibadan, particularly Mr. S. O. Oderinde, for assisting me to locate materials in this collection.

not mean that we never attack individuals; we do this when it is necessary, but never vilely or with personal animosity showing in every line of it. We concentrate on trying to raise the general standard of behaviour among students, and at the same time, give them the most interesting articles to read.[7]

In the first two issues he edited, Soyinka remained true to this policy by using his editorial column to scold fellow students for failing to turn up at meetings on time, to thank faculty and staff for giving student hitchhikers lifts to and from campus, to congratulate the Dynamic Party for its decisive students' council election victory, and to reprimand *The Sword,* another campus publication, for indulging in smear tactics against its critics. However, by the time the third issue of *The Eagle* materialized, Soyinka's patience with the antics of some of his peers had been exhausted by a personal incident which he took very seriously and which prompted him to let loose the full fury of his tongue in an editorial entitled "Reptiles." The piece is worth quoting in toto, for it reveals the impassioned rhetoric of which the nineteen-year-old Soyinka was capable:

I hate snakes. I hate all reptiles with a hatred that is born of fear. That is why I'm writing this. That, in fact, is why I have stayed on this term merely to write this Editorial, which is about the only thing I have done in the production of this issue.

I'd rather face an infuriated bull—then, at least, I can see what's coming to me. But a snake, a vile venomous, slimy, disgusting creature who will strike and disappear before you can say "Jumping Rattlesnakes". . . .

Some days ago, a student killed two snakes and a scorpion—all in one night! He was quite amazed, for he hadn't believed that there were so many reptiles in the Campus. How many people think the same way! And that is precisely what makes reptiles so dangerous. Until the last holidays I, too, did not realize that the college had so many of them. But we do! They exist in shirts and trousers, they browse in the library and behave like gentlemen.

When the BISI TAIWO—BOZO gang, hiding under the cloak of anonimity [sic], scored personal hits off the "Embassy" members, several students said it was "Fair Comments." I ask such students if they will still make the same defence for them when they learn that these cowardly

<hr>

[7] *The Eagle* 3, no. 1 (1953): 2.

creatures, or members of the same 'genus,' wrote letters to friends of the Embassy maligning the members most callously, and concocting stories, compared with which Russian propaganda is child's play. These letters, I may add, were written mostly to girl-friends of the Embassy Clubmembers.

I called them snakes. Yes, only a snake's brain could have thought of a description like "wriggling her waist like a wounded snake." I know that BISI TAIWO is a jilted aspirant, as were many of the horrified "Puritans." But surely it was carrying vindictiveness too far, *to write an anonymous letter* to that girl's principal, embellishing and painting luridly an incident at which civilized people would not have batted an eyelid. What did you hope to gain? The credit of having ruined a girl's career by engineering her dismissal from her school?

Contemptible creatures—too mean to be noticed, too dangerous to be ignored! The fountain-heads of morals, uprightness and virtues. Self-imposed judges, most competent, since, being master of all vices, you can smell a little fault one mile off and, what's better, placard it 120 miles toward the Coast. Your cowardice threw the former Editor of "Bug" into disrepute; for a long time he was thought to be the writer of the anonymous letter. Rather than correct the opinion, you encouraged it, because it put you above suspicion.

But I warn you, stop playing with poison gas. We have enough snakes in this college without your belly-crawlers who fawn in public and strike behind.[8]

Vituperation of this sort, however, was rare in *The Eagle*. Most contributions were light-hearted and amusing, even when they were jabs at the absurdities and bad manners of fellow students. Since many of these pieces were anonymous or signed with pseudonyms, it is likely that a good number were written by Soyinka's friends and acquaintances, but he himself set the dominant tone with his editorials, regular columns and numerous witty vignettes and fillers. One can use his signed contributions as a guide to identification of the articles he wrote incognito. Here, for example, is an unsigned anecdote which is characteristic of his playful style:

SORRY PARTNER

Once upon a time, I went to play tennis on the tennis court (some play it on the table, you know.) Well, my partner was just as good a player as

---

[8] *The Eagle* 3, no. 3 (1954): 2.

I—that is, the very worst. He wielded his racket like a blunderbuss and once or twice sent his racket into the football field. That didn't worry me. It was when I saw that he was a confirmed die-hard sorry-partnerer that sweat began to stand out on my forehead like icicles.

I was embarrassed. Why? Because I was playing just as badly as he and there he was, apologising for every bad stroke he played. In vain I assured him that the essence of tennis is not in apologies, but he insisted, and poured out his Sorrys as if he had all the sorrows of Satan in his pocket.

The short of it was that, in the long run, he became so effusive that I took the offensive. Boy oh Boy! Did I sorry-partner him or did I? When, (he standing at the net) I hit the ball into his rudder, I porry-sartnered him. When, attempting to take a fast one, I skated, jitter-bugged and eventually landed on my cusher, I torry-parsnered him before he could open his mouth. When, (a liver fluke it was), he hit a super-tonic one that took our opponent on the kisser, I Tory-gardenered him. (You see, by this time I didn't know what I was talking again.)

Even when he groaned (as he always did when hitting a ball), I sorry-portnered him. I'm telling you that I very-pestered him so ruthlessly that he capitulated and took refuge in a passing car.

That's what to do to them![9]

Also, as far as anonymous poetry is concerned, one would be willing to swear, based on the evidence of "Thunder to Storm," that the following rhymed lines bear all the earmarks of the wild and Wole idiom:

THE BANJO'S BROKEN STRING

A Hall Three disaster
Hapt after siesta.
Ukele Banjo
Woke with the cry, "My Joe!
I'll betcha my last dime
For high tea it's high time."
He went for a quick bath
Gave his tooth a quick bruth—
That is how he said 'brush'
When his tooth had—but s-sh!
His brush played a bad joke
His false tooth in two broke.

---

[9] *The Eagle* 3, no. 1 (1953): 4–5.

The poor lad his tooth eyed,
Said, "Thou wasth my great pride."
He fixed back the top half
To tea went with a loud laugh.

But worse hapt at tea quaff,
The top part too came off.
My lad thought 'twas sugar
Or hardened vinegar,

And being a good Christian,
He swallowed his pride. When
this Banjo was ex-rayed,
This was the report made:—

"Long after a ray-look
Up and down his stommick,
We found his false fangus
In his oesophagus."
Signed—X-Ray Man, Tagus.[10]

Even if these two attributions are incorrect, even if Soyinka never wrote inspired trivia about tennis or teeth, he must be given credit for having encouraged such nonsense in *The Eagle*. The quality of the humor in the three issues he edited was far higher than that in any of the rival campus publications of his day and infinitely superior to what can be found in similar academic publications in Nigeria today. Soyinka was one of the quickest of the campus wits at University College Ibadan in the early fifties, and he earned his reputation as a clever word-monger by making people laugh. He had an antic imagination.

If one wishes to seek clues to his literary opinions at this period, *The Eagle* provides a few rewarding hints, especially in an article entitled "Ten Most Boring Books," which Soyinka had culled from an American magazine. After reporting that a poll of hundreds of editors, booksellers, authors and librarians in America had revealed that Bunyan's *Pilgrim's Progress,* Melville's *Moby Dick,* Milton's *Paradise Lost,* Spenser's *Faerie Queene,* Boswell's *Life of Samuel*

---

[10] Ibid., p. 6.

Johnson, Richardson's *Pamela,* Eliot's *Silas Marner,* Scott's *Ivanhoe,* Cervantes' *Don Quixote* and Goethe's *Faust* were regarded as the ten most boring classics of literature, Soyinka added: "A good choice I would say, except in Scott's *Ivanhoe* and Cervantes' *Don Quixote.* How the latter in particular was included in the list beats me completely. And evidently those lucky people have never heard Newman's *Idea of a University*—oh, maybe it isn't a classic."[11]

It is perhaps significant that Soyinka, as a young student, was turned off by all but the prose chivalric romances on the list. In the following issue of *The Eagle* he wrote, under the pseudonym "The Gallant Captain," a mock-heroic poem which spoke of longing for the old days of King Arthur when it was possible to rescue damsels in distress with romantic flair.[12] Soyinka, who had written many gallant articles in defense of "ladies" maligned, heckled or in some way abused by his peers at the university, may have responded to the ideals and courtesies of courtly love, even while perhaps adopting a more down-to-earth approach in his own personal entanglements. As well as being a humorist, the teen-aged Soyinka appears to have been a pragmatic romantic.

The importance of *The Eagle* in Soyinka studies is that it gives us a bird's-eye view of the vitality, creativity and intellectual energy that animated this extraordinary young man long before he developed into a full-fledged writer. We can see a sample of what he thought, what he did and what he wrote at this very formative period in his life. He once invented this motto for his contributors:

> A plateful of criticism
> With a spice of witticism
> Makes the correct article
> of food for the "Eagle."[13]

One could say that all of Soyinka's creative concoctions have been a

---

11 *The Eagle* 3, no. 2 (1954): 5.

12 *The Eagle* 3, no. 3 (1954): 6. This poem is quoted in full in my "Popular Literature for an African Elite," *Journal of Modern African Studies* 12, no. 3 (1974): 471–86.

13 *The Eagle* 3, no. 2 (1954): 8.

blend of witticism and criticism, but it is clear from reading his earliest writings that over the years the emphasis has gradually shifted from light witticism to heavy criticism. In his youth he could still indulge in innocent laughter.

After leaving for England in 1954, Soyinka appears to have settled down to his studies for a year or two. At least there is no extant published evidence from mid-1954 until 1956 to show that he continued to engage in such extracurricular activities as creative writing and campus polemics while making the initial adjustment to undergraduate life at the University of Leeds.[14] He occasionally composed humorous "Epistles of Cap'n Blood to the Abadinians" which he sent to his friends Pius Oleghe and Ralph Opara, the new editors of *The Eagle* and *The Criterion*, where at least one of these letters was published in 1955; from this sample it is clear that he enjoyed regaling his friends with tall tales about life in the British Isles:

Hallo Ed.,

I'm sure you must be hoping that I'm dead—and when I say you I mean of course your readers (usually no more than six or seven) who must be glad that I no longer smear the pages of the "Eagle" with my nib. No such luck, I'm afraid. You ought to know I'm pretty hard to kill. Why, only yesterday a car bumped into me and had to be taken to the Scrap-Iron Dealer, while I walked home with no worse damage than some engine-oil on my trousers.

Well, I suppose that story is as good as any to begin with but I'm sure you never believe it—just because you fellows never believe me when I'm telling you the truth. You'll want to know what I think of England, no doubt. Well, it's a wonderful place to live in. Even the climate is not unbearable. The only thing I quarrel with in the climate is the frequent gales. These gales, you'd better know, don't come once in a grey sun; they come without warning (except when B.B.C. Weather forecast has remarkable luck) and they are strong enough to blow your teeth into your throat. But I must admit to myself that it does me a world of good to watch men and women (the fatter the better) chasing their hats or shawls for a couple of thousand of yards.

---

[14] The record, of course, may be incomplete. It would be interesting to examine student publications from the University of Leeds to see if any contributions by Soyinka can be found there.

Only yesterday I stood at the bus-stop and one of these gales was fooling around just then. Well, a friend of mine came along, and he stretched out his hand for a handshake. D'you know what happened? The wind bent his hand gradually backwards, and before he knew where he was, he was shaking hands with the person standing behind him. If that doesn't give you an idea of the strength of these "breezes", nothing ever will.[15]

Though Soyinka did not start writing for the stage while he was at Leeds, Gerald Moore states that some of his early satirical poetry, such as "The Other Immigrant," was written there before he obtained his B.A. in 1957.[16] What is not generally known is that Soyinka also wrote a good deal of fiction in his late undergraduate years. In 1956, for example, he was awarded second prize in the Margaret Wrong Memorial Fund writing competition for a fiction entry entitled "Oji River."[17] He also published at least two short stories in a University of Leeds magazine called *The Gryphon* and contributed another to *New Nigeria Forum*, a Nigerian students' journal based in London. Since it would take too much space to reproduce these stories in full, here is a brief synopsis of each.

"Madame Etienne's Establishment," which appeared in the March 1957 issue of *The Gryphon*,[18] is a hilarious Chaucerian tale of sexual duplicity. Told in the leisurely, familiar style of a witty confidante, it describes how a clever Parisian madam contrives to marry a foolish provincial barber in order to convert his barbershop into a prosperous rural bordello. This is accomplished without the husband ever realizing what is going on. Persuaded to believe that she has merely changed the place into a high-class hair dressing salon, he goes off to his farm each day, leaving all the hairy details of the new business to his wife and her numerous buxom assistants from the metropole. The establishment thrives and becomes a major French tourist attraction. Only toward the end of the story does a crisis threaten.

---

[15] *The Eagle* 4, no. 2 (1955): 4.

[16] Moore, *Wole Soyinka*, p. 6.

[17] *West Africa* (13 July 1957), p. 670. Manuscripts submitted for this competition were to be "not less than 7,500 and not more than 15,000 words," according to *Universitas* 2, no. 1 (December 1955): 3.

[18] *The Gryphon* (March 1957), pp. 11–22. I am grateful to Tony Harrison for bringing this and the following story to my attention.

Monsieur Etienne returns home early one day and finds Petjones, the ex-Mayor of the town, in the waiting room.

"What are you doing here?" demanded Etienne.

"I came for a hair-cut of course," replied the miscreant.

"A hair-cut?" laughed Etienne. "Why, you haven't a hair on your head!"

It was true indeed. Petjones's head shone with the bald brilliance of fifty years' careless living. But at that moment, it also housed a measure of active matter, which was now working furiously, and eventually succeeded in producing the outrageous lie that, "It was a mere slip of the tongue. I really come here every week for a scalp massage. It is meant to make my hair grow again."

Etienne looked at the man and he pitied him. Then he looked at the terrified girls, and he despised them. He looked all round the room, at the expensive furniture, and the plush-carpeted floor. And he smiled bitterly. For he knew at last what vile methods had been used to pay for the luxury.

He had always considered his business and his name impeccable. But now a huge light shone on the rottenness, and he realised at last the dishonesty of the foundation on which his reputation as a hair-dresser had been built. This was what Valeise had meant by her Parisian methods.

He felt disgraced and polluted for ever, and the veins of anger swelled in the muscles of his bull neck.

"Send Madame to me at once," he snapped at the girls. "I shall be waiting for her in her private room."

Soyinka then allows suspense to build up for a few paragraphs while Petjones tries to take French leave of the establishment. Finally there is the climactic confrontation scene:

Monsieur Etienne wasted no time at all when he stood face to face with his wife. He seized her by the shoulders, and the scared and guilty look on her face confirmed the very worst of his suspicions. Valeise gasped with pain and terror as his powerful fingers dug into her flesh and brought her mercenary face within an inch of his own livid countenance:

"Madame," he spat, "Have you thought of what will happen to us when Monsieur Petjones, and the others you have swindled, discover that you have no means of making their hair grow!?"

It was marvelously orchestrated scenes such as this, scenes which swell up magnificently until Soyinka suddenly deflates the melodrama by letting it burst into comedy, that gave evidence of Soyinka's maturing theatrical instincts. He obviously knew how to keep an audience entertained.

Soyinka's next story for *The Gryphon* was a mock fable set in Africa in the early nineteenth century.[19] Entitled "A Tale of Two Cities," it told of court intrigues and missionary conspiracies in the palace of King Kupamiti of Abeolumo. This young king, an early convert to Christianity, had been persuaded by the missionaries to give up four of his five wives and to take on a private tutor named Oddy Summers so future princes and princesses could be instructed in the ways of Western life. One of the first services Summers is called upon to perform for the royal household is to provide secret assistance for Kupamiti's queen who discovers she is barren. Both are aware that this news must be kept from the king lest the queen and Christianity be expelled from the kingdom. Summers carefully arranges for a twin baby discarded by a pagan village to be retrieved from the forest and pronounced the queen's miraculously conceived son. The strategem works, the bastard heir is christened Prince James, the kingdom rejoices and celebrates the immunity from British taxation that this continuation of the royal line ensures, and King Kupamiti and his queen are presented with a special gift from the British crown to commemorate the historic event and to create an indissoluble link between the dynasties of the two nations. The gift is a bed-warming pan.

Soyinka tells this zany tale with characteristic wit and ebullient imagination. Again he opts for amusing rather than instructing his audience.

The third story from this period, published in the *New Nigeria Forum* in May 1958, also had the somewhat incongruous title of "A Tale of Two Cities."[20] It recounts a harrowing episode in the life of Raymond C. Pinkerton, Esq., a young British civil servant assigned to a colonial post in Lagos. To prepare for his stint in Africa, Pinkerton had heated his London apartment to a super-tropical temperature, had borrowed all the books on African travel and adventure

---

[19] *The Gryphon* (Autumn, 1957), pp. 16–22.
[20] *New Nigeria Forum* 2 (May 1958): 26–30.

from the municipal library, and had put in long hours at local cinemas watching Tarzan films. After three strenuous weeks of sweating and swotting, he boards the plane exhausted and soon falls asleep while reading yet another true-life adventure about a "mammoth spider which swallowed a whole cow alive and crushed wooden huts with its tentacles." When the plane arrives in Lagos, Pinkerton is still sleeping, and the official who has come to welcome him, thinking he has been overpowered by the heat, quickly conveys him to his flat and puts him to bed. Pinkerton awakes the next morning puzzled, then alarmed, then terrified and panic-stricken to discover that he and his bed are completely surrounded by a gauzy film tapering to a point directly above him.

> . . . his mind went back to the book which he had read on his plane journey. Spiders! African spiders! A spider which would swallow a cow, and crush wooden huts could surely spin such a web as that. Pinkerton began to sweat. His imagination was fired. He could see it all . . . . The dead of night, and the spider stalks into his room, and finds him lying helpless in his bed. Perhaps the monster had just dined and finds a juicy morsel like Pinkerton too large for dessert. So he spins a web round him, intending to return after he has digested his last meal. That could be any moment now!

In a blind and desperate fury Pinkerton flings himself at the web, finds he can't break through, and struggles frantically to disentangle himself from its clinging folds. When he screams for help, an African steward rushes to his aid and quickly extricates him from the spider's terrifying white shroud, which of course turns out to be nothing more than a mosquito net.

Given this evidence of Soyinka's pronounced predilection for merriment, it is not surprising that three of his earliest plays, all of which date from his London years, were comedies—*The Lion and the Jewel*, "The Invention" (an extravagant political satire), and *The Trials of Brother Jero*.[21] Since his career as a neophyte dramatist at

---

[21] Pieterse and Duerden, *African Writers Talking*, pp. 170–74; Moore, *Wole Soyinka*, pp. 7–15; Ricard, *Théâtre et nationalisme*, p. 228; Jones, *Writing of Wole Soyinka*, p. xiii. For a description of "The Invention," see Charles R. Larson, "Soyinka's First Play: 'The Invention,' " *Africa Today* 18, no. 4 (1971): 80–83.

the Royal Court Theatre has already been traced by a number of commentators,[22] let us now turn our attention to his activities in the months following his return to Nigeria early in 1960.

Soyinka leapt back into Nigerian life with gusto. Awarded a fellowship by the Rockefeller Foundation for research on African drama,[23] he was able to buy a Landrover and travel about Western Nigeria with ease. However, he appears to have spent most of his time in Ibadan where he held a position at the university as research fellow in African drama.[24] From this base he made frequent jaunts to Lagos, at times commuting between the two cities almost daily in order to rehearse with those members of his newly formed acting company "The 1960 Masks," who lived in the capital. Gerald Moore and others have sketched in the outlines of this very busy period in Soyinka's life.[25]

What has not been discussed or even mentioned in the literature on Soyinka is his work in Nigerian radio and television in 1960 and 1961). The *Nigerian Radio Times* (later called the *Radio-TV Times*), a program journal of the Nigerian Broadcasting Corporation, provides a gold mine of information on his performances and productions for the electronic media during this period. As early as March 6, 1960, he was on the air participating in a dramatic reading of his first one-act play, "The Swamp Dwellers," which had been performed in London and Ibadan the year before. His program notes for the occasion yield interesting theatrical data. After giving a brief synopsis of the plot and warning listeners that it would be "futile to seek a central character or action" in this "play of mood," Soyinka describes the earlier performances as follows:

---

22 See especially Moore, *Wole Soyinka*, pp. 7–9, and James Gibbs, "Wole Soyinka: Bio-bibliography," *Africana Library Journal* 3, no. 1 (1972): 15–22.

23 Moore, *Wole Soyinka*, p. 9. Moore says Soyinka was awarded a "research fellowship which would enable him to travel widely in Nigeria, studying and recording traditional festivals, rituals and masquerades rich in dramatic content," but an account in Nigeria's *Radio Times* (3 July 1960) states, "A grant was made recently by the Rockefeller Foundation to enable 'Wole to make a survey of Nigerian drama in its modern development." It appears that he was studying modern development in traditional theater.

24 Gibbs, "Wole Soyinka," p. 16.

25 Moore, *Wole Soyinka*, pp. 14–15; Gibbs, "Wole Soyinka," pp. 15–16.

"The Swamp Dwellers" was first produced in London at the Annual Drama Festival of the National Union of Students on New Year's Eve, 1958. It turned out that there was nothing significant about the date. We called ourselves the Nigeria Drama Group, but this included a Ceylonese (Tamil), two West Indians, an American with a jaw breaking German name, and three Britishers.

We also had some Nigerians. Miss Francesca Pereira was our First Lady of the Stage—listeners here are already acquainted with her talents.

Mr. Jide Ajayi provided unexpected comic inventions with his creation of the part of a goofy drummer, and Banjo Solaru—of "Calling Nigeria" fame— paralysed the audience for five minutes, during our second performance, by giving vent to a subterranean, earthy, odorombustious belch after the cane-brew swilling scene of the play.

It was the briefest but windiest ad-libbing I was ever priviledged [sic] to hear on any stage.[26]

Five months later, in the *TV Times and Radio News,* an entertainment publication spawned by the *Daily Times* of Lagos, there is a report on Soyinka's first television play, which was broadcast on August 6, 1960. This may be the only account available of this still unpublished play:

The Western Nigeria Television organisation reaches a significant milestone on Saturday August 6. On that day (at 8.45 p.m.) WNTV will screen the first full length play produced in their studios in Ibadan. The play entitled "MY FATHER'S BURDEN" was written by the Nigerian playwright, Wole Soyinka and has been produced and directed for television by Segun Olusola, WNTV Producer.

"MY FATHER'S BURDEN" is a human interest drama about the struggle between an idealistic young man and his father whose philosophy of life, in an age where every man tries to grab the most he can, is "live and let others live."

The part of Chief Nwane, the sixty-year-old father, is played by Nigeria's stage and screen star Orlando Martins.

This will be Orlando's first public appearance on the stage since he returned to this country about a year ago after nearly forty-five years abroad.

Chief Nwane is an aristocrat. He is enlightened, influencial [sic] and a former minister of state. He loves his son, Onya, and sees to it that he is

---

[26] *Radio Times* (March 1960), p. 5.

well provided for to enter the world. But Chief Nwane is also pompous, proud, authoritative and blunt. . . .

Wole Soyinka, author of the script, assumes, perhaps, the most burdensome role—that of Chuks, ostensibly Onya's friend. Chuks does not know a thing about Onya's character neither are they of the same temperament. He is no more than Onya's drinking companion.[27]

Soyinka wrote at least one other script which has never been printed. This was a play called "The Tortoise" which was broadcast on NBC radio in mid-December 1960 and again in late January 1961. It appears to have been a rather unusual Anansi story. The first account of it in the *Radio Times* states: "The Tortoise in Wole Soyinka's play is different. This Tortoise is in business—big business. In actual fact, this story is about the days of prospecting. I know nobody will believe that the Tortoise can ever have any saving grace, but this play is about one Tortoise who turned out to have a heart of Gold."[28] A later account gives more details:

In Wole Soyinka's play, the Tortoise appears under the name of Anansi. The change in name or rather the adoption of a pseudonym has not effected any change in character. The Tortoise is always the Tortoise. One would have expected Anansi (The Tortoise) to be a little bit out of his depth with so much (shoot'n) going on. But no sir! Anansi had his own "one shooters" even if he did not use it too often. He did not have to, you see. After all he had got himself interested in research work and by diligently experimenting with all sorts of home-brewed wine, he had discovered the most lethal weapon of all—the Anansi Milk-Shake. You may well ask "what on earth is that?" My answer will be "The first ever invented homemade bomb," and the recipe is very simple!

In all his exploits, the Tortoise has always had one family or the other as his target. In this play, it is the unfortunate Ajantala family. Yes, the Ajantalas and the Anansi were perpetually feuding. . . . "You can take all your Western badmen and put them together—the Kelly's, Bill and Kid, Cimarron Kid, Jesse James and all other what-nots—and I tell you that none of their exploits will come near the havoc which the Ajantalas and the Anansi reaked [sic] on one another. Two out of every three murders which were committed in Plateau Dry-Gulch Saloon could be notched on the one-shooters of these two clans."

---

[27] *TV Times and Radio News* (28 July 1960), pp. 12–13.
[28] *Radio Times* (18 December 1960), p. 3.

That was a long time ago. It all happened in Plateau Mining Town in the days when stories were *not* stories but part of every-day life. In other words, it happened ONCE UPON A TIME."[29]

Soyinka's first TV drama, "My Father's Burden," may have been intended as a serious work or a "play of mood" similar to "The Swamp Dwellers," but this mock "Tortoise" from the Wild West obviously was meant as a free-wheeling farce. Soyinka was back to his old antics again, trying to corral belly laughs.

The *Radio Times* also makes mention of one other unknown Soyinka play entitled "The Roots," which was "played during the British Drama League" in 1959, presumably in London.[30] No further details are given but one imagines Soyinka must have been active in the production since he was still in England at that time. Later, on September 25, 1960, just one week before the ceremonies marking Nigeria's full political independence, the *Radio Times* announced a forthcoming radio production of Soyinka's "Camwood on the Leaves," which had been "specially commissioned by Radio Nigeria for INDEPENDENCE."[31] This play, broadcast five years later on the BBC's "African Theatre" program and finally published in 1973,[32] was introduced in program notes by Abiola Irele as having been "inspired by some traditional Yoruba songs," especially "one of the best known traditional songs of the Yorubas, 'Agbe',," which concerns "Camwood (*Osun*), a bright red dye with which the new child is bathed."[33] These traditional songs apparently were incorporated in the play without substantial textual modification by Soyinka.

In addition to writing radio and television playscripts, Soyinka was quite active in 1960 in developing a new series of radio talks called "Talking through Your Hat."[34] Several of his light-hearted contribu-

---

[29] Ibid. (22 January 1961), p. 7.
[30] Ibid. (3 July 1960), p. 6.
[31] Ibid. (25 September 1960), p. 6. Soyinka mentions this fact in an interview in Pieterse and Duerden, *African Writers Talking*, p. 171.
[32] See Shirley Cordeaux, "The BBC African Service's Involvement in African Theatre," *Research in African Literatures* 1 (1970): 153; Soyinka, *Camwood on the Leaves* (London, 1973).
[33] *Radio Times* (25 September 1960), p. 6.
[34] Ibid. (3 July 1960), p. 6.

tions to this series were later published in the *Radio Times*: first a hilarious medley of parodies on after-dinner speeches as delivered by a patronizing American, a pompous government minister, a long-winded "small-fry" master of ceremonies, and the oldest alumnus in attendance at the Sir Milton Mackenzie Grammar School Eve of Independence Old Boys' Dinner;[35] then an amusing glance at the lives of lorry drivers and their scrapes with the law (a theme to which Soyinka returned in his play *The Road*);[36] next a personal travelogue telling of the wonders of Paris, "land of flesh and bread";[37] and finally an attack on the concept of the "African Personality," which Soyinka found as demeaning to Africans as previous stereotyped notions of the "African mentality."[38] All these topics, even his serious indictment of the shortcomings of the Negritude ideology, were treated comically.

Although writing for radio and television must have kept him quite busy, Soyinka also managed to find sufficient time in his first months home to play a leading role in a University of Ibadan production of *The Good Woman of Setzuan;*[39] to complete the manuscript of *The Trials of Brother Jero,* which had its première performance in Ibadan that same year;[40] to script, produce, direct and act in his most ambitious play, *A Dance of the Forests,* which had been commissioned for the Nigerian Independence Celebrations;[41] and to publish a number of poems and critical essays in *The Horn,* a University of Ibadan poetry magazine founded a few years earlier by J. P. Clark and Martin Banham.[42]

Soyinka was a regular contributor to *The Horn* between 1960 and 1962. Among his poems dating from this period are two dealing

---

[35] Ibid. (11 September 1960), p. 7.
[36] Ibid. (18 September 1960), p. 7.
[37] Ibid. (4 December 1960), pp. 6–7.
[38] Ibid. (22 January 1961), pp. 6–7.
[39] *Ibadan* 9 (1960): 20; Moore, *Wole Soyinka,* p. 15.
[40] Ibid.
[41] Moore, *Wole Soyinka,* p. 15; Gibbs, "Wole Soyinka," pp. 16–17. Reviews of the performance can be found in *Ibadan* 10 (1960): 30–32, and *African Horizon* 2 (January 1961): 8-11. Moore said it was *Caucasian Chalk Circle,* also by Brecht.
[42] For a history of this magazine, see W. H. Stevenson's article in a forthcoming issue of *Research in African Literatures.*

with aspects of the theater, "Stage" and "Audience to Performer," one written in pidgin English, "Okonjo de Hunter," one entitled "epitaph for Say Tokyo Kid" (a driver and captain of thugs who re-appears later as a character in *The Road*), as well as the earliest printed versions of his now famous "Season" and "Death in the Dawn."[43] His major critical contribution to *The Horn* was a 1960 essay "The Future of West African Writing,"[44] in which he argued that the real mark of authenticity in African writing was indifferent self-acceptance rather than energetic racial self-assertion. Early African writing, he claimed, was dishonest because it either imitated literary fashions in Europe or pandered to European demands and expectations for the exotic and primitive. The first West African writer to produce truly African literature was not Léopold Senghor but Chinua Achebe:

> The significance of Chinua Achebe is the evolvement, in West African writing, of the seemingly indifferent acceptance. And this, I believe is the turning point in our literary development. It is also a fortunate accident of timing, because of the inherently invalid doctrine of "negritude." Leopold Senghor, to name a blatant example. And if we would speak of "negritude" in a more acceptable broader sense, Chinua Achebe is a more "African" writer than Senghor. The duiker will not paint "duiker" on his beautiful back to proclaim his duikeritude; you'll know him by his elegant leap. The less self-conscious the African is, and the more innately his individual qualities appear in his writing, the more seriously he will be taken as an artist of exciting dignity.

Soyinka's famous put-down of Negritude ("a tiger does not have to proclaim his tigritude") apparently originated in this remark on the duiker and duikeritude, of which it must have been a perversion, tigers being no more indigenous to Africa than surrealist French

---

43 "Stage," *The Horn* 4, no. 1 (1960): 1; "Audience to Performer," *The Horn* 4, no. 1 (1960): 4; "Proverb: Okonjo de Hunter," *The Horn* 3, no. 3 (1960): 6–7; "epitaph for Say Tokyo Kid," *The Horn* 4, no. 5 (1962): 10–11; "Season," *The Horn* 4, no. 2 (1961): 2; "Death in the Dawn," *The Horn* 4, no. 6 (1962): 2–3. Other poems of his in this magazine are "Poisoners of the World, Unite," *The Horn* 3, no. 3 (1960): 4–5, 9, and "Committee Man," *The Horn* 4, no. 3 (1961): 10–11.

44 *The Horn* 4, no. 1 (1960): 10–16.

poetry.[45] In any case, this early articulation of Soyinka's artistic credo is interesting when placed beside the creative writing he was doing at this period in his career. In his serious works Soyinka evidently aspired to create authentic African art of "exciting dignity." His aesthetic philosophy was based on total acceptance of his Africanness.

Soyinka's impressive literary and dramatic accomplishments in London and Ibadan soon won him a measure of recognition in Nigeria. In March 1961, after he had been back home only a year, the twenty-six-year-old author was made the subject of an illustrated feature article in *Drum,* probably the leading African popular magazine in Nigeria in those days. The headline read "Young Dramatist Is Earning the Title of Nigeria's Bernard Shaw."[46] The comparison was apt, probably more apt and more prophetic than the journalist who made it could have realized, for Soyinka hadn't yet displayed some of his most Shavian qualities. He was known primarily as a humorist, a public entertainer, a campus wit, a high-spirited clown. And he was known almost exclusively in his homeland, where he addressed his own people through the most popular of the public media—theater, radio, television and, much less often, print. It was not until 1963, when his first three books were published (two of them in England) that he became—instantly and forever—one of the most important writers in the English-speaking world.

---

[45] Janheinz Jahn quotes Soyinka's later elaboration of this concept at a conference in Berlin in 1964 in his *History of Neo-African Literature: Writing in Two Continents* (London, 1966), pp. 265–66.

[46] *Drum* (March 1961), p. 27.

THE ROLE OF THE PUBLISHER IN ONITSHA MARKET LITERATURE

Don Dodson

Onitsha market literature—a proliferation of chapbooks with such titles as *How to Speak to Girls and Win Their Love, Mabel the Sweet Honey That Poured Away, No Condition Is Permanent, How to Write All Kinds of Letters and Compositions,* and *Money Hard to Get But Easy to Spend*—is usually portrayed as a true popular art written by the common man for the common man.[1] The chapbook writer is the mouthpiece of his readers: he voices their own concerns in their own English vernacular with little regard for monetary reward.[2] As Donatus Nwoga has written:

> The success of many of these authors lies in their closeness to their subject and their audience. They know what their audience wants. They too are part of that audience and they share the same problems, and in the mode of expression, they also know how to put things to catch the interest of the audience.[3]

The relationship between author and audience, however, is not as close as most of the research on Onitsha pamphlets implies. Field research conducted in 1971 points to more attenuated links.[4]

Pamphlet writers generally have more schooling than their readers. Out of sixty-one readers who answered a questionnaire sent to eighty-three mail order customers throughout Nigeria, forty-four had completed Primary VI or VII. Eight had less schooling and nine had some secondary education. Between ages twelve and thirty, their average age was eighteen. Twenty were students, eleven were traders, six were soldiers or policemen, seven were unemployed, and seventeen had occupations ranging from fisherman to houseboy. Twenty-four earned no money. The twenty-three who specified their monthly earnings said they made between £1 and about £28 with an average of £8. These findings are supported by a second nonprobability sample of 141 Onitsha residents.

Most writers are more advanced students or provincial journalists with secondary schooling. Wilfred Onwuka, one of the most prolific pamphleteers, wrote his first pamphlet in 1963 after he had completed one year of secondary school as well as a battery of courses at a stenographic institute and evening adult classes on the British constitution, economics, and English. Ogali A. Ogali had completed Form V eight years before his first pamphlet, the immensely popular *Veronica My Daughter*, was published in 1957. He used his profits to attend the Ghana School of Journalism and the London School of Cinematography. Thomas Iguh was in secondary school when his first pamphlet, *Alice in the Romance of Love*, was published. He later studied law at the University of Lagos and he still writes pamphlets. Other pamphleteers, including E. U. Anya, Okwudili Orizu and J. N. C. Egemonye, also went on to attend universities.

Thus it is debatable that the authors are part of their audience. It might be more accurate to say that they have grown out of their audience to a higher level of education and social status.

Nor are the pamphlets a direct link between authors and audience. Authors usually surrender control over content to get their pamphlets into print. Lacking the capital to pay printing expenses, the typical author sells his manuscript to a publisher who pays for printing, handles distribution, and reaps all the profit. One of the few authors to rebel against this system is Chude Graham-Akus Jr., who grumbles that "If I have to sell my works to them, I think they will have to make money out of my sweat. . . . If I sell my works to them, I'm cheated. I wouldn't mind if the work is out and doesn't sell well. I wouldn't care." His second pamphlet, *International Knowledge*, gathered dust at the City Press for weeks after it was printed because Akus could not complete payment. Other authors are not so dogged. Forsaking any further control over their manuscripts, they sell them outright.

Although the publishers play a pivotal role in pamphleteering, they are shadowy figures in most research on Onitsha chapbooks. Emmanuel Obiechina, whose *Literature for the Masses* is the most ambitious study of the pamphlets, writes that

> the publishers band themselves into a kind of guild with regulations and rules of conduct. They have common practices for commissioning works to would-be authors and they have evolved entrepreneurial techniques for regulating the pamphlet business and making money out of it.[5]

Who are these publishers? What kind of "guild" do they have? What are their common practices? The answers to these questions have been sketchy because scholars have studied Onitsha pamphleteering more as a cultural phenomenon than as an entrepreneurial one.

The cultural aspect—however significant—is inseparable from the entrepreneurial. Pamphleteering is a major business in Onitsha. Hundreds of titles were published in the decade before the Nigerian civil war. More than seventy-five titles, many of them new, are available in the market today. Pamphlets usually go through several printings. *Veronica My Daughter*, the greatest best seller, has been reprinted so many times since 1957 that publisher Appolos Oguwike says he cannot keep track of the number. He states that he sold more than 80,000 copies in one year alone and that he printed another 10,000 shortly after the war. C. C. Obiaga, the owner of All Star Printers, estimates that he used to print about eight pamphlets a month with an average run of 6,000 copies—a total of well over three million copies in the six years before the war. Although All Star was probably the biggest pamphlet printer before the war, it had to compete with more than a dozen other presses.

The roots of this proliferous pamphleteering go back to the late 1940s, but it was not until it flourished in the 1960s that its commercial structure stiffened. The reconstruction of the Onitsha market, the rapid growth of literacy, the availability of printing equipment, and the vitality of a new "democratic" spirit all fostered the feeling that any man could make a name and money by writing a story. This creative anarchy crystallized into an organized business as bookselling in Onitsha became highly competitive. With as many as forty separate booksellers on New Market Road and many others in the market by the 1960s, Onitsha booksellers confronted a problem described by Margaret Katzin:

> At Onitsha, a common complaint of traders who formerly carried on a profitable business in a particular line is that so many others have taken it up that the margin of profit has been reduced. The search for new ways of earning a profit is unremitting.[6]

Besides facing heavy competition, the booksellers were engaged in a seasonal trade. Their profit came chiefly from the sale of schoolbooks at the start of the school year in January and February. Noticing the popularity of such forerunners as *Money Hard*, *Veronica My Daughter*, and Okenwa Olisah's publications, some booksellers decided they could increase their profits by publishing their own pamphlets to sell throughout the year. "If I stop publishing pamphlets, after three months I will have nothing to sell," says bookseller Michael Ohaejesi. "So I keep publishing these pamphlets for the little money they will bring in."

When Ohaejesi published *Teach Yourself Hausa, Ibo, Yoruba and English* in 1962, he was one of the last booksellers to jump on the bandwagon without falling off in the lurch of competition. Most of the major publishers started in 1960. It was in that year or earlier that Maxwell Obi published *The Gentle Giant "Alakuku," Our Modern Ladies Characters Towards Boys*, and *Guides for Engagement* under the pseudonym Highbred Maxwell. Appolos Oguwike came out with *Alice in the Romance of Love* and *Life Story of Zik*. A. N. Onwudiwe entered the fray with *The Labour of Man*. N. O. Njoku produced *Man Suffers, Beware of Women*, and *Half-Educated Court Messenger*. J. C. Anorue followed with *The Unnatural Death of Chief Mambo* and *Never Trust All That Love You* in 1960 or 1961. Gordian Orjiako, popularly known as Gebo, started with *Learn to Speak English, Hausa, Ibo and Yoruba Languages* in 1963.

These seven booksellers, who accounted for a large proportion of the pamphlets produced before the war, are the only major chapbook publishers who have resumed trade in Onitsha. (Their addresses are listed in Appendix I.) The others died, embarked on other projects, or could not recoup from the war. Bookseller J. O. Nnadozie sold his copyrights (including the famous *Money Hard to Get But Easy to Spend, Beware of Harlots and Many Friends: The World Is Hard*, and *What Women Are Thinking About Men: No. 1 Bomb to Women*) to J. C. Anorue after the war and became a medicine trader in Lagos; Okenwa Olisah, who operated a stenographic institute, died before the war; bookseller C. N. Aririguzo died under suspicious circumstances during a legal suit against a competitor; B. A. Ezuma, the proprietor of Chinyelu Printing Press, was wiped out by the war and is now selling mirrors and holy pictures next to his damaged shop.

Although the seven major pamphlet publishers face new competition from several younger entrepreneurs, they still produce most of the pamphlets. Each buys manuscripts from authors for £3 to £20. Assuming complete ownership of the manuscript, he makes any changes he wants: he can alter the title, revise the content, or put his own name as the author. Next he takes the manuscript to a printer and "beats price" or haggles over terms. For £225, he might order 6,000 copies. Selling these to vendors at a fixed rate of eighteen shillings per dozen, he stands to make a profit of more than £200 on each impression. The vendors take the pamphlets to markets, motor parks and thoroughfares in small villages and big cities all over Nigeria. While most pamphlets are now marked to sell at five shillings, the normal price is two shillings or two-and-six unless the purchaser is unusually meek or aggressive as a bargainer.

Thus the publishers are the central figures in pamphleteering. The system can be described more fully by elaborating on the relations of publishers with one another and with other key figures.

RELATIONS WITH ONE ANOTHER

The publishers are able to operate as a kind of guild, as Obiechina puts it, because they share close ties transcending the rifts of competition. Most of the scores of booksellers in Onitsha are from the town of Urualla in Nkwerre Division southeast of Onitsha. Just as the sale of motor parts is dominated by traders from Nnewi, bicycle parts by traders from Awka-Etiti, and used clothing by traders from Abiriba, so the sale of books is dominated by Urualla traders.

The typical way to enter trade is to become an apprentice to an established trader who is a townsman or a kinsman. The apprentice (called "boy") is both a ward and a servant who helps his master at home as well as in trade. Usually unpaid throughout his service, the apprentice is "settled" by his master when he has the maturity and skill to go into business on his own. The settlement may be cash, credit on goods, support for education, or some other reward.

All the pamphlet publishers have "boys" and all of them except J. C. Anorue, who began as J. O. Nnadozie's partner, started that way themselves. Michael Ohaejesi describes the process:

> Really first year I was just doing some domestic works. Washing clothes, keeping the house clean, cooking—and at times I go to the market to help in selling. That was the first year. Then as for the second year I started staying in the market, went and travelled to Lagos to collect books, and then I continued although by then I was under somebody in the market. We are all serving one person but there is one somebody who is the senior servant. Then the third year I was left with a full shed. And I started managing one. . . . That wasn't my shed but still I am serving the man.

Finally he got his own shed. Ohaejesi will not say what he received when he was settled, but other publishers mention a variety of practices. N. O. Njoku was able to enter school after he had served his master for five years. Appolos Oguwike started business with £60 from his master and his father. A. N. Onwudiwe's master gave him £30. They all started business between 1954 and 1963.

It is through the apprentice system that the dominance of Urualla booksellers persists. Such prominent businessmen as Alaka, Anebere, Ugoji, Ibetu, Mogu and Dike (none of them pamphleteers) are among the many booksellers from Urualla. Three of the seven publishers are also from Urualla: Highbred Maxwell, Michael Ohaejesi, and Gebo. Maxwell and Ohaejesi both served under T. A. Obi, a pioneer in the book trade, who came to Onitsha in the 1940s. When Maxwell earned his independence, he trained Gebo. After Gebo got his own shed, he brought Peter Udoji from Urualla to be his apprentice. Udoji started publishing pamphlets in 1971. The system continues.

The other four publishers are not from Urualla—J. C. Anorue is from nearby Ihioma, Appolos Oguwike and N. O. Njoku are both from Ogwa in Owerri Division to the south, and A. N. Onwudiwe is from Ogbunka to the north—but they share close ties with one another and with the Urualla group. (These ties are schematized in Figure 1.) Ohaejesi and Anorue are partners in the Do-Well Press. Anorue has also teamed up with Appolos to produce 10,000 register books. Appolos and Njoku are kindred: a wife of Njoku's father is the sister of Oguwike's father, and Njoku's senior brother married Oguwike's sister. Onwudiwe, whose Trinity Printing Press produced several pamphlets for Highbred Maxwell, used to share a market shed with him. Maxwell lives in the same compound as Gebo. Maxwell, Gebo, and Ohaejesi meet monthly for the Urualla Progressive Union and for a singing club called the Urualla Choral Party. Gebo and Ohaejesi belong to another social club called the National Social Board Movement. Besides the formal connections, friendships—some close, some casual—tie the publishers together. Anorue and Ohaejesi are "tight" friends who are frequent companions. "We are all friends. We are very friendly," affirms Njoku. "Oh yes, sometimes we argue and fight, but we are friends. You know, birds of a feather flock together."

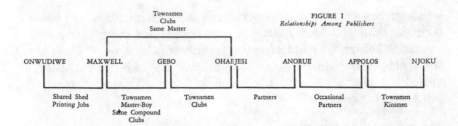

FIGURE I
Relationships Among Publishers

The arguments rarely get as bitter as the one that ended with the death of C. N. Aririguzo. Although squabbles about underselling or plagiarism sometimes erupt, the publishers enjoy remarkably amicable relations. Grievances can be aired at meetings of the grandly named Pamphlet and Novel Publishers Association of Nigeria. The aim of the association is to set fair trade practices (such as the rate of eighteen shillings per dozen pamphlets for vendors) and to plan joint projects. Founded in August 1971, the group met with uneasy camaraderie every other week until the fifth meeting was postponed and then disbanded for lack of a quorum. Appolos is chairman, Anorue secretary, and Njoku financial secretary. The other members by early 1972 were Ohaejcsi, Maxwell, Gebo, and Udoji. The only major holdout was Onwudiwe. This stirred the resentment of the others, who interpreted his obstinacy in different ways. While one thought Onwudiwe did not have to join because he "is very wealthy," another muttered with the didacticism that pervades the pamphlets:

> I think he's a little soft in the head. He doesn't keep up his shop. He is more interested in showing that he has a car than in staying in his shop and working. But if he rides around in his car all day and doesn't keep it in repair, then one day he won't have it any-more, will he?

Onwudiwe, naturally, offered different reasons:

> I don't have the money now. . . . You see, we are all from different areas, so we don't think alike. We have different kind of view, different kinds of ideas. We have different responsibilities. . . . They told me they was going to open a meeting, but many a time I wasn't in . . . The position is this: It is very difficult to control books or prices.

His real reason seemed to be suspicion of the others. Onwudiwe admitted to underselling them. For a "large quantity" of pamphlets he sometimes charged vendors seventeen shillings instead of the usual eighteen shillings. Such independence annoyed his competitors, who wanted to bolster the guild aspects of pamphlet publishing. "There are some publishers who refuse to join and we are going to hit them," vowed one member of the association in 1971. "The printers won't print their books again."

RELATIONS WITH PRINTERS

The printers used to have their own association that set uniform prices and salaries. Efforts to revive it since the war have floundered. With inflation and the generally chaotic state of business after the war, publishers must "beat price" with the printers. Estimates for printing 6,000 copies of a 72-page pamphlet in 1971 ranged from ninepence to one-and-ten per copy. Ninepence to a shilling was the usual response. The more copies, the lower the rate. Although 6,000 copies is the typical print run today, it is often as low as 2,000 or as high as 20,000. Printers, who used to be willing to print impressions of 1,000 to 2,000, will not print less than 2,000 today.

All presses do jobbing: printing handbills, business cards, labels, wedding announcements, and the like. Only a few still specialize in pamphlets. Many of the pamphlet printers (including Popular Printing Press, New Era Printing Press, Eastern Niger Printing Press, Chinyelu Printing Press, and Onwudiwe's Trinity Printing Press) were either destroyed in the war or so enfeebled that they are struggling to revive. Oguwike's Appolos Brothers Press and the Do-Well Press of Anorue and Ohaejesi are operating again. But even Anorue and Ohaejesi farm out many of their jobs to the two biggest pamphlet printers: Providence Printing Press, which has moved to Awo-Idemili, and All Star Printers, which has moved to Nnewi.

Providence owner G. O. Onyenwe and All Star owner C. C. Obiaga say they are good friends with the publishers. "When they come to me," says Onyenwe, "it's like doing business with one of your friends." Obiaga concurs: "They are very good friends to us. We used to go to their home town when they need us to go." Most of the publishers reciprocate the warm words, but the friendship does not run as deep as it does among the publishers themselves. Although one publisher says "Providence" and "All Star" are his good friends, he does not know their real names. J. C. Anorue says of the printers: "They don't know much of the publishers. They only print what we send to them."

Printers find the publishers hard bargainers. Says Onyenwe:

> Publishers will get lower rates . . . because they will resell their product, so they have to get their costs down. . . . It is difficult to get profit from these type of publishers because bargaining is the thing they do day and night.

Transactions, however, are informal. Obiaga asks for a third of the bill in advance, the rest payable at any time. He explains:

> They used to pay gradually. Some of them don't even pay this advance. One man now hasn't given anything on two pamphlets. If he have, he pay us. If he have not, we have to give him some copies until he can pay us gradually.

Onyenwe asks for a fifty percent deposit with the rest payable on delivery, but he too is flexible: "We can let him take and then pay out of his profits." Like most of the pamphlet printers, he finds J. C. Anorue the most reliable customer. But he describes another regular customer this way:

> He's not a first class gentleman, but he's somehow good. If he owes you £100, he will pay £90. When he comes to pick up the order he can ask how many extras you gave him. You can tell him that you used all the papers and there is only one or more extra. Then he will say, "Ahh! Take £10 from it."

And Onyenwe took one publisher to traditional court for default of payment. Such open conflict between publishers and printers is uncommon.

RELATIONS WITH WRITERS

Relations between publishers and writers are more strained. There are few personal friendships to ease the natural tensions. "Many of these authors are hungry writers. . . . I can say that the authors who write pamphlets are much more after making money than making name," asserts a publisher. One of his writers, screwing up his face in distaste, counters: "He is a cheat. Why? He pays a few pounds for your labor and he becomes rich off it."

While a publisher can expect to make at least £200 off of each large printing, the author rarely sees more than £15. The payment varies widely depending on market appeal and the author's bargaining skill. Gebo says he paid 15 shillings for *Chains of Love*; Appolos says he paid £100 for *Veronica My Daughter* after it had proved itself as a best

seller; two of the most popular writers, Thomas Iguh and Wilfred Onwuka, say they usually receive between £15 and £20 for a manuscript;
lesser writers can expect between £3 and £10; some have never received
any payment beyond promises.

Publishers usually buy manuscripts outright. There are two ways this
is done. Sometimes the author seeks out the publisher. Both Iguh and
Onwuka sold their first manuscripts this way. Iguh recalls:

> I wasn't really sure who to approach with my manuscript initially.
> I simply walked into the market, found the book section,, con-
> fronted one man [Appolos] with my manuscript and he agreed
> to print it. Later, traders became interested in me and started
> coming to me to scout for these manuscripts.

The publisher just as often seeks out the writer and commissions him
to write a pamphlet to his specifications. Although many authors like
Iguh or Ogali Ogali or Ahanotu Umeasiegbu write primarily for self-
expression, some who accept commissions feel they are doing hack work.
Armand Odogwu, assistant editor of the *Nigerian Mirror*, says he sold
a manuscript to Appolos for £10 so he could finance the typing of another story, *Anger Behind the Trigger*, which he took more seriously.
He recalls:

> I met Appolos just surprisingly—he was introduced by some-
> body—and he said, "You are Armand Odogwu!" I said, "Yes."
> "Why don't you do me some pamphlet? I would like it."
> I said, "Okay, I'm in need of cash. I could give it to you in a
> few days time."
> This is my own approach: If I want to imitate trash, and you
> say give me a pamphlet and I need £5, as soon as I make sure that
> you are serious about publishing it sometime I'll put it out, give it
> to you, you pay me £3 out of the £5, I leave the manuscript with
> you—and that's exactly what happened.

While his motivation for *Anger Behind the Trigger* was "the irresisti-
ble urge to write," his motivation for the Appolos job was "purely for
the money."

Occasionally publishers give royalties. Peter Udoji offered the author
of *Ideal Friendship Between Boys and Girls*, Ahanotu Umeasiegbu, a
royalty of twopence on every copy sold. Thomas Iguh sometimes asks
for royalties as well as a lump sum. "But there," he chuckles, "you see
the Nigerian businessman is a subtle character: He will never tell you

how much he has printed."

Many authors can point to such abuses. Some of them are never paid the full amount promised. Others have been victims of plagiarism. Iguh says he submitted *Dr. Okpara (The Power) in Political Storm* to a bookseller who could not pay the price he demanded. The bookseller paid another writer to make some changes and published it under a different name without paying Iguh. Iguh then sold the manuscript to Highbred Maxwell, who published the legitimate version. Plagiarism is fairly common. Publishers blame writers; writers blame publishers. The attitude of most is aggrieved tolerance. Claiming that several of his pamphlets have been copied, Wilfred Onwuka says he doesn't care

> because I have sold the manuscript to a publisher. . . . If they want to take action they must do it themselves. But they will not take action because they do the same thing themselves. When I copy your book, you will know that you have done the same thing worse, so you will be embarrassed to take action. They are after money, that's all.

Publishers, on the other hand, complain about "hungry" writers. One author admits accepting £7 for three manuscripts from a bookseller, then printing one of them on his own. He justifies his action by asserting that he never signed a final agreement.

A few publishers sign contracts only if the author demands it. Gebo says he signs contracts only occasionally. "We are all Igbos," he remarks. "You can sell a land without even a receipt according to Igbo customs." Other publishers always sign contracts with authors. Appolos, for example, insists on contracts specifying that "the author has given up all rights and benefits in the book to the publisher." This is the usual understanding even if it is not certified on paper. When an author sells his manuscript to an Onitsha publisher, he relinquishes control over it. The publisher can do whatever he wants with it.

While Gebo and Highbred Maxwell make minimal changes in manuscripts, others make extensive changes. There are three kinds of changes: title, attribution, and content.

Publishers almost always change titles to underscore the themes of romance or success.

Publishers sometimes use their own name or a pseudonym in place of the real author's. Highbred Maxwell acknowledges he has never written a pamphlet even though his name appears under such titles as

Our Modern Ladies Characters Towards Boys, Wonders Shall Never End, and *The Gentle Giant "Alakuku,"* which was copied from *The Sunday Times*. Several of his pamphlets were written by his junior brother Charles. Most of the pamphlets published by J. C. Brothers Bookshop are attributed to J. C. Anorue, J. Abiakam, or R. Okonkwo. Asserting that Abiakam and Okonkwo are his own pseudonyms, Anorue swears he has written everything published under those names. Some of his acquaintances scoff at this claim. It is clear that at least a few of his pamphlets, including *The Complete Story and Trial of Adolf Hitler* by J. C. Anorue and *The Complete Life Story and Death of Dr. Nkrumah* by J. C. Abiakam, were actually written by Wilfred Onwuka. But Onwuka, like almost everyone else who has dealt with Anorue, is unstinting in his praise: "J. C.'s an honest man. He's very kind. . . . He wouldn't mind paying higher. He's a man of justice."

Although some authors resent such changes, others have asked their publisher to use his own name. Okwudili Orizu did so because "I considered the stuff very low." N. O. Njoku, who published *A Guide to Marriage* with his own name in place of the real author's, has turned down similar requests. He says he refused to take credit for John Uzoh's *Love Shall Never End* "because of the grammar there. The book contains some Latin words and I don't know why to speak Latin. If I am questioned as the author, how can I answer?" Felix N. Stephen wanted him to take credit for *How to Behave and Get a Lady in Love*, Njoku recalls, "But the grammar there! In fact it's above my own."

It is difficult to ascertain authorship because of such practices and because all of the publishers except Highbred Maxwell have done some writing themselves. As Onwudiwe says, "You know, I write a bit, I write small." The writing of the publishers generally consists of revising the manuscripts they buy.

Few authors complain about changes because they recognize that their work has become the property of the publisher. "They have the right to take away what they doesn't like and put their own," Onwuka says of the publishers. "They never say anything about it after they have sold it," says Appolos of writers, "because you ask him to write this thing. It's not his own sense. It's not his own creation." The pamphlet is viewed as a commodity in which the creator has no inherent rights. It is manufactured for the market.

The publisher standardizes the product by adhering to successful conventions. If he has solicited the manuscript in the first place, he may not make any changes. Explains Appolos: "I usually get a title, jot down the contents, give you the key notes and then say 'Write on this.' " If he is not satisfied with the result, he may ask the author to make changes: "You've got to sit down and say, 'Look, this thing you have written is not appealing to the public. You've got to make more valuable points, more appealing points.' " Or he may make the changes himself: "Sometimes the author will write something that won't interest the public. I will like to change it. I will substitute more interesting amendments. . . . If one writes with very academic English, we can bring it to normal English."

N. O. Njoku often makes alterations for new editions of a pamphlet. He says he expanded Okenwa Olisah's *No Condition Is Permanent* by adding everything from "24 Charges Against Wives" on page 25 to the end of page 48. Changing the title of Felix N. Stephen's *How to Get a Lady in Love* to *How to Behave and Get a Lady in Love*, Njoku added the first ten pages and made some other alterations:

> I only arranged it in a way that will suit the public. Seeing that the ending is not attractive or is not so good, I added some pages to conclude the whole show. Now what matters in a pamphlet is the beginning and end, and the title.

Juggling content does not bring publishers into conflict with authors like Onwuka who are happy to write on demand. But sometimes there is conflict with writers who see their work as a calling rather than a business. Okwudili Orizu, who has dropped pamphleteering, comments: "My ideas are in conflict with the requests of the publishers. That is because the publishers, as businessmen, are trying to make money while I, as a writer, am interested in changing things in society." Armand Odogwu, a dedicated member of the Scripture Union, declares:

> When you start talking about morals in what you write, as soon as they buy off the copyright the booksellers may decide to remove it. Because these pamphlets published locally are for a certain grade of people. In *Man Must Work* and *Love in the Bunker* I was forced to bring in pidgin English by the booksellers, and a lot of rotten romantics because one, it is the taste of the majority of their customers.
>
> So you wouldn't be surprised if you see the final thing, they have removed the moral aspect of it. They publish what they want to publish.

What they want to publish is what they think readers want.

RELATIONS WITH READERS

What the publishers think readers want are love stories and letter writing handbooks. The great majority of pamphlets are in these categories. Pamphlets on money or politics are also popular.

A few publishers perceive changing tastes. Onwudiwe says the main criterion of popularity is topicality:

> One, if it is a story that connects the present wave, the immediate wave, which connects the country, like this Nigeria civil war now, you know this connects the country now. If it's anything on the civil war, it will sell. If the book is published during that period, it will sell like hotcake—as I published that book on Lumumba during his death—it sells.

Njoku finds that readers are not as interested in love as they used to be: "I don't put more importance to that yet. After the war, what they want now is only money—how to rehabilitate themselves." Gebo articulates the variety of public taste most sharply. "You know, minds are not steady," he remarks. "Perhaps you like eating foofoo today, tomorrow you like rice." In 1965, says Gebo, the public was interested in letter writing; in 1966, political dramas; after the war, "nothing yet, they aren't interested in anything." Gebo thinks tastes also vary from area to area: Onitsha buyers like pamphlets about business, Northerners like love, Westerners have more general tastes. But love and letter writing remain the dominant themes of Onitsha pamphlets.

Closely mirroring the responses of readers who were questioned, the publishers seem to perceive public taste accurately. How do they know what the public likes?

The most important clue is sales. If something "moves" well, it will be reprinted and imitated until all profit is drained from it.

Another basis is contact with readers. There is little direct contact because the readers generally buy from vendors. Although Njoku maintains that "I don't have any association with readers, I don't have anything in common with them," he suggests that public tastes can be sensed by a kind of osmosis: "Psychologically, I'm a social man. So when we go to functions and gathering, from there you know the opinion of people." This ambivalence toward the public is typical of the publishers. When asked to describe their contact with readers, most mention correspondence. They used to receive many fan letters and requests for advice. Ohaejesi recalls: "Some want to know how one will operate a lover after quarrelling—how he or she should contact the opponent for reconciliation." Njoku received this letter after the war:

> Dear Sir,
>
> I am indeed very happy to congratulate you about what you have wrote about "NO CONDITION IS PERMANATE." I am very happy about it and it shows a good thing in my future life because I am very young and I also praised the author of the book. The author is the Master of Life exactly because you wrote many things which shows you are a good man.
>
> I want you to send me one of your best catalogue in which important things are written.
>
> Please I beg you not to fail me. May God be with you where ever you go and as far you are good man. You are among the chosen people and Jesus explaining this said, "For many are call but few are chosen."
>
> With love from
>
> . . .

The flow of letters has subsided since the war and now consists largely of orders.

The third way publishers gauge public taste is to assume that their own taste approximates the average. Appolos explains: "Myself, I know what I like. And through myself I know what I like and other people may like it, you see." Feeling that their writers tend to get lost in ivory towers, the publishers think they can speak to their "semiliterate" audience more effectively. This attitude has some justification. Although they are wealthier and older than the average reader, the publishers share his level of literacy and education. All of them stopped schooling after Standard VI. They are common men who have succeeded in the hurly-burly of trade—as their readers hope to do—rather than in the halls of learning. They are men of the world whose advice on *How to Get a Lady in Love and Romance with Her* or *How to Start Life and End it Well* is earthy and pointed. The publishers emphasize both education and entertainment in the pamphlets. J. C. Brothers pamphlets sometimes carry this blurb:

> Read J. C. books for the following reasons:
> 1. It will teach you many things which you do not know,
> 2. Constant reading will improve your knowledge in education,
> 3. Interesting novels will inspire happiness in you.

Echoing the claims of the publishers, many readers praise the pamphlets for their educational value. Some cite pamphlets as moral authorities. "Since I read *Money Hard*," says Albert Mbadugha, a cosmetics trader, "I have learnt to beware of women with stricted measure. Women are generally after money. One must know this in order to succeed in business." Some read them to improve their English. Michael Olumide, a Yoruba soldier, says: "I read them mostly to gain a good conduct of English language. It has given me help." Others utilize the pamphlets more directly. When asked whether *How to Write Love Letters* is useful, army clerk Ezekiel Onanoga replies, "Yes yes yes . . . yes yes yes. I have copied the letter." An Onitsha trader says he read *How to Write Love Letters* because "I just got a new girlfriend. There are some good letters in it which are exactly what I wanted to write." Sometimes two rivals unwittingly copy the same love letter to send to the same girlfriend.

This may be the most embarrassing but least important way readers are led astray. Wavering fact and fractured English make the pamphlets shaky guideposts. They are guideposts nonetheless. Even their exploitation of romance answers real problems of sexual conduct created when marriage is postponed by the collusion of poverty and brideprice. While *How to Behave and Get a Lady in Love* is not the most urgent social issue in Nigeria, it is a pressing personal problem. The commercial basis of Onitsha market literature forces the pamphleteers to focus on the stuff of common dreams: success in love and money.

CONCLUSION

Onitsha market literature, as the term implies, is a commercial as well as a cultural phenomenon. Commercial constraints mold the cultural conventions. The pivotal figure in the commercial system is the publisher. He takes the risks and makes the profits. He minimizes risks by standardizing the product. What has sold before is what is published again. Like other traders, the publisher is more concerned with salability than quality.

A few publishers who control most of the pamphlet trade are interlocked in a kind of guild with common practices for buying and selling their product. While the links between them smooth some of the competitive ruffles, their pursuit of profit has been complicated by new competitors in a tight post-war market. Some of the older publishers are seeking new ways to make a profit. Appolos Oguwike, for example, wants to concentrate on printing and selling stationery:

> I don't expect to invest much more on pamphlets. It absorbs your money and fluctuates it too much. It takes a long time to realize your gain. If I am going to invest £1,000 to print four pamphlets it is better to put it into something that will bring immediate liquid cash. I will continue printing pamphlets, but just on a small scale. I will concentrate on postal orders because there you get the full price for the pamphlets.

Appolos says he made £2,000 producing Christmas cards in both 1968 and 1969. Many booksellers were producing Christmas cards in 1971. Michael Ohaejesi alone printed 44,000 in his first effort to carve out a niche in the Christmas market. The unremitting search for profit continues as each innovation is threatened by imitation.

Appolos sums up the driving motive of all traders, whether they sell pamphlets or cosmetics or bicycle parts, when he muses:

> I like business. All I want is to chop one fowl a day, to get a nice car, to build a nice house in town, and at home a nice country house, and to educate my children to whatever level they want.

Publishing pamphlets is a means to those magnetic but elusive goals.

FOOTNOTES

[1] See, for example, Nancy J. Schmidt, "Nigeria: Fiction for the Average Man," *Africa Report*, 10 (August 1965), p. 39, and Emmanuel Obiechina, *Literature for the Masses: An Analytical Study of Popular Pamphleteering in Nigeria* (Enugu: Nwankwo-Ifejika & Co., 1971), p. 3.

[2] Emmanuel Obiechina, *Onitsha Market Literature* (New York: Africana Publishing Corporation, 1972), pp. 9–19.

[3] "Onitsha Market Literature," *Transition*, 19 (1965), p. 29.

[4] The research was supported in part by the National Science Foundation, and the African Studies Committee and the Center for International Communication Studies at the University of Wisconsin. An earlier version of this paper was presented at the Fifteenth Annual Meeting of the African Studies Association in 1972. When the research was conducted, Nigeria had not yet converted to a decimal currency. For the sake of simplicity, therefore, pounds and shillings are used in this paper.

[5] Obiechina, p. 4.

[6] "The Role of the Small Entrepreneur" in *Economic Transition in Africa*, ed. Melville J. Herskovits and Mitchell Harwitz (London: Routledge & Kegan Paul Ltd., 1964), p. 189.

APPENDIX I

Established Pamphlet Publishers

Appolos Oguwike	Academy (Nig.) Bookshops 75 Upper New Market Road Onitsha
	Appolos Brothers Press 18 Modebe Avenue Onitsha
Maxwell Obi (Highbred Maxwell)	Students Own Bookshop 58 Venn Road South Onitsha
Gordian Orjiako (Gebo)	Same mailing address as Highbred Maxwell
A. N. Onwudiwe	Membership Bookshop 87 Upper New Market Road Onitsha
N. O. Njoku	Survival Bookshop 81 Upper New Market Road Onitsha
J. C. Anorue	J. C. Brothers Bookshop 26 New Market Road Onitsha
	Do-Well Press 29 Francis Street Onitsha
Michael Ohaejesi	Minaco Bookshops 13 Iweka Road Onitsha
	Do-Well Press

New Pamphlet Publishers

Peter Udoji	Udoji and Brothers Bookshop 54 Moore Street Onitsha
Shakespeare C. N. Nwachukwu	Nwachukwu Africana Books P. O. Box 585 Onitsha
Donatus Adikaibe	Dona Brothers Bookshop 8 Yahaya Street Onitsha

G. C. Osakwe

Pacific Correspondence College
71 Old Market Road
Onitsha

THE HORN: WHAT IT WAS AND WHAT IT DID

W. H. Stevenson

The Horn was a Nigerian student poetry magazine that was begun in January 1958 and continued to appear at varying intervals, sometimes two or three times a term, sometimes only two or three times a year, until the end of the session in 1964. Vol. VII, No. 3 (May 1964) was the last, and then *The Horn* went into oblivion, overtaken by more ambitious (though less successful) magazines of comment and criticism. The anthology *Nigerian Student Verse*,[1] selected from *The Horn*'s first three years, however, attracted quite a lot of attention. Poems from it were translated into Polish by 1962,[2] for example, and it was mined by several editors of anthologies of African verse in the 1960s. Occasional references to *The Horn* began to appear in footnotes, introductions, and similar little-read places, and now the interest that is shown by scholars of African literature amply justifies this brief critique of such an unassuming magazine. To begin, then, at the beginning.

In the late 1950s, University College, Ibadan, had less than a thousand students all told. (This was one of its advantages.) According to the system traditional at the University of London (to which U.C.I. was affiliated until 1963), Arts and Science students took a three-year General degree in three subjects, unless they were admitted to a specialist Honours course (also three years). Many students, lacking the formal qualifications for entry to a degree course, took a two-year Preliminary course first. In the Department of English, with a teaching staff of eight or nine, "General" classes numbered up to twenty, and "Honours" classes seven or eight. With national independence in the air (it came on October 1st, 1960), students in such small classes were very much aware that they belonged to a highly-selected group from which much was expected and for whom anything seemed possible. It was not felt shameful to belong to such an élite.

In October 1956, Martin Banham came from England to take up a post in the Department of English at Ibadan. He soon came to feel that Ibadan needed an undergraduate poetry magazine, run by students, to encourage student writing. As a student at Leeds University (and, incidentally, an M.A. contemporary of Wole Soyinka) he had known such a magazine, *Poetry and Audience* (which still exists). In 1957 he persuaded one of his students, J. P. Clark, to start one. Clark gathered a committee of three—Bridget Akwada, Aigboje Higo, and John Ekwere —and so in January 1958 the first issue of *The Horn* appeared. The organization of the committee, and the format of the magazine itself, were informal and amateur. But neither these things nor the irregularity of its appearance should mislead the reader, for in these typewritten and cyclostyled pages he is witnessing an essential stage in the creation of modern Nigerian poetry.

The Horn had to be virtually self-supporting. There were no official funds for such a venture. Martin Banham himself provided enough cash to start it; the English Department's typewriter was borrowed, and in later years the Department provided paper also (see Vol. III, No. 3, p. 2). But funds had to be raised, and so *The Horn* was sold at two-pence a copy (raised after the third issue to threepence, a price maintained to the end). It could never afford to appear in any but the most modest form—which was probably just as well, if it were to remain a genuine student magazine. There was a printed heading on the first page, giving title, price, issue number, and names of the editor and committee. Beneath the heading was the first poem, typewritten as was the rest of the copy. The first issue was broader than it was high, but after that every issue was made up of foolscap sheets folded in two and stapled together, book-fashion. The page size was therefore 8 inches high x 6½ inches wide.

Such a slight, typewritten, amateur, student production seemed destined for oblivion. Its value in encouraging students to write poetry was not doubted; that it was worth saving did not occur to anyone. I have not been able to find anyone with a complete collection. Student editors came and left; the Department of English and the University itself had no official connection with the magazine; even those among the teaching staff[3] who were actively interested in the venture did not trouble to keep all their copies. The University Library received copies only sporadically, when an editor thought of it. My enquiries have produced copies of most of the issues, but there are still some gaps. One cannot always be sure that the last issue discovered in a given session is the last that actually appeared. However, the collection I have made is now almost complete, and I have set out in the Appendix to this article the tally of copies I have been able to assemble, with suggestions as to how near to completion the collection may be.

I have a total of twenty-five issues from seven annual volumes, 170 poems altogether. Seven are anonymous; fifty-six authors contributed the rest. Of these, ten were expatriates, contributing eighteen poems.[4] These will not be considered further, and all the following remarks will be concerned with the forty-six Nigerian contributors. All of these were students at Ibadan, with two or three notable exceptions: Christopher Okigbo and Wole Soyinka (who was a postgraduate fellow from 1959 to 1961) in particular. In the last issues, Nelson Olawaiye writes from Ahmadu Bello University in Zaria ("Silence, my Art" and "My Pen"), and Glory Okogbule Nwanodi[5] from the University of Nigeria, Nsukka ("Salute to Songhai" and "A Memorial").

Of these writers, twenty-seven contribute either one or two poems each. Nine contribute between three and five poems, and only another nine more than five. J. P. Clark is much the most prolific, with sixteen poems. Mac Akpoyoware has nine; Aig Higo, Pius Oleghe and Wole Soyinka have eight; Frank Aig-Imoukhuede seven; and Dapo Adelugba, Onyema Iheme and Abiola Irele six. These figures are of course not strictly accurate, as two or three copies are missing, but they are as accurate as need be.

Not only poems were printed. Many issues had some editorial comment. Reviews were soon added, since University College, Ibadan, was ambitious in drama as in many other ways.[6] The first review of a local production appeared in Vol. 1, No. 3, covering *The Magic Flute*, as presented at the college Arts Theatre, conducted by Peter Konstam, a consultant surgeon at the University College Hospital, and produced by Geoffrey Axworthy, lecturer in Drama in the Department of English. (A controversy over the availability of tickets caused more stir in *The Horn* than the performance itself.) Reviews soon became a staple of *The Horn*, especially at times when the committee had collected few poems good enough to print. For our purposes, a more important feature was the occasional appearance of articles discussing the nature of Nigerian poetry. Vol. 1, No. 4 contains an article by Kay Williamson, the linguist (then a research fellow, now a Professor at Ibadan) on "Metre in Traditional African Poetry." Vol. III, No. 2 (December

1959), p. 3, says, "we have something in store: a symposium on *The Future of African Writing*. The series will be started off by Mr. Obia-junwa Wali in our first number next term." This article duly appeared: the next was to be by Wole Soyinka, but a note in No. 4 puts it off until "early next term." A similar notice appears in No. 5, but the essay did appear at last in Vol. IV, No. 1. Any discussion of this theme by Soyin-ka would be important; I wish his early comments on the future of Afri-can theater, prepared for his sponsors in the Rockefeller Foundation and now lying in a file in the University of Ibadan Library, were also avail-able in print. The *Horn* article is very valuable—I shall return to it later in this essay—and characteristic. The playfulness: "I would say that poets like Leopold Senghor, and—blast, who was it again who wrote 'Give me back my dolls' and something else about the 'childish games of my pristine youth'?—are a definite retrogressive pseudo-romantic in-fluence on a healthy development of West African Writing"—should not blind us to Soyinka's seriousness.

The "symposium" was not continued, however (see IV, 2, p. 12). Vol. IV, No. 3 contains on page 12 a quotation from Edward Blishen's BBC review of *Nigerian Student Verse*, but thereafter most of the prose, apart from editorials, was in the form of reviews.

The Poetry

As may be expected, the 152 poems we are concerned with vary widely in quality. At one extreme there is the small group of "Bad Verse" in-cluded to pad out Vol. 1, No. 2 and to act as a goad, and at the other Soyinka's superb "Death in the Dawn," first published in early 1962 in Vol. Vc. The contributions of J. P. Clark (who was a student) and Christopher Okigbo and Wole Soyinka (who were not) will be treated separately. For the rest, although this is a collection of *student* verse, where it would be mistaken to expect to find sustained high quality, there is real poetry and insight here, and it is only occasionally that one is embarrassed by what one reads. An apparently simple poem, Frank Aig-Imoukhuede's "Sinner," for example, contains a skill, and a dis-guised assimilation of different techniques, that are easily underesti-mated:

        I reach out
            hand
        to clout
            enemy
                on the head.

    Hand, hang
        helpless.
            o hapless,
                That was
                    God
                at the
                receiving end.

The first editorial (I, 1, p. 11) points out that these young poets are not writing in their own language:

> Of course, the difficulties are immense, since we have neglected almost from childhood our vernacular to affect a foreign language.

In Vol. VI, No. 1, Abiola Irele, in his review of *Nigerian Student Verse*, says:

> Few writers have been able to create lasting work in any alien language, and however conversant we have been with English, it still remains for us something of a second language, if not less . . . The truth is that we not only study in English, we study it—we do not, like an English undergraduate, come up to *read* it.

It is a considerable achievement that this fact scarcely ever obtrudes on the reader. The awkwardness that is quite often encountered is usually a result of the writers' inexperience as poets, their clumsiness with poetic tools, rather than linguistic failure in a second language. One finds exactly the same awkwardness in any collection of student verse, even when the authors are writing in their own language.

If any fault derives from the difficulties of a second language, it is the failure to find a consistent style. A foreign student, who has never heard the language spoken in its homeland, inevitably finds it hard to recognize the registers of the language; specifically, in poetry, in recognizing what is formal and what is colloquial, what is contemporary and what is old-fashioned. There is a good deal of old-fashioned poetic diction in these poems. John Ekwere's "To Sunrise" (I, 5, p. 2) begins strikingly, but fails in the end by falling into archaic inflections and inversions:

> What in ancestral days was fear,
> In me is grandeur;
> What in ages gone was dread,
> In me is splendour; . . .
>
> Thy glory shed and let it stay,
> And mock me not at end of day.

It is interesting to see what themes these young writers chose. There are, for example, only a few love poems, and most of them are bad, derivative both in sentiment and style:

> Your fingers made the furrows on my face
> When you were striking the chords of love.
> No matter now . . . I should have known better.[7]

This is one of the better ones. Most are out of Romanticism by F. T. Palgrave. J. P. Clark's "Darkness and Light" (III, 5, p. 1), by contrast, is on another plane altogether.

Unexpectedly, perhaps, there are not many political poems. Those that appear deal with one of two general themes: racial politics in various countries, and the Nigerian political situation. The nature of the first group is indicated by some of the titles—"Katanga," "Lumumba," "Alabama"—but although the strong feeling expressed in these poems is clearly genuine, there is little good poetry in them. Truth is being expressed in clichés. The writers are writing from ideas rather than from experience, so that they are not mediating experience:

> . . . But they who abuse
> With hate-tilted tongue the wearer of black
> Pour malediction
> Upon the same who even created white—
> That Cosmic Painter
> Who knows that opposites make complete whole . . .[8]

220

Of the shorter poems, in fact, the best is the very first, Aig Higo's "Helplessness," which appears on the first page of the first issue. Its diction is clumsy in places, but it avoids, by its sensitivity, the ephemeral superficiality of most of the political poems:

> Homeless winds waft me about
> From desert to kraal.
> I cry for help from cape to cape,
> The echo lingers on Ruwenzori. . . .

Yet this is not by any means a great poem. There is really only one outstanding political poem—Clark's "Ivbie" (II, 2, pp. 2–15). This poem (dated, on page 15, 28 October 1958 and republished in whole or in part in his Mbari volume of 1962, his *A Reed in the Tide* [1965], and the *Présence Africaine* anthology, *Nouvelle Somme de Poésie du monde noire*, ed. L. G. Damas [1966?]) spreads across the boundaries of my two groups. In so far as it is a "political" poem, it takes up one of the themes of Achebe's *Things Fall Apart*—a point not missed by Obiajunwa Wali in his review of "Ivbie" (II, 3, p. 3ff.)—the disruptive effect of an alien culture on Clark's own homeland in the Delta. No other poet in *The Horn* takes up this theme, though it might have seemed an obvious one, especially after Achebe. Wali, who regarded "Ivbie" as an interesting failure, thought that Clark's error was to use the theme stated in the alternative title "The wrong done to you without any hope of justice" as "a thesis, a scaffolding, which the poet is to stuff with life and blood" (II, 3, p. 8), a theme more suitable for the novel than for poetry. Perhaps other writers thought so too. In any case, almost all the other poems on Nigerian political themes deal with the great perennial problem of the corruption of politicians. Again, these are most successful when ironic:

> His struggles over,
> Freedom has come
> What! Popular class?

> But a 403 is
> A good car.
> In two years' time
> An Oldsmobile.[9]

"Man an' Equality," by Frank Aig-Imoukhuede, is a satirical companion-piece to his better-known poem in pidgin, "One Wife for One Man":

> You say dem born you equal with me? Sure?
> Den tell me why your fingers long pass my own? . . .
>
>   Okay Oga,
> Make you talk now. Any time I say make 'A
> Rise for reach only your chest, you low me down;
> Any time I try run pass you, you give me back stud.[10]

There are some "political" poems that do not concern themselves solely with corruption. The only poem in the whole collection not in English is a celebration of the proclamation of Nigeria as a Republic in 1963, and the independence of the University of Ibadan from the University of London, through the figure of Sir Abubakar Tafawa Balewa:

> Le voici magnifique devant les gens académiques,
> Sir Abubakar, premier premier ministre de la République,
> Maintenant premier chancelier de la première Université. . . .[11]

The same issue contains the more sophisticated "Salute to Songhai," by G. Okogbule Nwanodi, which was published again in *Black Orpheus*, No. 16, p. 32:

> we walk on toes, shivering,
> like the chameleon
> treading the infant earth,
> shaking,
>   changing . . .
> fearful . . .

The last issue contains a poem on the sinister theme of tribalism. The issue is dated May 1964; this was the time when the prime minister of Western Nigeria was talking about the "constitutional extermination" of his non-Yoruba opponents, and it is probably no accident that the author of "Afterwards" was Ibo:

View a single hand
of ligaments divergent
you scouting stranger,
five we are avowed . . .

'but single whole', they affirm.

It is not a good poem, but it shows the new and threatening trend of
events at the time the last issues of *The Horn* were appearing:

The ethnic fraternity rears
the façade—that bulwark
of enervating glowing hope
that pretends to unify . . .[12]

This is a theme of the middle 1960s, however. *The Horn* was
founded, and flourished, in the years when these dangers had not yet
been fully realized. Students of the late 1950s and the first years of
independence felt themselves to be living at the beginning of a new
era—as indeed they were. Their poems can be expected to reflect their
self-awareness at such a time. Three themes are worth studying, for
their relative frequency: *alienation*, that common disease of the modern world, *Negritude*, then a popular concept among black writers, and
self-awareness.

Alienation

The word is not "conflict," so common as a theme among the novelists.
This may seem surprising. One might expect poetry illustrating the
mental struggles of undergraduates, coming from the villages (as so
many of them did) into the sophistication of a modern university, and
a town of a million or more inhabitants.[13] Many were indeed townsfolk,
but it would seem natural to find poetry contrasting the ways they had
known and the ways they now found themselves in: poetry of the conflict between the demands of the family at home and of the Westernized world they were entering; between the traditions they had been
brought up in and the indeterminate morality of this new world. These
are the themes of a hundred novels, and it is natural to look for them
in *The Horn*.

Yet there are very few poems directly contrasting the new and the
old. One is Frank Aig-Imoukhuede's "Life in the Country . . . Life in

the Town," and the mark of this poem is irony, rather than nostalgia:

> Night-birds (or witches!) cawing
> To beats of tom-toms,
> Half-clothed virgins with rhythmic buttocks
> Daring the lads to beat 'that' . . .
> And on the morrow
> Almost beating the cock to its crow
> Work!
> Work again in the blistering sun? . . .

But in the town's night-spots:

> Respectability shamelessly rubbing buttocks with harlots
> To immoral tunes by depraved band-boys;
> The usual flight of guided chairs and missiles . . .
>
> The arrival of authority and law and order;
> The slinking off of the delinquent father
> To the respectability of his home and his wife;
> Or of the hardened 'regular' with a daughter of Eve.
> Aw! I don't like this life either
> It is filled with constant fear of the law
> And the thought of next meals.[14]

This is one-half serious; the poet's tongue is visibly in his cheek when he talks of the "immoral tunes" of the "depraved band-boys," yet it is one of the few to deal with Ibadan life at all. There are a few poems about the University, but they are nearly all slight verse about the burden of essays or examinations laid on them by unsympathetic teachers. For example: "History or Mystery," by Minji Karibo (I, 1); "Penitence," (anon., II, 1); "Road Closed" by Yetunde Esan (II, 4); "Dream-in-Life" by Obi Wali (II, 6); "College at Night" by Abiola Irele (II, 6).

Almost all the "college" poems are found in the first two volumes. There is a solitary exception in one of the last issues of *The Horn*, Emeka Okonkwo's "They Sleep Not" (VII, 1 [Jan. 1964], pp. 9–10). It describes the consolation found by the student, forced to leave college for lack of fees, in the thought of his ever-present ancestors. The style is awkward, and the rhythm broken, but the theme is ingeniously handled. Okonkwo does not underline the "moral," that the student is finding the strength of tradition when the new world has failed him, but simply states it, and lets the ancestors speak:

> Exiled—we are salvaged—from the greed and hypocrisy
> Of your human state, believe we live
> Your unsleeping guides.
> We live in every form—
> Not as hired mourners that must weep
> For father-Tiger in order to eat:
> Maybe as the perfect foreigner that mollifies
> All fee-thirsty mourners with obtuse sympathy.[15]

This, however, is not "alienation," but self-rediscovery. Something more recognizable as "alienation," in the usual sense, is found in certain introspective poems where the authors express their doubts and hesitations about their present and future states in this strange world. Obiajunwa Wali, in the very first issue, considers the state of the apparently futile intellectual scorned by his more "productive" peers:

> Surely it's leprosy to them but gem to me: . . .
>
> But our gem is thought and thought is power;
> We shall gather them in one mighty heap
> And in our day invade their cheap
> Citadel, their bankrupt soul, their tottering tower.[16]

Mac Akpoyoware writes:

> This is the resolution, to walk
> My way down the dried-up riverbeds
> To seek the mountain streams. Perhaps
> I shall be following a desert caravan;
> I am used to losing my way.[17]

And J. P. Clark's "The Cry of Birth," "Agbor Dancer," and "Tide-Wash" are well-known, as is Christopher Okigbo's "Debtor's Lane."[18] This style is caught from the English poets of the 1960s, and in particular from Robert Conquest's anthology *New Lines* (1956), which all students of English met as a set book. Sometimes their own efforts look like a pastiche, admirably done perhaps, but not necessarily profound:

> Repeated ripples on the map of the mind—
> Mere distortions of a serene thought—
> The jolting back and forth
> Of an expiring farce. . . .
>
> The shadows fade wearily into air
> The thread is lost in the dark.
> Where am I? afloat or arest?
> Too dizzy to know.[19]

These are poems which, without leaning heavily on any "objective correlative," speak symbolically of the author's state of mind. Nelson Olawaiye of Ahmadu Bello University, Zaria, catches exactly the post-Eliotean idiom of English poetry in his "Silence, my art":

> You will find me there
> wherever
> cells hatch
> in silence:
> in the moment of
> every creative spell
> in the marrow of
> every growing cell;
> I should be there, my shadow
> hunched between the boughs of
> life's e'er-maturing tree . . .[20]

It is only in the last line that he gives himself away, technically speaking.

And yet these are not characteristic poems. As one turns the pages of *The Horn*, one comes across such poems from time to time, but only as one by no means dominant kind among many. The pastiche of modern English poetry can blend with poetry of another age to produce, as this poem produces by crossing the seventeenth with the twentieth century, something different from either:

Who calls me
    To his side?
    I am a god
Of exquisite lusts
    to havoc on the sense
        and go
Where life finds
    tongue to tell the odd
        from even,
Perfect from imperfect tense.
    Yet they dread
        Me.
I must die.[21]

Negritude

This concept, on the other hand, seems closer to *The Horn*'s poets. In in the 1950s, students keen on independence, both political and cultural, might have been expected to catch hold of the Negritude of Césaire and Senghor. And in fact *The Horn* gives us a picture of the rise and fall of Negritude in Nigeria. There are only a few references to the word and the concept, but they are adequate to show how the students felt about it. The editorial in the very first issue, presumably written by J. P. Clark, declared, "We venture to submit 'Negritude' as a most compendious word! . . . it stands for . . . that new burning consciousness of a common race and culture that black men in America, the West Indies, and Africa are beginning to feel towards one another." Later he says, "It is to arrest such subtle imperialism [i.e., by Westernized education] that we join those already fighting to preserve our heritage by launching this magazine." John Ramsaran, in Vol. 1, No. 3, put in a warning against this sentiment, saying that it "is a negative view of things, a passive acceptance without that inner conviction which comes with the glimmering of truth." In Vol. I, No. 5, the editorial, "Looking Back," accepted this, pointing out, "Of course, we have flown with the harmattan, swum with mermaids in the creeks and besides being caught in a tornado, have won fame for even the blind beggar. The point however is that we also met Oxford punters, uncanny robots, and Russian sputniks and satellites—all fellow-passengers. . . . And here lies the great realisation: human contact with men everywhere. For what is poetry that lacks that?"[22]

The note of Negritude, as distinct from this note of universal humanity, was occasionally struck again. In the introduction to Clark's "Ivbie"
(II, 2, p. 2), Abiola Irele said he hoped the poem "will contribute to
that spirit of 'Negritude' which he [Clark] so ably championed as the
first editor of this paper." And again, in the closing editorial of the
volume, "Bend in the River" (II, 6, pp. 15–16), Irele wrote that the
famous black authors are like a river "flowing towards the great ocean—
the great ocean of *Negritude*."

Many of the poems in *The Horn* can be seen as supporting the concept—the poems that consciously recall the cultural heritage of the
writers. But Negritude was an idea that took only shallow root in Nigeria, and it soon withered. When Wole Soyinka, coming to fame as
Nigeria's first internationally-known playwright, attacked it (Vol. IV,
No. 1) in his essay "The Future of West African Writing," its doom
was sealed. "The significance of Chinua Achebe is the evolvement, in
West African writing, of the seemingly indifferent acceptance" of the
"West African subject-character." There follows what is, I believe, the
first appearance in print of a famous saying:

> The duiker will not paint 'duiker' on his beautiful back to pro-
> claim his duikeritude; you'll know him by his elegant leap. The
> less self-conscious the African is, and the more innately his indi-
> vidual qualities appear in his writing, the more seriously he will be
> taken as an artist of exciting dignity. But Senghor seems to be so
> artistically expatriate that his romanticism of the negro becomes
> suspect and quite boring sometimes.

After this, the word is, I think, never again used in *The Horn*, except
once, and poetry clearly dependent on the concept almost disappears.
The "once" is a satiric poem by Frank Aig-Imoukhuede in Vol. IV, No.
2, "The Poor Black Muse" (which was reprinted in *Black Orpheus*,
No. 10, under the title "Negritude"):

> I cannot continue in a strain that's both forced and unnatural.
> The sounds, if you think they're 'negritudine', make the 'idiot
>   boy' of me.
> O Ne—negri—gri, gri—tud—thud! (does that sound well?)
>   —tudes!
> Why can't you leave the black Muse alone?

The common feeling among Nigerian writers and critics has always been that they can do without the "self-consciousness" of Negritude, which has always seemed to them a foreign concept. But in one poem towards the end of the magazine's life ("Insomnia," VI, p. 1), Irele brings Negritude briefly back. Sent in from Paris, where Irele was carrying on his postgraduate studies, it reads almost like a translation from the French:

> A single persistence in the abyss of my white nights
> Harassed by the nightmares of my feebleness
> Coughed upon the gulf of my dilemma profound tenacious . . .
>
> *　*　*　*　*
>
> The light snore of my dark brother in the heaviness of his African
> sleep . . .
> And here I am rocked on white sheets of punished innocence . . .

These phrases show the influence of Negritude, but Irele was in Paris.

Self-rediscovery

Negritude, or the intellectual atmosphere that encouraged it, was however invaluable in disposing of one error to which the students were prone. Their "upward mobility," and the belief that such mobility was necessarily "progress," had been inculcated in them as schoolchildren, not only by their Westernized education but also by their relatives, who could see all the benefits that such education brought to the pupil and to the family. One result of this was a deprecation of tradition and the old ways, of indigenous art and culture. One young man in the Peace Corps, Max Brandt, conducted a survey of music teaching in schools. He found that about 95% of the music taught was English folksong. When he asked why Nigerian folksongs were not taught, he was repeatedly given the shocked answer, "That's bush music!" (Ironically, the reason why English folksongs were available for such misuse was that, a century ago, English musicians determined to teach indigenous folk music to English children, rather than bringing them up on, say, German lieder.)

The students were now engaged in a fascinated and delighted rediscovery of themselves and their traditions. They were learning to look again at their surroundings, and to write about what they saw:

> . . . Below, the sea, burnish'd and turquoise,
> But for the flickering mirror of the western sky,
> Crawls past reluctantly.
> Beyond, the horizon breaks
> As distant sails appear
>
> To herald the rising wind;
> And presently, the expanse before me
> Ripples into a vast corrugation
> With the cool moist breath that breaks
> In a little murmur among the grooves . . .[23]

The carefulness and precision are Conradian, but the poem shows a genuine feeling for what is being described.

Not everyone was happy about such poetry. Its Romantic origins were suspect, especially among those who sought "modernity" in poetry. Edward Blishen, who gave a B.B.C. talk on poetry from Africa, quoted in Vol. IV, No. 3, p. 12, said that "*modern* English verse . . . would, I should think, be a far better starting-point than our romantic verse for the journey towards a truly African poetry." He is no doubt right as far as diction is concerned, but otherwise he has missed the point, which is that, for these young writers, Romanticism was in some ways much more relevant than the tired disillusionment of the postwar English intelligentsia.

In particular, Romanticism led the students to express their own experiences. Most Nigerians, like farming people the world over, have more of an eye to the work that Nature brings than to her beauties. Now the students made the double Wordsworthian discovery: that the metropolis was not the only source of art, and that great poetry can, and probably does, reside in peasants' homes. The discovery was supremely releasing. Some of the poems it produced are simply vividly descriptive:

> The wind howls, the trees sway,
> The loose house-top sheets clatter and clang,
> The open window shuts with a bang,
> And the sky makes night of day. . . .
>
> Home skip the little children;
> 'Where have you been, you naughty boy?'—

The child can feel nothing but joy,
For he loves the approach of rain. . . .[24]

The preceding poem in the same issue, Mac Akpoyoware's "Olokun"
(I, I, p. 8), is less simple. It begins like a Romantic, or perhaps even
Georgian poem on the pleasures of Nature and youth. But the second-
hand diction fades into something more direct as the experience becomes more real:

We will go again to that easy Place?
To plunge, to frolic in the noontide sun,
Drift on rafts to midstream and vie
For the shore and bask and lazily dream
Those little lovely things of youth.

Some say she wraps three goddesses
In her dark sultry waters . . .
We know in her we store up, too,
At least our fears; in that queer coldness
We know she must be there.

It is an idle place and you hear
That unanswered calling note; you watch
That eddying leaf: sometimes it breathes;
Exudes votive offerings brought by the dozen
As they take home the rare catch.

We have sat in the canoe and watched
The sun skip and dodge beneath the mangrove,
We have heard wings beating the silence
And the dark: we've heard children suddenly cease
To laugh and run for home . . .

Such poems as these are the essence and the best of *The Horn*. It
would have been easy for those young men and women to have con-
cocted occasional verse, moralizing on the obvious themes that I have
outlined—the old and the new, freedom and colonialism, the conflict of
traditions. It would almost certainly have been bad verse, like most of
the political poetry in *The Horn*. In fact, the best poems embody the
reconciliation, rather than the conflict, of the divergent elements in their

lives, not by talking about them, but in another way. Their lives had hitherto been spent largely in the villages, and this foundation therefore provides the *themes* of much of the poetry. Their hopes and fears, yet unformed, provide the *mood* and direction. University College, Ibadan, its Department of English, and its teachers, syllabuses, books and examinations, provides not another piece of subject-matter, but a *method*. In these poems the students are expressing their vision of life, African life, through the mediums provided by their Western education, and it is this conjunction of themes, moods and process that relates the divergent elements.

That, perhaps, is why confidence, rather than doubt, is the dominant note of *The Horn*. Even such poems as "Olokun" show it, because the important thing is not whether the poet is at ease with the legends of the spirits or not, but the fact that he is at ease with himself. He knows where he is, where he came from, and where he is going. Minji Karibo, for example, treats a similar subject to "Olokun" in her "The Waterman" with a similar acceptance both of the traditions of her home and the viewpoint of her rationalist education:

> Twinkles from the dim shore beckoned us home,
> And our smoke-seasoned baskets full of fish
> Heaved sighs of relief when we at last sought
> Our faithful dugout, patient in bondage:
> Eager feet hurrying over white sands.
> Dusk was our escort.
> And suddenly He was there—the Waterman.
> Like a lone palm in an enchanted lake;
> White as the sand, long hair his only wear.
> Yet majestic power held us hypnotized
> Till gooseflesh and swelling head gave us the cue
> To turn to fly on wings of fear—speeded by
> His magic song converging with the wind.
> 'O come and pass!
> My heart too is as white as the sand.
> Do come and pass!
> I am not luring you to evil end.
> We Watermen serve the Water Spirits.
> Our errand is sometimes to mortals
> Sometimes from gods.

But mournful Night unfolds her black wrapper—
Our summons back to sandy depths;
The oil lamps yours to the marshy flats.'
And suddenly He was no more—the Waterman.
But the rhythm of wind and waves remained.
And our fear and wonder.[25]

Frank Aig-Imoukhuede is better known for his pidgin poems, but he too can be more serious, as in "The Olori" (IV, 4 [May 1961], p. 8):

The face that once lightened a king's palace
Is now supplanted—fallen out of grace.
The figure that once was for proud display
Is now a slumplace to be got out of the way.

No ochre; no, not even antimony
Can now bring back her lost beauty,
For the face that once was the chief's delight
Has been blackened by age's blight.

She tells no tales of woe or of misery,
But teaches her rivals the art of wifery:
And wishes—like all mothers—her daughter's
Lot would be better and nobler than hers.

A study of *The Horn*, however, soon demonstrates one thing—that the flowering of talent belongs chiefly to the students who came to Ibadan during the late 1950s. From 1961 on, the quality of the verse is lower, and mediocrity is less often balanced by talent. There are about thirty poems in each of the first four volumes; in Volume V this number is halved. Editors become more insistent and more apologetic in their search for usable poetry, and the quantity of prose (mostly reviews of Arts Theatre productions) relative to poetry increases. A few good poems appear, such as Nwanodi's "Salute to Songhai," and Olawaiye's "Silence, my Art," already quoted, but the best poetry of *The Horn* undoubtedly belongs to the first four volumes, and comes from writers who began to write in the first two. Without Aig Higo, Frank Aig-Imoukhuede, and especially Wole Soyinka and J. P. Clark, Volume IV would be negligible.

What is the reason for this? Why should these young people, with

Mac Akpoyoware, Minji Karibo, Pius Oleghe, and their friends display poetic ability while their student successors did not? The explanation has been hinted at in the opening paragraphs of this article, and it boils down to two incentives: the mutual encouragement of a small group of enthusiasts, and the sense of beginning. J. P. Clark and his friends created *The Horn*; their successors merely found it, and in spite of the efforts of Juliet Udezue (now Okonkwo—herself almost a founder-member of the group though, strangely, never a contributor), Molara Ogundipe (now Leslie) and Onyema Iheme (who spent a good deal of effort in maintaining *The Horn* in its last years), students from 1960 on never felt the enthusiasm that the founders had known. Numbers had a lot to do with it. In 1959 there were seven Honours graduates in English. Between 1960 and 1963 the class was eleven or twelve. The last Honours class as such was the twenty-two who graduated in 1964. Then the system changed, classes were much larger, and the cross-fertilization by which students had brought poetry out of one another in 1958–1960 began to fail. Student interests noticeably changed. The desire to *write* Nigerian poetry shifted into a desire to *study* it—an easier option.

The Horn was essentially a family affair; the members of the family are named on the pages of those first issues. After about 1961, whatever attempts were made to keep the tradition alive, it was bound to wither away, as all but the most massive student societies do. That it existed so long was due to its avoidance of the error of most Nigerian student organizations—obsession with the workings of a constitution and a vast committee. Because it was always in the hands of three or four enthusiasts, working only half-formally, it was able to survive long enough to encourage poetry from the universities at Nsukka and Zaria, which at that time were at that stage of first beginning which had nurtured *The Horn*.

Major Poets in The Horn

Wole Soyinka and Christopher Okigbo had studied their art in Britain before *The Horn* made use of them. Their poems add greatly to the value of *The Horn*, but they would have published anyway. The same may perhaps be true of J. P. Clark, but it remains a fact that *The Horn* gave him his first opportunity to circulate his poems to a critical audience. The single most important feature of *The Horn*, in other words, is the appearance of J. P. Clark. Sixteen of his poems appear in the copies of *The Horn* that I have, and all but two were good enough to be reprinted in more permanent form, in the Mbari collection of 1962, or in *A Reed in the Tide* in 1965. "Ivbie," his most ambitious early poem—and, indeed, the longest and most ambitious poem by anyone to appear in *The Horn*—was reprinted in its entirety in the Mbari collection, and selections have appeared in both the above collections and in *Présence Africaine*, No. 57, *Nouvelle Somme de Poésie du monde noire*, ed. L. G. Damas (1966?). The popular student anthology, *Modern Poetry from Africa*, edited by Gerald Moore and Ulli Beier (London: Penguin Books, 1963), contains three Clark poems from *The Horn*: "The Cry of Birth," "Fulani Cattle," and "The Imprisonment of Obatala."[26] Langston Hughes's *Poems from Black Africa* include "Agbor Dancer" and a surprisingly bad text of "Fulani Cattle," among other poems from *The Horn*. The Clark who contributed to, and first edited, *The Horn* was clearly no hesitant beginner.

It is interesting, nevertheless, to follow through the emendations of Clark's poems as they travel from *The Horn* through various reprintings in different collections. "The Cry of Birth" and "Fulani Cattle," because they have been reprinted so often, provide many interesting comparisons. The differences are as follows (not including Hughes's version, which contains too many copyist's errors to be useful):

(A)   *Fulani Cattle*

	The Horn (1959)	Mbari *Poems* (1962)	Moore & Beier (1963)	*A Reed in the Tide* (1965)
Title line	The Fulani Cattle	Fulani Cattle	Fulani Cattle	Fulani Cattle
9	So mute, so fierce and wan	So mute and fierce and wan	So mute and fierce and wan	So mute and fierce and wan
10	or	nor	nor	nor
21	town	towns	towns	towns
22	last[27]	least	least	least
23	vouchsafe	vouchsafe	reveal	reveal

(B)   *The Cry of Birth*

line	*The Horn* (1959)	Mbari *Poems* (1962)	Moore & Beier (1963)	*A Reed in the Tide* (1965)
3	brilliant	piquant	piquant	(not in this collection)
8	ere	before	before	
12	glimpse—the		glimpse, the	
12	of all our see	of our see	of our see	
13	Ah, the souls	The souls	The souls	

16	whose treacherous motions bedevil	with wanton motions bedevilling	with wanton motions bedevilling
17	But all night, through	All night, thro'	All night, through
18	Io	Yo[28]	Io
19	have, alack	have at my back	have at my back
21	O it comes	It comes	It comes
22	commingled	conmmingled[28]	commingled

It is easy to see what has happened. In the two years between the first writing and the first real public appearance in the Mbari *Poems*, Clark has been refining his art. Almost all these alterations are directed to one end—to a greater immediacy of poetic effect. One method is to make the verse more compact. Hence the very small changes in lines 12 and 17 of "The Cry of Birth," which look trivial in the list above, but make a notable difference to the run of the verse when it is read aloud. The other method is to eliminate the Romantic rhetoric. The vague "brilliant" becomes the less obvious and more precise "piquant"; the overstated "treacherous" becomes "wanton"; the exclamatory ejaculations of lines 13, 19 and 21 are cut out. In "Fulani Cattle," likewise, a simple syntax replaces rhetoric in line 9, and a direct word replaces a "poetic" one in line 23.

The variation between "last" and "least" in "Fulani Cattle," line 22, is interesting. I find the word "last" preferable; it is appropriate to the long journey, and quite colloquial enough. "At least" is a strange alternative, even though all the later versions prefer it. It implies that the beast is hoping to get more than rest, although he wishes "at least" for that. Instead of which the poet is delaying the "rest" (of death) that is coming. Perhaps that is the point: the bull is saying, "Can't you *at least* let me rest?" The point will bear no more laboring, though it is interesting enough. Of such is the substance of scholarly inquiry made; let us avoid Scriblerus.

Other poems by J. P. Clark show the same development between *The Horn* and later versions. The cases of Christopher Okigbo and Wole Soyinka are different. Both were already older, more finished poets when they contributed to *The Horn*. Okigbo contributed only two, "Debtor's Lane" (III, 2, pp. 6–7), reprinted in *Black Orpheus*, No. 11, p. 6, and "On the New Year" (III, 4, pp. 4, 9) which has not, I believe, been reprinted, although it is not without the familiar Okigbo power:

Now it is over, the midnight funeral that parts
The old year from the new;
And now beneath each pew
The warden dives to find forgotten missals
Scraps of resolutions and medals;
And over lost souls in the graves
Amid the tangled leaves
The Wagtail is singing: . . .
Cheep cheep cheep the new year is coming;
Christ will come again, the churchbell is ringing
Christ will come again after the argument in heaven . . .

                                        (lines 1–11)

By contrast with the reissue of almost all Clark's sixteen poems, Soyinka has, I believe, reprinted only two of the eight poems that he contributed to *The Horn*. The two are "Season," and the justly famous "Death in the Dawn," both of which appear in the anthologies of Moore and Beier, Donatus Nwoga[29] and *Présence Africaine*, as well as Soyinka's own *Idanre*. This is a great pity, for some of the poems are very fine.

They are certainly varied. There is Soyinka's contribution to pidgin verse (which he normally seems to disparage) in "Proverb: Okonjo de Hunter" (in III, 3). The same issue contains the rather loose—for Soyinka—political poem, "Poisoners of the World, Unite," which should have been reissued recently when it returned, unfortunately, to topicality: its theme is the French insistence on exploding "atomic devices" in the Sahara:

We whom you tattered Powers condemn
To slow, unmeaning future fears
Regret we cannot furnish instant
Proof, by dropping dead.

It seems a pity that Soyinka has not channeled his abilities into such satiric journalism as well as into the less widely-reaching satiric play. He might have been more effective in such a role than as an "Interpreter," a would-be leader of Nigerian intellectual thought.

Two poems in Vol. IV, No. 1, "From the red silk lining . . ." and "Audience to Performer" are more subtly and more personally satiric.

237

When he wrote them, Soyinka seems to have been suffering disillusionment with his audiences, who are likened to the still watchfulness of a chameleon or a frog, apparently asleep, but actually looking for something to destroy:

> The eyes of a chameleon turn
> Endlessly, a globe on rheumy axis
> But the chameleon said
> I'm not awake
> Just looking for a fly.
>
> ("Audience to Performer")

Another brilliantly witty, semi-political poem is "Committee Man" (IV, 3, pp. 10–11):

> Juggler of colons, definer of semi-, full
> And missing stops, Master-Serf
> Oh 'ohs' and 'sirs', begetter of the arch-
> 'suppose', Janus at obsequies,
> Toastmaster to my lords and ladies—yes
> You'll be there. At the celestial session
> You'll be there, your forms in order . . .

But the finest poem of all those that are still in limbo is "Epitaph for Say Tokyo Kid" (Vb [Feb. 1962], p. 10). The passenger lorry is one of the most homely features of life for those who belong to West Africa, and one of the quaintest and most exotic for those who only visit. Soyinka puts over its comedy, simplicity, power, crudeness and pathos in a manner that presages *The Road*. The driver likes carrying timber, hates carrying women passengers:

> Slow fingers probing depthless caches for
> A haggled fare. Screams curbed his speed until
> The forest taught him refuge. Timber was
> A male clerk passenger. Disdain filled him
> With silence. And he asked no change. . . .
>
> *   *   *
>
> In thrilled accents, touts, apprentices, garage
> Driftwood and worse predators tell surreal

Tales of Mile Forty-Six. Of the wild
Rebellious wood whose savaged earth unleashed
Its primal spirit, summoned
Death by the centrifuge. They found the Kid,
Say Tokyo Kid, Shatanooga Stomp, alias, alias . . .
Alias Cimarron plus Billy the plus Say Tokyo Kid
Lay up-axled, his head ungeared, his proud
Dakar-to-Yola lungs, rudely decarbonised.

(lines 10–14, 30–39)

It is to be hoped that Soyinka will soon reissue the complete poem. It makes an excellent companion-piece to the more personal "Death in the Dawn," which also was first published in *The Horn* (Vc [Jan. 1962], pp. 2–3).

The Horn does not reveal many great poets who have since been lost to the Civil Service, commerce or academia. It is a pity that Mac Ak-poyoware did not write more, or that Frank Aig-Imoukhuede is known to the world at large only by one comic poem, since he shows more *variety* than any other poet, not excepting Clark and Soyinka. But the same would be true of any university coterie: of the number of promising student poets only a few ever go on to give their lives to poetry. In this light, *The Horn* must rate very high indeed. There can be few student poetry magazines that have produced so much printable—and readable—poetry. Abiola Irele, in his review of *Nigerian Verse*, Martin Banham's selection from *The Horn*, concludes, "This is certainly not a collection of great poetry . . . but I venture to say, fully aware of the risk, that this collection holds within its pages some *poems*."[30] Ten years and more later, the claim stands.

APPENDIX: THE COPIES

This is a summary of the copies I have collected, and my conclusions about their dating. My collection seems to lack only two issues, and if any reader can supply either of these—or any I have missed—I shall be most grateful, especially because the lack of these issues is the first major obstacle to a possible reprint of *The Horn* as a whole. I would also like to hear from any reader who can amplify or correct my bibliographical data.

Volume I (Session 1957–58, ed. J. P. Clark): Nos. 1, 2, 3, 4, 5. No. 1 is dated by hand (I believe by someone in the University Library) "Jan. 31, 1958." No. 5 contains an editorial showing that this is the last issue of the session.

Volume II (Session 1958–59, ed. Abiola Irele): Nos. 1, 2, 3, 4, 6. No. 5 is missing. The editorial at the end of No. 6 again concludes the volume.

Volume III (1959–60, ed. Abiola Irele): Nos. 1, 2, 3, 4, 5. No. 5 seems to have appeared early in the third term, but was probably the last for the session. My photocopy is dated by the acquisitions stamp of the University Library, Ibadan, 20 May 1960. The "Editorial Comments" on the last page refer to "our next issue" but imply that the session is drawing to a close by a reference to forthcoming examinations (which began at the end of May). The material promised for "our next issue" appears in Vol. IV, No. 1.

Volume IV (1960–61, ed. Juliet Udezue): Nos. 1, 2, 3, 4. No. 4 contains a review of plays produced "in the last week of April." This issue, therefore, appeared in May, and it is unlikely that another issue would appear after this one.

Volume V (1961–62, ed. Omolara Ogundipe). There is an anomaly here. I have three copies edited by Miss Ogundipe, but labelled "Vol. IV." I have no copies from any source labelled "Vol. V." One can only conjecture why the three issues from the first half of 1962 were not described as "Vol. V." Perhaps the printer of the title-block made an error, and the committee could not afford to rectify it. I have not yet been able to get in touch with Mrs. Leslie(Miss Ogundipe), but I am indebted to Dapo Adelugba, who graduated in July 1961, but was still at U.C.I. in late 1961 while waiting to go abroad. During this time he collected poems for *The Horn*, which he passed on to Miss Ogundipe when she became editor early in 1962.

The three issues are numbered by hand. I have one original, with "6" pencilled in, and two photocopies, both numbered by hand, and both at first sight "5"; however, one figure is overwritten and may be "3." They can be dated thus: the issue beginning with "An Apology," by Saidu Angulu, contains a review of *King Lear*, which was performed in December 1961. It can therefore be dated January 1962, and in the body of this article I refer to it as "Va." Similarly, my issue No. "Vb," beginning "Sinner," can be dated by its review of *Agamemnon*, to late January or early February. This leaves Vc, beginning "Snake Charmer," which cannot be so conveniently dated; but as it is numbered 6 (albeit illogically), we may suppose it followed the other two.

Volume VI (1962–63, ed. F. Onyema Iheme): I have one copy, labelled "Vol. No. VI." An editorial (pp. 7–8) complains of the shortage of material and dates this issue in the third term. Presumably this was the only issue of the session.

Volume VII (1963–64, ed. F. Onyema Iheme): Nos. 1 and 3. These are dated in print on the title block, January and May 1964 respectively. Presumably No. 2 is missing, but probably no more.

Summary. Volumes I, III, IV, and VI appear to be complete. Volume V may be. The only issues certainly missing are Vol. II, No. 5 and Vol. VII, No. 2.

FOOTNOTES

[1] Martin Banham, ed., *Nigerian Student Verse* (Ibadan, Nigeria: Ibadan University Press, 1959).

[2] *Poezja Czarnej Afryki* (Warsaw: Państwowy Wydawniczy, 1962).

[3] In particular Mr. Banham, Dr. J. A. Ramsaran, Mr. G. J. Axworthy and Professor J. Ferguson, all of whom were at Ibadan throughout the journal's life, and who have been very helpful in providing me photocopies of issues in their possession.

[4] The ten are: Mary Alexander, Martin Banham, Ronald Dathorne, John Ferguson, Norman Gary, Harold Guite, Christine Maney, C. A. Newbury, John Spencer, Kay Williamson. For stylistic reasons, I believe that the owner of the pseudonym "Samsara," who gave one poem to Volume V, was also an expatriate.

5 I give the spelling as it appears in *The Horn*. The more recent spelling is, of course, Wonodi.

6 These reviews are not substantial enough to absorb much time, but it may be worthwhile listing some of the dramatic fare which was being provided for and by students who had no other opening into the theater. There are plays from the Western stage: Chekhov, Brecht, Ibsen, Sartre, Fry, Synge and *King Lear*, as well as Aeschylus, Aristophanes, and Plautus. There are operas—*The Magic Flute*, *The Beggar's Opera*, *The Bartered Bride*, as well as occasional instrumental recitals covered by Abiola Irele. Thirdly, there are plays by Nigerian writers: *The Gentle People*, *The Trials of Brother Jero* (reviewed on its premiere with Remi Adeleye as Jero), *That Scoundrel Suberu* (an adaptation from Molière), Ayo Ogunlade's *Anatomy of Folly*, Frank Aig-Imoukhuede's *The Curse*, and Nkem Nwankwo's *The Heritor*. One Yoruba play, *Love of Money*, by the Ogunmola group is also reviewed in Vol. VI (1963). The variety shows once again the vitality of the cultural life of University College, Ibadan, and one must remember that there was a good deal going on that *The Horn* does not report.

7 Aig Higo, "Complaint," III, 4, p. 2.

8 I. B. Mmobuosi, "Alabama," VII, 1, p. 1.

9 Yetunde Esan, "His Very-Highness," VI, 1 (Oct. 1960), p. 3.

10 IV, 2 (Dec. 1960), p. 4.

11 Chidi Ikonne, "La tête de la tête," VII, 1 (Jan. 1964), p. 7.

12 A. T. C. Anamelechi, "Afterwards," VII, 3 (May 1964), pp. 8–9.

13 Ibadan is virtually uncountable, since many people live half in town and half in satellite villages; but it is commonly said to have over a million inhabitants.

14 IV, 3 (Feb.–March 1961), pp. 4–5.

15 (One imperfect foreigner who had to mollify more than one "fee-thirsty mourner" as sympathetically as possible wonders if this is after all a compliment.) This word is printed "moolfies" in the original, an evident typing error. As I note that this particular issue was typed on my typewriter, I may be allowed the emendation.

16 O. Wali, "They say I'm a leper," I, 1 (Jan. 1958), p. 3.

17 "Dejection," II, 1 (Nov. 1958), p. 9.

18 Respectively in I, 3 (April 1958); III, 1 (Nov. 1959); III, 3 (Jan.–Feb. 1960); and III, 2 (December 1959).

19 I. Oduah, [no title], III, 1 (November 1959), p. 1.

20 VIII, 3 (May 1964), p. 7.

21 Jim Nwobodo, "Death," Va (January 1962), p. 4.

22 In a poem by Kay Williamson, then a graduate student engaged in linguistic fieldwork. The poem, in Vol. I, No. 1, is called "The Punters."

23 B. Akobo, "Sundown at the Beach," I, 3 (April 1958), p. 4.

24 Pius Oleghe, "A Sudden Storm," I, 1 (Jan. 1958), p. 9.

25 I, 5 (April 1968), p. 7. In *Nigerian Student Verse* the quotation marks surround only the first line of the Waterman's speech. This is a faulty correction of an error in the original copy of *The Horn*, which has closing quotation marks both there and after "marshy flats," which is self-evidently the end of the speech.

26 In issues I, 3 (ca. March 1958); III, 2 (Dec. 1959); III, 5 (May 1960) respectively.

27 The typescript has *least*, but in two separate copies that I have seen, there is a manuscript alteration, presumably authorized and probably asked for by Clark, to "last."

28 These are clearly typographical errors, which Moore and Beier correct. I include them for completeness' sake.

29 *West African Verse* (London: Longman, 1967), pp. 64, 66.

30 *The Horn*, IV, 1 (Oct. 1960), p. 9.

THE "COMMUNALISTIC" AFRICAN AND THE "INDIVIDUALISTIC" WESTERNER: SOME COMMENTS ON MISLEADING GENERALIZATIONS IN WESTERN CRITICISM OF SOYINKA AND ACHEBE

J. Z. Kronenfeld

Many African intellectuals—politicians, writers and other professionals —have been concerned with establishing the value of precolonial African life, in the face of hundreds of years of Western condescension towards and misunderstanding of "primitive" peoples. This essay concerns the use made of the terms of these African intellectuals in Western discussion of modern African literature, a use that sometimes leads the literary critic and the social scientist alike, away from, rather than into the actual nature of the works he is examining.

This attempt to establish a "positive" African identity, indeed to stress the unique values of African societies, has been intimately involved with the struggle for independence, and with nation-building. It has been characterized by the use of a series of contrasts between African and Western cultures, which are, by now, very familiar to the reader of modern African fiction and nonfiction, of Western discussion of African literature, and, finally, of African commentary, both on African literature itself and on Western criticism of it. Perhaps the most familiar of these contrasts is that between "communal" African society and "individualistic" Western society, which is often linked to the contrast between the "traditional" and the "modern," the "rural" and the "urban," and often closely associated with a distinction between a mystical attitude toward nature that does not separate the individual from the cosmos, and an empirical or rational attitude toward nature. The contrast between "communal" African society and "individualistic" Western society has become a touchstone for Western criticism of African literature; it has been put into service in the explanation of apparent differences between Western literature—in particular, the nineteenth and twentieth century novel —and African fiction, which, for example, less frequently involves conventions of extensive introspection.

The intellectual history of these familiar contrasts might plausibly begin with the distinction in nineteenth century German social theory between Gemeinschaft and Gesellschaft, originally found in Tönnies, buut also present in Max Weber, and anticipated in Marx, who is certainly an influential figure in modern African thought. On the one hand, there are collectivist, cooperative, small-scale, homogeneous societies governed by divine sanctions, in which there are close personal bonds between individuals; on the other, individualistic, secular, heterogeneous societies in which it is the "cash-nexus" that controls relationships among individuals.[1] In many ways it is this kind of distinction that is passed on in Jan-heinz Jahn's influential works on "African" values and that appears in Léopold Senghor's writings. For the African intellectual and for the African politician, the positive connotations associated with the cooperativist side of the dichotomy are crucial: connotations of brotherhood, a nonmaterialistic outlook, of sharing, of a mystic closeness to nature, not an exploitation of it.

The question of the truth value of these distinctions between kinds of societies is a complicated one which belongs to the discipline of anthropology. However, one does need to keep in mind that these generalizations have been applied to the great range of African cultures, when it is not clear whether the "collectivist" description holds for anything but, say, hunting and gathering societies, and in what senses even, there. Though I cannot go into detail here, I would like to suggest the possible usefulness of a distinction between the ideology of the "communal" society, with all its positive associations of sharing and absence of conflict, and the nature of "communal" society. For example, it is true that many African societies have communal "ownership" of land—that is, the "lineage," not the individual, "owns" the land.[2] "Ownership," as we think of it, involving rights of alienation on the part of the individual, is actually an inapplicable concept here. However, this does not mean that there is idyllic sharing of all valuables, that there is no differential access to valuables, that there are no disputes. We are very likely to associate such a situation with communal land tenure, because "ownership," as we think of it, is clearly an area in which disputes and tensions exist in our own society. However, individuals do matter in the African situation; they do have "use rights," which they inherit, and may sometimes procure in other ways. There may indeed be political squabbling about who gets what, as well as differences among individuals as far as the ability to procure such rights goes, not to mention differences in wealth resulting from the nature of the land a person has rights to, among other factors. To put it bluntly, because people in different cultures do not dispute over exactly the same things, in exactly the same ways, does not mean that they have no disputes!

Similarly, the Western sense of the overall "religious" orientation of African, or non-Western, societies—a commonplace—may result from our particular perspective, from invalid comparisons, rather than from as great a difference in human behavior as is sometimes supposed to exist. What *we* call religious activities are relatively discrete, formalized and isolated from the rest of our activities, which we consider secular. However, an alien observer might consider that our religion is capitalism—involving such rituals as formal speeches about the virtues of the free enterprise system—which would then be seen to pervade all aspects of our lives. As alien observers looking at small-scale societies in which institutions overlap, we may see the same set of people involved in religious activities involving the supernatural, social activities involving arbitration of disputes, and economic activities—sometimes at the same time—and we may consequently think of these societies as pervaded by religion, and fail to make the necessary distinctions. We may then classify activities that are not primarily involved with the supernatural (e.g., visiting a herbalist, which is often pragmatic or empirical) as religious, because they have no exact counterparts in our society—given *our* classifications—even though they are in fact closer to medicine in our sense than not. Or, we may fail to see that activities in our own society which we exclude from the rubric religion (for example, psychoanalysis) have a great deal in common with activities in other societies that we think of as related to religion (for example, visiting a priest who may diagnose and suggest a remedy for a purely "social" illness such as tension among certain kinsmen, even if his supernatural sanctions *may* give him the power to make such a diagnosis).

The critic anxious to define African values as the basis for a discussion of African literature often makes use of the kinds of contrasts I have been discussing. However, he may fail to understand the facts upon which the contrasts need to be based in order to be valid, and thus may overstress the differences between cultures. He may fail to adequately distinguish between philosophical, political or celebrative aims and other kinds of aims that the artist may have, even when this distinction is necessary; he may fail to distinguish between the ideology of the nature of African society, and African society, when there is a distinction that should be made. That is, although these contrasts do not necessarily have a very

clear content in his mind, the critic may impose them, with their valu-
ations, on the works he is examining. While such terms are crucial background for the poetry of Senghor, for example, they are quite misleading
when forced on most of the plays of the satirist, Wole Soyinka. Furthermore, the Western critic sometimes seems to be attributing the differences
he observes in African literature as opposed to Western literature to an
absolute difference of the African and Western psyches. Thus, the noted
absence of introspection in some African novels (one need only mention
the novels of Ayi Kwei Armah and Soyinka's novel, *The Interpreters*, as
exceptions) is linked with the supposedly communal character of the
African mind, rather than with the special political situation of the African writer which makes him more likely to deal with societal problems
than with uniquely personal ones. The absence of "introspection," insofar
as it exists, is more related to the absence of a developed literary tradition
of introspection than to an eternal feature of the "African Mind."

From the sociological point of view, perhaps there is a correlation of
the less urgent need to establish uniquely African values, with such factors
as the achievement of independence, or with the absence of a settled,
landed colonial population in some parts of Africa, or with the degree
of comfortable assimilation or acceptance of his own culture on the part
of the African writer himself, which, in turn, would relate to the other
factors. Certainly, once nations achieve their independence, their writers
are more likely to become concerned with injustices *within* their own society. Even if a desire to create viable *art* might have to await conditions
in which people can afford to care about art *per se*, there certainly are
African writers who object to the overly polemical as incompatible with
their growth as artists or the creation of art. Insofar as art involves fidelity
to truth—as envisioned by the individual artist—even in order to be
credible, we might expect some artists to take off from different assumptions than those involved in the familiar contrasts outlined here. Human
conflict is the stuff of literature; sometimes those critics who find African
literature "simple," do so because they assume the absence of conflicts, in
accordance with their presumptions about African thinking about African society, when, in fact, those presumptions are not applicable.

The actual variety of opinion as to the nature of their own societies, of
the influences of opinion, and of personal experiences of Africans in
differing circumstances and cultures should encourage a healthy reluctance on the part of Western critics to turn uncritically, and without some
of the caveats outlined above, to individual sources for the "essence" of

African culture on which to base a theory of the nature of African literature. If Senghor was influenced by Lucien Lévy-Bruhl concerning the
"pre-logical" mentality of primatives, modern African intellectuals show
an awareness of the works of more recent anthropologists, such as E. E.
Evans-Pritchard, who have gradually corrected the rather extreme views
of Lévy-Bruhl by pointing to the logicality of "primitive" systems of
belief within their own assumptions, to the attentions of people everywhere to pragmatic as well as supernatural concerns.[3] "Primitives" are
aware of empirical causation just as we are; it is events that cannot be
controlled empirically that require other means of control, just as in our
own culture. Some African intellectuals find the presumed close association of drama and ritual (as in Francis Cornford's theory of Greek comedy) attractive, interesting, and in some cases exploitable for experiments
in modern drama, since their own societies have ritual performances and
animal sacrifice.[4] However, others suggest that the mimetic instinct is
universal, that acting out is inherently pleasurable, and thus, that there
is no intrinsic relation between religious feeling, and drama; rather, a
"religious" occasion may simply provide the necessary formal circumstances for drama to take place uninterrupted, in small societies where
everyone knows everyone else.[5] Such writers are in effect suggesting
that the African is no more inherently and totally mystically oriented than
anyone else.

Even though there is certainly a great deal of competent criticism of
African literature, there still is something of a tendency to think uncritically in terms of these contrasting categorizations—especially "communalistic" vs. "individualistic"—without the necessary distinctions and
caveats in mind. These categorizations encourage the misrepresentation of
certain literary works, the underestimation of their human complexity and
ambiguity, and the diminishing of their merit, when they are imposed on
literature structured in different terms. I would like to examine the comments of two critics who serve as examples of these tendencies: first, a
social scientist commenting on Wole Soyinka's *The Lion and the Jewel*,
among other African works; second, a literary critic discussing Chinua
Achebe's *Things Fall Apart*.

In his article, "Behavior and Cultural Value in West African Stories:
Literary Sources for the Study of Culture Contact,"[6] Austin Shelton argues
that Wole Soyinka's play, *The Lion and the Jewel* (one of four African
works he considers), reasserts the value of traditional, communally-based
society. Soyinka's comedy concerns the victory of a chief over a super-

ficially Westernized schoolteacher in a rivalry for a village belle—whose head has been a bit swelled as a result of the appearance of her photograph in a glossy Lagos magazine. The play is assessed as follows, along with the other works Shelton considers: "The value most clearly approved . . . is traditional communal responsibility, revealed partly in the condemnation of self-seeking individualism" (p. 411). Now the play does mock "modern" ways, but particularly insofar as they are espoused superficially, naively, or hypocritically by Lakunle, the village schoolteacher. In this sense, what is being exposed, as in comedies generally, is pretension. The categories of approved traditionalism involving positive qualities ("responsibility") and disapproved modernism involving negative qualities ("self-seeking") may derive from the literature that celebrates or seeks unique ethical values in African social institutions, but they are not the categories that structure this play. To come to the play with these preconceived notions in mind is to miss the *comedy*. The comic stance is a more objective one. As comedy, *The Lion and the Jewel* exposes self-seeking and inconsistency—beneath various guises—in *all* the characters. It shows how people use the "traditional" for "modern" purposes, and the "modern" for "traditional" purposes, in accordance with universal human motivations of pride, power, and sex, rather than out of loyalty to an abstraction such as "tradition," or even primarily out of religious or moral conviction. If "tradition," as exemplified by chief Baroka, wins (in the sense that Sidi the belle becomes his youngest wife), it is mainly because he is wilier than Lakunle, not because he has appealed to better values, which in themselves motivate behavior. Baroka and Lakunle may not be equally good choices as mates, for economic and other reasons, but the chief is equally subject to the penetrating comic glance that distinguishes the eloquent speech from the mundane motive.

As the play opens, Sidi, a young village girl, is being courted by Lakunle, the village schoolteacher, who offers her a "Western" monogamous marriage. However, she will not marry him until he pays the brideprice; she will not have people say she "was no virgin / that [she] was forced to sell [her] shame."[7] We soon learn that Sidi has been photographed in various exotic poses for a magazine by a "Lagos man," who seems to have exploited the idea of "bush" beauty. After she has seen the photographs, her sense of her importance grows and indeed she does become more significant in the village. But, her inflated ego piques the village chief, even more than the pictures attract him to her charms. Although the chief's eldest wife brings Sidi her husband's offer of marriage, and explains the advantages of being the youngest wife in a polygamous household, Sidi does not jump at the chance. In fact, she is quite suspicious of the chief's motives. Baroka has manipulated events in the past to preserve the status quo and his own comfortable position; he bribed some roadworkers to encourage them to see the wisdom of not building a motor road through the village. Now he arranges a trap which both squelches Sidi's inflated ego and wins her as his youngest wife. He allows the rumor of his impotence to circulate through his gleefully unaware eldest wife, with the result that Sidi comes, uninvited, to his house, in order to enjoy this blow to his pride, to scoff. However, and partially because she is off her guard, believing she has the upper hand, he is able to seduce her by alternating a show of power and scorn with overwhelming eloquence and flattery, not to mention the aid of some available palm wine. The flattery includes a promise to print stamps with her glorious image on them right there in the town on a machine obtained for the purpose. Whether or not Baroka really intends to use the stamp machine is not clear. But it certainly would not be inconsistent with his character for him to turn the "modern" to his own uses by collecting a local stamp tax. And it is part of the conception of human behavior in the play for him to use the same kind of flattery to win Sidi for himself as was involved in the photographs which made her think herself more important than him, rather than for him to appeal to her directly in terms of the value of traditional life and institutions. After Sidi has lost her virginity to him, although at first angered and humiliated, she decides to marry him. He has won in a show of strength and cleverness; it is best to make good one's losses.

This brief plot summary should make clear that the play does not really operate in terms of a simple antithesis between the modern and the traditional, and certainly not in terms of an antithesis between "self-seeking" modernism and "responsible" traditionalism, unless some explanation is forthcoming! Now, let us consider the comedy in more detail in order to see how its comedic aspects in fact undercut so simple a conception. Lakunle is in love with Western ways, and he attempts to make his "knowledgeableness" a selling point in his courtship of Sidi. Recent writings on West African popular culture suggests that Western styles of courtship, as observed in the cinema, for example,[8] are aspired to, imitated and enjoyed by some West Africans who, like Americans trying out "alternative life styles," get pleasure from being *au courant*. But Lakunle is presented by Soyinka with purely mundane motivations

as well. It is suggested that he was unskillful at rural occupations (p. 36);
it is not uncommon in rural situations for African children who show
little aptitude for farming or fishing to be sent to school. His rejection of
traditional customs has a strong economic cause; he simply cannot afford
the bride-price (p. 36). Like the other characters in the play, he uses or
abuses the "traditional" in accordance with his own needs and situation.
Thus, he adopts a misinformed Western attitude toward bride-price ("To
pay the price would be / To buy a heifer off the market stall. / You'd be
my chattel, my mere property." p. 8) partially because he is in a bad economic position. If that position encourages his fascination with Western
values, the espousal of such values also compensates him—at least in his
eyes—by boosting his low social status in the village. Yet, he is not above
using a *traditional* argument when it suits his purposes. After Baroka has
successfully seduced Sidi, Lakunle, at first reacting with shock, recovers
himself (his love is "selfless—the love of spirit / Not of flesh."); besides, she will agree:

> it is only fair
> That we forget the bride-price totally
> Since you no longer can be called a maid (p. 60).

Shelton's view of the play, as asserting the *value* of one way of life over
another, would seem to require that the author or the characters—
especially the "traditional" characters—be concerned with value judgements. However, the comedy clearly operates in terms of the characters
adjusting ideology, or selecting convenient aspects of it, in accordance
with their situations and their psychological needs, as Lakunle does here:

> 'Man takes the fallen woman by the hand'
> And ever after they live happily.
> Moreover, I will admit,
> It solves the problem of her bride-price too.
> A man must live or fall by his true
> Principles. That, I had sworn
> Never to pay (p. 61).

Sidi's concern with bride-price makes her no more self-consciously an
upholder of traditional values for their own sake than Lakunle's abuse of
it makes him a sincere believer in "modern" ways. Neither traditional
nor modern values and institutions are treated as abstractions, but in their

relation to people's universal needs, which clearly can be met in a variety of ways. Sidi participates sufficiently in the village society to feel that marriage without bride-price would seriously undercut her self-esteem, making her a "laughing-stock," a "cheap bowl for the village spit" (p. 7). However, her self-esteem can be served equally well by modern means; once her ego has been flattered by the photographs, she becomes Westernized in her own way. She may reject the abandonment of bride-price, but she is quite willing to give up carrying firewood—which many West African women do—and to allow Lakunle to behave in a courtly, "Western" manner in this instance (p. 19). We might indeed call this an example of the selective adaptation of new customs! Although she rejects Lakunle's equation of the custom of bride-price with the concept of "property," she does seem to use his ideas in rejecting Baroka's offer of marriage. Indeed, "property" in a more generalized and universal sense *is* involved in Baroka's interest in her:

> Why did Baroka not request my hand
> Before the stranger
> Brought his book of images?
>
> . . . .
> Can you not see? Because he sees my worth
> Increased and multiplied above his own;
> Because he can already hear
> The balled-makers and their songs
> In praise of Sidi, the incomparable,
> While the Lion is forgotten.
> He seeks to have me as his property
> Where I must fade beneath his jealous hold (p. 21).

In their different ways, both men want Sidi as extensions of their pride or self-images. Most ironically—not in accordance with a dialectic of pure tradition as opposed to impure modernism, but with the more universal and realistic terms in which the play operates—Sidi finally ends by taking from Baroka, the supposed traditionalist, what she refused from Lakunle, the supposed modernist: marriage *without* bride-price. Although the "fox" seduced her (like Volpone, by playing at impotence), she still would not be granted bride-price because of her loss of virginity, as has already been made clear (p. 7), and furthermore, she might not care to have her gullibility mocked at great length. She goes in the direction that salvages her pride. Like Lakunle, when it suits her situation and purposes, she makes light of "traditional" customs. As reported by Sadiku, Baroka's eldest wife, her comment is "leave all that nonsense to savage and brabararians" (sic, p. 62). In any case, the traditionalist in power—that is, Baroka—may always dispense with tradition, and more easily than someone like Lakunle. And, from Sidi's point of view, marriage to a chief upon whom she has some claim because he seduced her, even marriage without bride-price, is certainly a better choice than no marriage or marriage to a person poorer in status and wealth, or one who might use her "shame" as a bargaining point, to her disadvantage. In her present situation, she is indeed, to quote Shakespeare, "not for all markets."

Baroka's negative attitudes toward modernization stem as clearly from the threats it poses to his authoriy and status, as from his fondness for the old ways; they certainly do not stem from a moral preference unrelated to vested interests. His desire to "get" Sidi, apart from her evident attractions, is a desire to squelch an upstart, a "little fool" (p. 59), who would mock him and dare to think herself more important than him, and it is an aspect of the eternal war between men and women. Although his speech on the sameness of modern life (p. 52) is appropriate to the superficiality of modernization evident in Lakunle and is concordant with Soyinka's general dislike of the *unassimilated* facile imitation of other cultural styles,[9] Baroka's words are comically undercut in the dramatic situation. Baroka is, after all, trying to overwhelm Sidi with eloquence, and at the same time, enjoying her lack of comprehension of the joke he is about to play on her. His metaphors concerning change and tradition are so patently sexual, his posture so clearly a situation-related pose (the "body-weighed-down-by-burdens-of-state attitude," p. 54), that whatever concern for the traditional *qua* traditional he may have is qualified—to say the least—by his evident enjoyment of duping her. *He* is the old wine and *she* the new bottle:

> Yesterday's wine alone is strong and blooded, child,
> And though the Christians' holy book denies
> The truth of this, old wine thrives best
> Within a new bottle. The coarseness
> Is mellowed down, and the rugged wine
> Acquires a full and rounded body . . .
> Is this not so—My child?
> [*Quite overcome, Sidi nods*] (p. 54).

The Lion and the Jewel, as comedy, depends on seeing humans in terms of their universal motivations of pride, power and sex, which culture provides various means of satisfying, not in terms of their allegiance to old or new cultural values *per se*.

Austin Shelton's brief comments on the characters seem to stem from preconceived notions about the concerns of modern African authors which are imposed on the play, rather than from the play itself. Shelton says that "Lakunle failed to obtain the 'jewel' because she had sense enough to succumb to the traditionalist Baroka . . ." (p. 411). However, we have seen that Sidi hardly has an unconstrained choice, that she does not make a self-conscious value judgment in favor of the traditional. *The Lion and the Jewel* is not a morality play in which Sidi is presented as freely assenting to "pure" traditional values, after having foolishly toyed with modernism, and having learned her moral lesson. Even were her choice unconstrained, Lakunle himself was not a very appealing example of a Westernized African, being too poor in goods and status. But there is nothing about Sidi's basic motivations, as they are presented by Soyinka, that would prevent her from responding more favorably to a government minister, albeit a virile one, who might offer her a monogamous marriage, should circumstances allow for such a possibility, just as there is nothing that prevents her from enjoying giving up carrying firewood, traditional as the practice may be for women. When Sidi does finally ceremoniously give up the magazine, she is capitalizing on the prestige and ego-satisfaction to be obtained from the choice she has been constrained to make. The same motives may be satisfied in the "traditional" and the "modern" situation.

Similarly, it does not seem appropriate to Lakunle's economic and psychological motives and his clear manipulation of "principle," to assess him simply in Shelton's terms, saying that he "possessed individualistic ideals, . . . and he extended these to Sidi, treating her accordingly" (p. 410), especially insofar as this description, taken in the context of Shelton's article, is meant to suggest a qualitative difference between the "self-seeking individualism" of Lakunle and the "communal responsibility" of Baroka. Again, there is nothing about Lakunle that would prevent his taking advantage of whatever combination of the "modern" and the "traditional" suited his purposes and situation. It is clear enough that he could enjoy the advantages of traditional polygamy, were he in the chief's situation, and that the fact that he cannot, encourages his attraction to the "modern."

> Ah, I sometimes wish I led his kind of life.
> Such luscious bosoms make his nightly pillow.
> I am sure he keeps a time-table just as
> I do at school. . . .
>
> . . . .
> . . . No! I do not envy him! (p. 26)

Alas, having several wives is expensive, and Lakunle cannot even afford one. Once again, the play seems to point out that people do not opt for the traditional or the modern as abstractions. The man who enjoys more privileges in the traditional situation than in the modern is certainly likely to be a "traditionalist." The traditional way is not inherently less likely to serve individual self-seeking than the modern. The plot alone makes clear that Lakunle did not fail to win Sidi because he did not "face the fact that what a young African woman really wants is to 'prove' her *raison d'être* through childbearing" (Shelton, p. 410). At the end of the play, Sidi does indeed look forward to "children, sired of the lion stock" (p. 64), but this comes after the fact, as it were, not before. The plot alone also makes clear that Baroka did not succeed by appealing to Sidi to consciously assent to her valued, traditional role, but rather, by coercion and by flattery. That flattery, which included the suggestion that there is a certain amount of prestige in carrying on the noble line, in assenting to the wisdom of the ancients, was particularly instrumental, since the only alternative was being thought "vain," with "a feather-light" head, and "always giddy/With a trivial thought" (p. 49). Bearing children is undoubtedly taken for granted as part of Sidi's idea of her future, but wanting to "prove" one's *raison d'être* requires more self-consciousness than she seems to possess, as well as a different sort of situation, in which the traditional as traditional *per se* is salient and chosen for ideological or political reasons alone.

Shelton's generalizations seem to be simply unrelated to the tenor of the play in that they suggest that it is primarily about the psychological and ethical value of the traditional way, which alone ultimately satisfies all the needs of the people, because of its inherent nature, and about which, the author, if not the characters as well, think in abstract moral terms of "right" and "wrong." "Change to the white man's way is 'wrong' even if necessary, but return to the African way is 'right.' . . . The individual . . . can regain 'wholeness' of self and proper orientation to behavior as well as obtain the deserved rewards only through his maintenance of traditions or a return to the traditionally sanctioned behavior"

(Shelton, p. 410). The play does not assert ಟಿಬ *moral* superiority of the old way of life, in fact making only a brief case for its esthetic superiority. Nor does it operate in terms of the possibility of a willed "return" to the "African" way, because it does not depend on the African way being qualitatively different, in the sense that it appeals to different motives, from the "modern" way. Rather, *The Lion and the Jewel* makes comedy out of human contingencies and inevitably mixed motives, in traditionalist and modernist alike. One wonders what the statement that Baroka "received full reward for his support of communal values" (Shelton, p. 411) can mean. Traditional ways, no more than modern, satisfy all the people all of the time. Indeed, Baroka's eldest wife, who had some good words to say about the advantages of being the chief's last wife, was not entrusted to win Sidi to the side of tradition, but played her role in accordance wih Baroka's knowledge that she would be delighted to make him a laughingstock because of his "loss" of vigor! The war between men and women pits the "traditionalist" against each other, and, indeed, aligns the "modernist" and the "traditionalist" (for even Lakunle has sympathy for his rival when it is a matter of seeing manhood being mocked). Insofar as the debate between the traditional and the modern figures in the play at all, it seems to revolve around questions of status, and vested interests—both psychological and economic—which are frankly understood as such, more than questions of value. All of the characters are more or less constrained by their situations, and all of them seek to enhance or maintain their power and prestige by taking whatever chances offer. Individuals will conflict as each has his eye on the main chance, but not necessarily within the same fixed alliances, and the alliances are in any case not determined by an overriding loyalty to the traditional or the modern *per se*. The Baroka, having more cards to play, succeeds in getting what he wants, but he is hardly acting in disinterested support of "communal" values, or out of any purer motives than anyone else. The play does suggest that traditional socialization is still operative, and that traditional institutions may still answer people's needs (not that they inevitably must), even that the older way of life is preferable to a superficial imitation of the new. But the traditional way of life has no monopoly on purity and nobility and does not inspire loyalty *on its own account*; the same kinds of human motivations and contingencies that result in its apparent preservation here, could as well result in significant modifications. *The Lion and the Jewel* does indeed tell us about culture contact and change, but in quite a different way than Shelton would have us think.

"Traditional" and "modern," especially as they are attached to positively-evaluated "communalism" and negatively-evaluated "individualism," may be rather meaningless and indeed misleading ready-made categories to use in the analysis of modern African literature. One suspects that such categories would also be troublesome for the social scientist. Soyinka's play seems very much related to the work of those anthropologists concerned with the selective adaptation to new institutions, and the incorporation of new ideas or practices into existent institutions, in situations involving rapid change, such as that of modernizing Africa. Soyinka's characters would easily fit into a world where a practitioner of folk medicine may live in an urban community and be saving money to send his son to college, or where bride-price becomes a matter of cash and is raised exorbitantly by parents of daughters. One danger of the categories is the assumption that change is an all-or-nothing experience. Another is that people act out of loyalty to abstractions, rather than in accordance with their needs, upon which many complex factors operate, including their socialization into their own systems. One might want to distinguish between situations in which people are likely to become self-conscious about "traditional" values conceived as such, or conservative for conservatism's sake, and situations in which they are not likely to act this way.

The tendency to use such concepts as "traditional" and "modern," "communalistic" and "individualistic" too carelessly and abstractly, without sufficient content in mind, and without regard for their fit with the literature being examined, is undoubtedly encouraged by the critic's awareness of what African intellectuals themselves have said, often for political purposes. Shelton does begin with the assumption that the African writer, like his society, is inherently communally-oriented, opposed to "any consideration of African literature as individualistic 'art for art's sake'." He asserts that the new African literature is reasserting a "traditional" African attitude toward art as "socially functional rather than merely aesthetically pleasing" (p. 406). In this he echoes the many statements made at African writers' conferences and by politicians such as Sekou Touré.[10] But politically motivated statements might overstress differences between cultures in this instance. A socialist or Marxist political leaning certainly encourages such an attitude toward art. The political need to establish a positive contrast between African values and Western values also would encourage such a position, especially when Western criticism has often been negative with regard to the lack of "individualization" in African literature. The African writer comes from a small intellectual class; he is rarely devoted to writing alone, but is often, as an educated person, a spokesman for his society, or pressed into the service of nationalism. His audience is both the local literate population and the rest of the world. The African literary movement in Western languages is of course very much tied up with self-explanation, identity-seeking and current conditions, hence the attraction of anthropology for so many authors. This is not unusual; in times of transition, writers often speak for their cultures. If these writers are more concerned with their societies and their nations than with unique experiences, this is a product of their circumstances, rather than an indication of their absolute nature as Africans, or of their inherent potentialities. Perhaps more literary reflection on uniquely personal experience needs to await a larger educated class and a more stable and diversified society, as well as a more stable political situation.

In any case, "socially functional," from the point of view of the political powers that be, can of course be quite different from "socially functional" from the point of view of the artist. Social purposes, in the sense of statements about one's society or its direction, often coexist with esthetic purposes and interests. Indeed, "socially functional" could cover the gamut from the sheerest propagandistic didacticism to the subtlest satirical attack by the author, as minority of one, on majority values. It is also probably a bit rash to assume that traditional African art is only socially functional, whatever is meant by that term, simply because we have tended to ignore its esthetic aspects.[11] The politician and intellectual, anxious that folk literature and art be credited with value in a world accustomed to written literature and signed sculpture, has stressed the values of "communal" and "anonymous" art. But individuals shape this anonymous art, even though their contributions do not get recorded as such, and the end result is constantly modified by performance in front of a general audience. More importantly, individuals have created modern African literature, and signed their own names to it. We cannot assume that they share precisely the same attitudes. We suspect that Shelton means that that African artist is "socially functional" in the sense that he voices "communally held" beliefs about the validity of ancient traditions and the corruption of the new civilization. But, even as a statement about what particular artists *say* they are doing, this is only adequate for some of the poets of négritude. Such a statement is particularly inadequate for those who reject excessively polemical or didactic straightjackets which they feel impede their development as *artists*, or which simply make for bad literature, which must delight, even in the service of teaching. Ezekiel Mphahlele has voiced such opinions; Wole Soyinka is notable for a consistent position of this sort.

For Soyinka, artistic concerns, which in large part involve a concern with truth, clearly are paramount. It is clear from his description of his position in "From a Common Back Cloth: A Reassessment of the African Literary Image,"[12] that he is concerned with art as the expression of the individual, not of the community in the sense that folklore and ritual are expressions of the community—that is, with the "validity of a creative imagination for the African, outside folklore and ritual" (p. 387). He finds that fiction is marred by sentimentality, inflation, "philosophical straightjacket[s]" (p. 389) of various kinds, including négritude, however politically useful it may be or have been. The African writer who accepts himself (p. 395) does not have to exoticize his past, does not have to share in or encourage the European critic's attitude, which he says too often becomes a condescending "Takes a simpleton to understand a child" (p. 387). When an author has been "selective to the point of wish-fulfillment" (p. 387), as he thinks Camara Laye has been in his nostalgic portrait of his African childhood (*The Dark Child*), such an attitude can be redeemed only by *art*: "Even if it grew precious, it carried an air of magic, of nostalgia, which worked through the transforming act of language" (p. 387). What Soyinka finds atractive in Mongo Beti, another African author, is instructive; simplification of human mixed motives is ultimately condescending.

> In the literary effort to establish the African as, first before all else, a human being, Mongo Beti with this novel (*Mission to Kala*) has leaped to the fore as the archpriest of the African's humanity. Mongo Beti takes the back cloth as he finds it, asserting simply that tradition is upheld not by one-dimensional innocents, but by cunning old codgers on chieftaincy stools, polygamous elders, watching hawk-like the approach of young blood around their harem, by the eternal trouble-making females who plunge innocents, unaware, into memorable odysseys. Hospitality is not, as we are constantly romantically informed that it is, nearly so spontaneous. There is a mercenary edge, and this, alas, is not always traceable to that alien corrupt civilization! (pp. 394-95)

This indeed sounds close enough to the situation in *The Lion and the Jewel* to reinforce the plausibility of the reading given. Soyinka rejects the simple formula that produces the kind of work that would fit Shelton's reading of *The Lion and the Jewel*: "A society, an intrusion, an all too predictable conflict" (p. 390).

Even if the writer in the emerging African national states understandably felt that he had to "postpone that unique reflection on experience and events which is what makes a writer—and constitute himself into a part of that machinery that will actually shape events," Soyinka suggests that the writer cannot be truly useful politically if, once again, he ignores the truth, becoming "blinded to the present by the resuscitated splendours of the past."[13] As he explains his attitudes about the political role of the writer in "The Writer in an African State," Soyinka is undoubtedly thinking of the Nigerian Civil War, during which he was imprisoned for supporting the Biafran cause.

> This was the beginning of the abdication of the African writer and the deception which he caused by fabricating a magnitude of unfelt abstractions. . . . The black tin-god . . . would degrade and dehumanise his victim as capably as Vorster or Governor Wallace. . . . The romancer and the intellectual mythmaker has successfully deleted this black portion of a common human equation. . . . The myth of irrational nobility, of a racial essence that must come to the rescue of the white depravity has run its full course.[14]

In accordance with these opinions, while some of Soyinka's plays do comment on materialism, they do not make "humanity" an inherent possession of Africans, nor do they associate the ethical life exclusively with traditional ways. As satirist, Soyinka shows the potential for exploitation in the older societies as well as the new—that is, he portrays *humans*. In *Kongi's Harvest*, both the traditional rulers and the new political leaders are clearly portrayed as subject to the same kinds of motivations. Furthermore, he may use the comparison of traditional and modern to touch on issues beyond it; in the *Swamp Dwellers*, neither the old religion (which is exploited by the cult priest) nor the new life in the cities can guarantee that there will be no risk, no loss in life.[15] Preconceptions about political or social attitudes and too hasty an attempt to generalize in terms of the "traditional" and the "modern," the "communalistic" and the "individualistic" can result in serious misreading of sophisticated literature, particularly when written by an author of Soyinka's cast of mind.

Chinua Achebe's novel, *Things Fall Apart*, although read most intelligently by such critics as Charles Larson and David Carroll,[16] has also been curiously misread on occasion. Once again, the reasons for the misreading lie in generalizations about "the African mind" or African society and too hasty an attempt to pin the nature of the novel on an "African" ethos. Perhaps because of his unfamiliarity with African societies, the Western critic is more likely to accept generalizations about "the African personality" without attempting to see them in context, whereas he undoubtedly would exercise more caution in the presence of generalizations about, say, the British or the American national character. It seems once again that an unexamined and unspecific notion of the "communal" nature of African society lends encouragement to this very tendency. Thus, for example, if told that Americans are ambitious, one knows the sense in which "making good" is an *ideal*, the many forms of "ambitiousness," and indeed, the senses in which it may conflict with other American values—more or less for different people and different situations—or, in fact, be rejected. One does not for a minute expect that all Americans will act as if they are molded of exactly the same materials. However, this complex sense of the variable responses to a cultural norm, of the discrepancy between ideal and reality, of the tensions that are inevitable because personality *is* variable, even if within culturally defined limits, seems to be abandoned when some critics confront African literature. Yet it is just this sort of awareness that is required for an open-eyed reading of Achebe's novel; anything less makes a naive polemic out of the fairly complex view of social change in the novel.

James Olney, in his recent critical work of considerable merit, *Tell Me, Africa*,[17] nevertheless serves as a significant example of these tendencies toward misreading. He begins with assumptions about the communal nature of African society based in part on what appears to be an imperfect understanding of clans and lineages. It is as if the mere existence of such kinship groupings is enough to guarantee a "community with one soul rather than a multitude of souls, held together by the will of the ancestors who speak group wisdom and timeless desires through the mouths of the present ruling elders" (p. 175), as Olney understands Achebe's portrait of Igbo society in the first part of the novel. Now, many peoples in the world have or have had extended families, lineages and ancestor worship—one might mention the Chinese—but no one has ever seen these mere facts as assuring no differences of interest within these groups, no conflict and no variation in personality, in short, a totally "homogeneous and coherent group character" (Olney, p. 175). Perhaps because of his lack of anthropological awareness—he does call the extended family "that uniquely African tie"! (p. 61)—Olney too readily attributes extra-ordinary significance to the mere existence of these forms of residence and affiliation, and ignores their contexts. Perhaps he grants these institutions more significance as indicators of African values of "community" than would automatically be granted them if he understood their specific roles in dictating residence patterns and inheritance, say, before leaping to their influence on an explicit or implicit African philosophy. In this, he follows uncritically, and here, irrelevantly, I think, those African writers who describe the "mystique" of lineage or ancestor worship. There is some point in this kind of background when the creative writer is himself speaking from such a position, as is the case, with qualifications, of Camara Laye. But Achebe, like Soyinka, takes a relatively objective stance. If Soyinka is objective as comic artist in *The Lion and the Jewel*, Achebe is objective as the anthropologist, or the documentarist might be in *Things Fall Apart*. He *is* concerned to "justify" precolonial African in-stitutions in a rather anthropological way, by showing that they *worked* to keep society functioning, although not always perfectly. Such a view counters the view of primitive societies as *irrational*, common enough until recently. "I would be quite satisfied if my novels (especially the ones I set in the past) did no more than teach my readers that their past—with all its imperfections—was not one long night of savagery from which the first Europeans acting on God's behalf delivered them. Perhaps what I write is applied art as distinct from pure."[18] But, Achebe's is an *analysis* that allows for imperfections, not a nostalgic or sentimental eulogy of the past.

> Will [the writer] be strong enough to overcome the temptation to select only those facts that flatter him? If he succumbs he will have branded himself an untrustworthy witness. But it is not only his personal integrity as an artist which is involved. The credibility of the world he is attempting to create will be called to question and he will defeat his own purpose if he is suspected of glossing over inconvenient facts. We cannot pretend that our past was one long, technicolour idyll.[19]

Let us look at an example of Olney's reading of his sources, in order to illustrate how he has perhaps forced the available material into his categorizations "communal" as opposed to "individualistic," with the end result that he, too, imposes these categories on the literature he analyzes, and consequently distorts it. The Igbo are commonly described as "individualistic," as Olney says, yet he wishes to emphasize their "communal" character in order to support his reading of *Things Fall Apart*, and of modern African literature generally. This causes some difficulty which he resolves by referring to Victor Uchendu's description in the latter's ethnography of the Igbo, which Olney curiously classifies as autobiography. "Victor Uchendu, for example, though he argues that the Ibo 'lay a great emphasis on individual achievement and initiative,' is quick to acknowledge that this individuality, when considered in a Western perspective, is a partial and non-extreme thing: it is *Ibo* individuality, not personal, private individuality. 'Igbo individualism is not "rugged" individualism; it is individualism rooted in group solidarity. . . . There is a great emphasis on communal cooperation and achievement'." (Olney, p. 177).[20] At this point the distinction gets a bit muddy. American individualism is equally "American." Uchendu's comments must be put in the context of his ethnography, where he also says: "[The Igbo world is] a world that is delicately balanced between opposing forces, each motivated by self-interest; a world whose survival demands some form of cooperation among its members, *although that cooperation may be minimal and even hostile in character.* It is a world in which others can be manipulated for the sake of the individual's status advancement—the goal of Igbo life." (Uchendu, p. 20, my italics). On the basis of Uchendu's ethnography as a whole and of other works on the Igbo, it appears that Uchendu is trying to give a picture that takes account of two facets of Igbo life that appear contradictory: on the one hand, they *are* very much oriented toward achievement and the gaining of status, on an individual basis—and status is *achieved* by individuals and not ascribed; on the other, the Igbo are unusual in the number of self-help organizations they have. The individual is motivated to achieve by such institutions as title-taking, in which Igbos compete on an egalitarian basis, yet his achievement may also redound to the credit of his group (town, family, age-group or whatever) and that group may facilitate his achievement as he in turn facilitates the achievement of other individuals within it. When put in these terms, the differences between our society and theirs *as regards self-seeking and cooperation* do not loom so large; "they" too appear to try to strike a balance. We too may in our individual achievements bring honor to our families or ethnic groups. We too have organizations—such as junior chambers of commerce—which encourage us to help ourselves by helping others. In fact, Uchendu presents Igbo society, not as a group with no conflicts of interest or unfavored people—he does of course mention the *osu* slaves, a group of outcasts, and mothers of twins who had to abandon them—but as a society that attempts to maintain a social and cosmological balance, a society that has to take different— even opposing—forces and claims into account.

> But the Igbo believe that these social calamities and cosmic forces which disturb their world are controllable and should be "manip-ulated" by them for their own purpose. The maintenance of social and cosmological balance in the world becomes, therefore, a domi-nant and pervasive theme in Igbo life. They achieve this balance, for instance, through divination, sacrifice, appeal to the countervailing powers of their ancestors (who are their invisible father-figures) against the powers of the malignant, and non-ancestral spirits, and socially, through constant realignment in their social groupings. . . .
>
> Indeed, whatever threatens the life of the individual or his security as well as society is interpreted by the Igbo as a warning that things must be set right before they get out of hand. . . .
>
> The Igbo individual balances his conflicts in one agnatic group with his privileges in another. His . . . (mother's agnates . . .) stand with him against the perennial conflicts he faces among . . . (his own agnates). Although he is exposed to physical danger among . . . his [own agnates] his person is sacred to his [mother's agnatic] group. . . .
>
> Domination by a few powerful men or spirits is deeply resented. A relationship that is one-sided, either in its obligations or in its reward system, does not last long among them. Imbalance, either in the social or the spiritual world, is considered a trouble indicator.
> (Uchendu, pp. 13–15)

Indeed, *Things Fall Apart* does reflect the attempt to balance cooperation and achievement, to balance the idea that one is perfectly free to shape one's own life—which would encourage achievement—and the idea that one has a preordained fate—which may be used to put a damper on inordinate ambition. It also reflects the actual balance between one's mother's patrilineal kin, who act as protectors in times of trouble and one's own patrilineal kin, as well as the attempt to balance the "mascu-line" and the "feminine" virtues. One misses all of this, if one comes to the novel prepared to find simply a celebrative account of "traditional," totally homogeneous and "communal" African society.

Things Fall Apart has been interpreted in terms of Achebe's presumed or actual social aims as a defense of "traditional" Igbo life; it has also been interpreted as a tragedy similar to *Oedipus*[21] and, as such, as a book beyond social considerations, which, in fact presents its hero as calling the fates upon his head. Insofar as the book is a tragedy, a better model is the *Hippolytus* which concerns the inevitable tragedy of choosing or aligning oneself with one of two necessary and opposed forces, which are extremely difficult to balance, but must be balanced. David Carroll's view of *Things Fall Apart* as a book concerning "competing claims," in contrast to Olney's view, is totally reconcilable with Uchendu's description of Igbo society, which clearly supports and probably helped shape it.[22] Such a view in fact takes all Achebe's statements about the novel into account and, when extended as I intend to extend it here, makes it possible to reconcile the view of the novel as an analysis of a social system with the view of the novel as a tragic statement of human and societal limitations, the role of the writer as ethnographer and the role of the writer as artist.

Olney makes two assumptions that drastically simplify what he has already called "a vastly simple tale of cultural conflict resolved in tragedy" (p. 166). For one, he claims that Achebe portrays a society that falls apart simply because of external influence, but which experienced no conflict because of the "attitudes" and "appetites" of individual members until that time (p. 175). "Until it begins to disintegrate under the impact of a foreign civilization, the old Ibo community, manifest in the person of Okonkwo, is untroubled by internal dissension or individual conscience, by moral hesitation or disunity of purpose. Conflict in such a fiction as this will always be large and simple, external rather than internal, intertribal or intercultural or even international rather than interpersonal or intrapersonal" (p. 181). Olney's second assumption is apparent in the above quotation; he claims that Okonkwo *exemplifies* Igbo society, that he is not individualized: "There is a virtual one-to-one relationship between Okonkwo as an individual and the Ibo as a people" (p. 170). From the point of view of common sense, it seems plausible that there may be less conflict of interest, one might say no competing world views, in smaller-scale societies in which most people do the same things or have similar experiences. Perhaps Olney has something like this in mind when he makes his broad statement about the necessary nature of conflict in the fictions he is considering. However, it is very clear in this particular fiction that there is *not* one cultural norm to which everyone fits, without difficulty, as if they are all cut from a master mold;

and it is equally clear that insofar as there is a dominant norm, it is not one to which Achebe gives his wholehearted approval. The Igbo past, "like other people's past," as Achebe has said, "had its good as well as its bad sides."[23] Okonkwo *is* a representative figure, but he represents one possible cultural type—albeit, perhaps, in a society with fewer possible norms that our own—rather than *the* Igbo type; everything in the novel reaffirms the idea that he overstressed manliness, when an ideal of balance was in fact available. And insofar as the norm he represents was a source of conflict in Igbo society, the destruction of that society comes as the result of the interaction of external *and internal* forces. As Achebe said: "This particular society . . . believed too much in manliness. Perhaps this is part of the reason it crashed in the end."[24]

David Carroll's penetrating analysis of *Things Fall Apart* makes it clear that Achebe analyzes Igbo society in terms of the polarity of the masculine and feminine virtues. Even if the masculine virtues of war and achievement define the dominant ethos of the society, it clearly also requires and gives a place to the feminine virtues of mercy and love. Just as Okonkwo did not *have to* suppress all feelings of tenderness, he did not have to internalize the shame he felt at his father's failure. Igbo society does not insist on heredity; both Uchendu (p. 12) and Achebe use essentially the same proverb to show that anyone can "get up": "As the elders said, if a child washed his hands he could eat with kings" (Achebe, p. 12). Carroll's analysis also makes clear that potential for change and actual changes, as well as conflicts between the individual and society, existed before contact with the white man. Rites had already begun to change on their own; cruel punishments for violation of the Week of Peace were modified because it began to be understood that they worked against their purpose. Individual characters show the existence of variations on cultural givens, and exemplify the senses in which cultural expectations were sources of conflict, or not all of a piece. Ezeudu urged Okonkwo not to personally participate in the killing of Ikemefuna because it would be a violation of an honorary kinship bond, and as such, a pollution of the Earth-Goddess. Obierika, a man of title (a masculine accomplishment) voiced the same opinion after the fact (although the men who refused to kill Ikemefuna were called effeminate) and questioned the exposure of twins, as well as banishment for an involuntary act.

To Carroll's analysis, I wish to add that the conflict in *Things Fall Apart* is not only a conflict between the individual and society, or human forces and divine, but a conflict within the divine realm as well, that is, to some extent, a conflict *between* the Oracle and the Earth-Goddess, which is to some extent congruent with the conflict between the dominant ethos of masculinity and the necessary balancing virtues of feminity. Furthermore, a full appreciation of the novel must take into account the crucial difference between balance, which is possible, if difficult, and reconciliation, which is impossible.

The Earth-Goddess is described as follows: "Ani played a greater part in the life of the people than any other deity. She was the ultimate judge of morality and conduct. And what is more, she was in close communication with the departed fathers of the clan whose bodies had been committed to earth" (*Things Fall Apart*, p. 37). The local Oracle, her messenger, is in a sense subordinate to her. Victor Uchendu's comments on oracles (p. 100), which suggest that they had to be in close touch with public opinion in order to be popular, support the idea that Okonkwo was wrong in obeying the Oracle. However, Uchendu also indicates that oracles could sometimes give publicly necessary but difficult acts a spiritual sanction, thus taking the responsibility away from men. There seems to be an understandable reason for Okonkwo's assertion that "the Earth cannot punish me for obeying her messenger" (p. 64), even if he is judged as acting wrongly. The Oracle, who orders the killing of Ikemefuna, is to some extent associated with encouraging the masculine virtues of war and solidarity; it is to some extent responsible for the unity of the village by urging it to acts that enforce its integrity, even to somewhat cruel acts. No one questions the necessity of obeying the Oracle, although one does question the necessity of *Okonkwo*'s obeying the Oracle. On the other hand, the Earth-Goddess, as both Achebe and Uchendu (p. 96) tell us, is merciful, slow to act, a source of morality—contrasting with the principle Okonkwo seems to represent: extreme quickness of action—and she opposes the slaying of Ikemefuna by Okonkwo. To some extent, then, although not perfectly, the roles of the Oracle and the Earth-Goddess overlap with the roles of the masculine and the feminine in the book. At the same time, as Carroll does indicate, there is conflict between these divine forces and individual humans: the Oracle is feared and causes suffering for Okonkwo when her priestess, Agbala, takes his daughter Ezinma, away; the Earth-Goddess who prescribes banishment for her pollution, even if accidental, allows the society to go on, since the offender is removed, but at a significant price to the individual.

As Carroll suggests, had Okonkwo agreed not to *personally* participate in the killing of Ikemefuna, he would have been able to strike a balance between "competing claims." But I wish to emphasize the tenuousness of such an equilibrium. Such an act only postpones the ultimate problem of reconciling conflicts in Igbo society, rather than merely balancing them. It would solve Okonkwo's immediate problem, but would it solve his son Nwoye's problem? The fact that his father did not participate in the killing of the friend he loved would not totally compensate him for the loss of the friend, whose *love* had inspired Nwoye to *manly* acts, thus temporarily reconciling the masculine and feminine polarities of Igbo society. For these reasons, the possibility of balancing claims is not the only context in which Okonkwo's behavior can be seen. That is, given the nature of Igbo society, Okonkwo does not represent a kind of behavior that can be modified in the direction of a community-accepted norm of moderate behavior, combining in one person, both the masculine and feminine virtues. Rather, from the tragic point of view, he participates in a society which is truly split. As in the *Hippolytus,* both of the opposing forces are necessary, and aligning totally with one at the expense of the other is dangerous, yet it is extremely difficult to take account of both, and impossible to reconcile them, since they conflict at the core.

Insofar as the masculine and feminine virtues tend to be associated with different people or sets of people, for example, discipline with one's father and "sympathy" with one's mother; one's "fatherland" with "good times" and one's "motherland" with "sorrow and bitterness" (p. 124), and insofar as the society encourages this sort of separation of functions and roles, balance is possible, however difficult. However, balance is not a solution for the *individual* who cannot exist comfortably in terms of the preferred role or norm assigned him in accordance with his situation and gender; he can find solace, but only at the price of loss of status. Reconciliation is what is required from the point of view of the individual—that is, the possibility of the acceptance of aspects of "masculine" and "feminine" behavior in the same person. Such a reconciliation *is* momentarily achieved in the friendship of Nwoye and Ikemefuna; it should be stressed again that it is the *love* of Nwoye for Ikemefuna (rather than his desire to achieve) that inspires Nwoye to *manly* acts. Persons such as Obierika are clearly asking the kinds of questions that might have changed the dominant norm of Igbo society. But, Igbo society as it is described in *Things Fall Apart* exists sufficiently in terms of the masculine virtues that it cannot *incorporate* the others without disintegration. As such, it is caught in a truly tragic dilemma. Insofar as individuals pay a personal price for community solidarity, the community is that much more open to threats from without, just as Nwoye's discomfort with Igbo practices such as the exposure of twins, make the religion of the invaders that much more attractive to him. On the other hand, without strictures on behavior that threatens the group, without punishment for certain crimes or without any encouragement of group solidarity in obedience to the local oracle, disintegration may take place from within.

Things Fall Apart, then, both describes a particular society and exemplifies a tragic dilemma of the type found in the *Hippolytus*. It describes a correctable situation, insofar as balancing claims was an available and meaningful alternative for an Igbo such as Okonkwo. But, insofar as *reconciliation* of such claims was what was needed from the point of view of the individual, although such reconciliation was incongruent with the very existence of the society, *Things Fall Apart* describes an insoluble tragic dilemma. This view accords with Achebe's comments on his book. The Igbo themselves are often given as a prime example of adaptation to modern circumstances. Yet the book itself and Achebe's comments make clear that he thinks of the Igbo society he portrayed as having experienced disintegration and downfall. He seems to think of the older Igbo society as fundamentally different from the new. "The weakness of this particular society is a lack of adaptation, not being able to bend. But I can't say that this represents the Ibo people today. I think in his time, the strong men were those who did not bend and I think this was a fault of the culture itself."[25]

In both the cases of critical misreading analyzed here, philosophical and political attitudes and categorizations seem to be imposed on particular literary works. It is possible that these categorizations, "communalistic," "individualistic," and so on, are also not very useful in generalizations about cultures, at least as they are used by the critics I have looked at. In any case, these critics do not seem to be sure enough about what they mean by these categorizations and hence allow them to encourage some simplistic readings. If the categorizations are useful, this must be shown in more precise definitions and more accurate readings of the works, achieved with their aid. As it stands, the roots of the misreadings discussed here seem to lie in a tendency to accept generalizations about other people that we would never accept about ourselves. It is with such generalizations in mind that James Olney comes to *Things Fall Apart* ready to find that the African author is inevitably synonymous with his culture, and the African individual, even in a novel, inevitably one with his group. He does not seem to feel the necessity to distinguish different groups and interests within a particular culture. It is hard to avoid drawing the conclusion that he assumes not only that African cultures are monolithic, but that they all can pretty much be summed up in the same way. And it is with such generalizations in mind that Austin Shelton argues for the relevance of abstract values appropriate to a political tract for a comedy that sees human behavior in all its contingent forms. Unfortunately, such critical assessments justify Soyinka's accusation that the Western critic is condescending: "Takes a simpleton to understand a child."

NOTES

[1] This distinction is summarized in Marvin Harris, *The Rise of Anthropological Theory* (New York, 1970), p. 192.

[2] See, for example, Paul Bohannan, *Africa and Africans* (New York, 1971), pp. 119–28.

[3] E. N. Obiechina makes just such an argument in "Transition from Oral to Literary Tradition," *Présence Africaine*, 63 (1967), 155ff.

[4] J. P. Clark takes seriously the idea that tragedy stems from a ritual sacrifice in his play, *The Song of a Goat*; an actual goat is sacrificed in the course of the play.

[5] Oyekan Owomoyela makes this argument in "Folklore and Yoruba Theatre," *Research in African Literatures*, 2 (1971), 121–33. The same argument may be found in the work of a British anthropologist, Robin Horton, in "The Kalabari Ekine Society: A Borderland of Religion and Art," *Africa*, 33 (1963), 94–114.

[6] In *Black Africa: Its Peoples and their Cultures Today*, ed. John Middleton (London, 1970), pp. 406–12. Page references to Shelton's article will appear in parentheses in the text.

[7] Wole Soyinka, *The Lion and the Jewel* (1963; rpt. London, 1966), p. 7. Further page references to *The Lion and the Jewel* are to this edition and will appear in parentheses in the text.

[8] E. N. Obiechina, *An African Popular Literature: A Study of Onitsha Market Pamphlets* (Cambridge, 1973), Ch. IV.

[9] See, for example, Soyinka's comment about those "contemporary interpreters of African themes [who] have not truly assimilated the new idioms. It is merely naive to transpose the castle to the hut. . . . There are the new poets in Nigeria who regroup images of Ezra Pound around the oilbean and the nude spear." In "From a Common Back Cloth: A Reassessment of the African Literary Image," *The American Scholar*, 32 (1963), 388–89.

[10] Cf. Claude Wauthier, *The Literature and Thought of Modern Africa* (New York, 1967), pp. 173–74. ·

[11] See, for example, Warren L. d'Azevedo, ed. *The Traditional Artist in African Societies* (Bloomington, Indiana, 1973).

[12] *The American Scholar*, 32 (1963), 387–96. Further page references to this article will appear in parentheses in the text.

[13] "The Writer in an African State," *Transition*, No. 31 (1967), 11, 12.

[14] Ibid., 12, 13.

[15] See Gerald Moore, *Wole Soyinka* (New York, 1971), pp. 16–19.

[16] See Charles Larson, *The Emergence of African Fiction* (Bloomington, Indiana, 1972), Ch. II, and David Carroll, *Chinua Achebe* (New York, 1970), Ch. II.

[17] Princeton, New Jersey, 1973. Further page references to Olney's book will appear in parentheses in the text.

[18] "The Novelist as Teacher," *New Statesman*, 29 January 1965, p. 62.

[19] From "The Role of the Writer in a New Nation," *Nigeria Magazine*, 81 (1964), quoted in G. D. Killam, *The Novels of Chinua Achebe* (New York, 1969), p. 10.

[20] Olney quotes from Uchendu, *The Igbo of Southeast Nigeria* (New York, 1965), p. 103. Further page references to Uchendu's ethnography will appear in parentheses in the text.

[21] Larson, *The Emergence of African Fiction*, p. 61.

[22] Cf. Carroll, pp. 26, 28 and n. 7 (p. 149).

[23] From "The Role of the Writer in a New Nation," quoted in Killam, *The Novels of Chinua Achebe*, p. 10.

[24] "Conversation with Chinua Achebe," *Africa Report*, 9 (July 1964), 19.

[25] Ibid.

NOTES ON CONTRIBUTORS

Notes on Contributors

Joel Adedeji, Acting Head of the Department of Theatre Arts at the University of Ibadan, has written numerous articles on African drama.

Tom Allen is a student in the Music School of the University of Wisconsin at Madison.

Robert P. Armstrong, Professor of Anthropology at the University of Texas at Dallas, is the author of *The Affecting Presence: An Essay in Humanistic Anthropology* (1970), *Wellspring:*_____ (1975) and numerous articles on African arts and esthetics.

Lloyd W. Brown, Associate Professor of Comparative Literature at the University of Southern California, has written *Bits of Ivory: Narrative Techniques in Jane Austen's Fiction* (1973) and has edited *The Black Writer in Africa and the Americas* (1973). He has also written many essays on African, Afro-American and Caribbean literatures.

Charles N. Davis is a doctoral student in Comparative Literature at the University of Wisconsin at Madison.

Don Dodson, Assistant Professor in the Department of Communication at Stanford University, has written extensively on the mass media, publishing and popular literature in Nigeria.

Michael J. C. Echeruo, Chairman of the English Department at the University of Ibadan, is co-editor of *Igbo Traditional Life Culture and Literature* (1971) and has written *Joyce Cary and the Novel of Africa* (1973) and numerous articles on African literature.

Ernest Emenyonu, Head of the English Department at the Alvan Ikoku College of Education in Owerri, Nigeria, is author of *Cyprian Ekwensi* (1974) and numerous articles on African literature.

J. Z. Kronenfeld, a Ph.D. in English, has taught English and African literature at the University of California at Irvine and the University of California at Riverside and has written articles on Joyce Cary, Shakespeare and Lévi-Strauss.

Bernth Lindfors, Associate Professor of African and English literature at the University of Texas at Austin, has written *Folklore in Nigerian Literature* (1973), and has edited *Dem-Say: Interviews with Eight Nigerian Writers in Texas* (1974), *Critical Perspectives on Amos Tutuola* (1975) and since 1970, the journal *Research in African Literatures*.

Donatus Nwoga, Chairman of the Department of English at the University of Nigeria at Nsukka, and has co-authored *Poetic Heritage: Igbo Traditional Verse* (1971) and has written many articles on African literature.

Oludare Olajubu, Lecturer in the Department of Education at the University of Lagos, has written a number of articles on Yoruba oral literature.

Oyekan Owomoyela, currently Lecturer in Communications at the University of Lagos and formerly Assistant Professor of English at the University of Nebraska, has co-authored *Yoruba Proverbs: Translation and Annotation* (1973) and numerous articles on African literature.

Neil Skinner, Professor of African Languages and Literatures at the University of Wisconsin at Madison, is the author of *Hausa Tales and Traditions* (1969) and many articles on African oral and written literatures.

W. H. Stevenson, who has taught at the University of Ibadan and Boston University and is now teaching at the Univeristy of Edinburgh, has edited *Studies in Romanticism* and has written articles on English and African literatures.

BIBLIOGRAPHY

Bibliography

Nigerian Literature in English:
A Selected List of Criticism and Commentary

Since information on literatures written in Nigerian languages can be located quite easily in the bibliographies cited below, the publications selected for mention here deal almost exclusively with Nigerian literature written in English. However, the list is far from complete. All essays and books devoted to individual Nigerian authors have been omitted, as have broad-ranging surveys which attempt to cover more than one nation's literary output. The intention has been to provide a fairly full sample of what has been published on Nigerian literature in English as a discrete and coherent body of African writing.

Bibliographies

For information on Igbo literature, see Mark W. DeLancey, "The Igbo: A Bibliographic Essay," *Africana Library Journal*, 3, 4 (1972), 3-30, and Joseph C. Anafulu, "Igbo Life and Art; Igbo Language and Literature: Selected Bibliographies," *Conch*, 3, 2 (1971), 181-203.

For information on Yoruba literature, a good introduction can be found in Adeboye Babalola and Albert S. Gérard, "A Brief Survey of Creative Writing in Yoruba," *Review of National Literatures*, 2, 2 (1971), 188-205.

For information on Hausa literature, see Frank A. Salamone, "A Hausa Bibliography," *Africana Journal*, 6, 2 (1975), 99-163.

For information on literatures in other Nigerian languages, see Nduntuei O. Ita, *Bibliography of Nigeria: A Survey of Anthropological and Linguistic Writings from the Earliest Times to 1966* (London: Frank Cass, 1971).

For further information on Nigerian literature in English, see Bernth Lindfors, *A Bibliography of Literary Contributions to Nigerian Periodicals, 1946-1972* (Ibadan: Ibadan University Press, 1975).

CRITICAL PERSPECTIVES

Criticism and Commentary on Nigerian Literature in English

Abasiekong, Dan. "Has the Nigerian Novel Run Out of Steam?" *Drum* (Nigerian ed.), August 1966, 11-13.

Achebe, Chinua. "The Role of the Writer in a New Nation," *Nigeria Magazine,* 81 (1964), 157-60; *Nigerian Libraries,* 1, 3 (1964), 113-19.

————. "The African Writer and the Biafran Cause," *Conch,* 1, 1 (1969), 8-14; *Biafra Review,* 1 (1970), 28-30.

Adedeji, Joel A. "The Church and the Emergence of the Nigerian Theatre, 1866-1914," *Journal of the Historical Society of Nigeria,* 6, 1 (1971), 25-45.

————. "A Profile of Nigerian Theatre 1960-1970," *Nigeria Magazine,* 107-09 (1971), 3-14.

————. "Oral Tradition and the Contemporary Theater in Nigeria," *Research in African Literatures,* 2 (1971), 134-49.

Adefemiwa, Akin. "Nigerian Creative Writers and the Preservation of Our Cultural Values," *Teacher's Journal* (Lagos), 3, 3 (1971), 17-19.

Adelugba, Dapo. "Nigeria—Theatre Survey," *New Theatre Magazine,* 12, 2 (1972), 15-16.

Agboro, James A. "Nigerian Poetry: Its Place in the Development of National Literature," *The Muse* (Nsukka), 2, 2 (1965), 25-26.

Amadi, Elechi. "The Novel in Nigeria," *Oduma,* 2, 1 (1974), 33, 35-37; *Afriscope,* 4, 11 (1974), 40-41, 43, 45.

Amankulor, Jas. "Postwar Theatre in Nsukka," *The Muse* (Nsukka), 4 (1972), 29-32.

Anon. "A National Theatre for Nigeria?" *Drum* (Nigerian ed.), August 1967, 21-24.

Anon. "Our Authors and Performing Artists," *Nigeria Magazine,* 88 (1966), 57-64; 89 (1966), 133-40. [Biographical sketches.]

Anozie, Sunday O. "Two Nigerian Poets," *African Writer,* 1, 1 (1962), 3-4, 26-28. [Osadebay and Clark.]

Armstrong, Robert P. "The Characteristics and Comprehension of a National Literature—Nigeria," *Proceedings of a Conference on African Languages and Literatures held at Northwestern University, April 28-30, 1966,* ed. Jack Berry et al. (n.p.: n.d.), pp. 117-32.

Asein, Samuel O. "Nigerian Literature and the Critics," *Bulletin of the Association for Commonwealth Literature and Language Studies* (Kampala), 10 (1972), 55-70.

Axworthy, Geoffrey. "The Performing Arts in Nigeria—A Footnote," *New Theatre Magazine,* 12, 2 (1972), 17-18. [Reply to Adelugba's essay above.]

Badejo, Kehinde. "Literature and Civil War: A Rejoinder," *African Statesman,* 4, 4 (1969), 35. [Reply to Bodurin's essay below.]

Banham, Martin. "Drama in the Commonwealth: Nigeria," *New Theatre Magazine,* 1 (July 1960), 18-21.

————. "The Beginnings of a Nigerian Literature in English," *Review of English Literature,* 3, 2 (1962), 88-99.

————. "Notes on Nigerian Theatre: 1966," *Bulletin of the Association for African Literature in English,* 4 (1966), 31-36.

————. "African Literature II: Nigerian Dramatists in English and the Traditional Nigerian Theatre," *Journal of Commonwealth Literature,* 3 (1967), 97-102; reprinted in *Insight,* 20 (1968), 29-30.

Beier, Ulli. "Nigerian Literature," *Nigeria Magazine,* 66 (1960), 212-28.

————. "Some Nigerian Poets," *Présence Africaine,* 32/33 (1960), 50-63. [Osadebay, Soyinka, Okara, Clark and others.]

————. "Public Opinion on Lovers: Popular Nigerian Literature Sold in Onitsha Market," *Black Orpheus,* 14 (1964), 4-16.

Bischofberger, Otto. *Tradition und Wandel aus der Sicht der Roman-schriftsteller Kameruns und Nigerias* (Einsiedeln, Switzerland: Etzel-Druck, n.d.).

Bodurin, A. "Literature and the Civil War," *African Statesman,* 7, 1 (1972), 15-20.

Bonneau, Danielle. "Le pidgin English comme moyen d'expression lit-téraire chez les romanciers du Nigéria," *Annales de l'université d'Abidjan,* 5D (1972), 5-29.

Carroll, Fr. P.J. "The Nigerian Novel," *Exiit* (Ibadan), 3 (1963), 5-8.

Chinweizu, Onwuchekwa Jemie, and Ihechukwu Madubuike. "Towards the Decolonization of African Literature," *Okike,* 6 (1974), 11-27; 7 (1975), 65-81; both parts reprinted in *Transition* 48 (1975), 29-37, 54, 56. [On Nigerian poetry and Nigerian literary critics.]

Clark, Ebun. "Ogunde Theatre: The Rise of Contemporary Professional Theatre in Nigeria 1946-1972," *Nigeria Magazine,* 114 (1974), 3-14.

Clark, John Pepper. "A Note on Nigerian Poetry," *Présence Africaine,* 58 (1966), 55-64.

————. "Aspects of Nigerian Drama," *Nigeria Magazine,* 89 (1966), 118-26; reprinted in Clark's *The Example of Shakespeare* (Evanston: Northwestern University Press, 1970, London: Longman, 1971), pp. 79-96.

————. "The Communication Line Between Poet and Public," *African Forum,* 3, 1 (1967), 42-53; reprinted in *The Example of Shakespeare,* pp. 61-75. [Considers Nigerian examples.]

Coulon, Virginia. "The Cultural Renaissance in Nigeria," *Commonwealth Miscellanies* (Pau, France), 1 (1974-75), 37-47.

Crowder, Michael. "Tradition and Change in Nigerian Literature," *Bulletin of the Associaion for African Literature in English,* 3 (1965), 1-17; *Tri-Quarterly,* 5 (1966), 117-28.

Dathorne, O.R. "Ibo Literature: The Novel as Allegory," *Africa Quarterly*, 7 (1968), 365-68.

Drayton, Arthur D. "The Return to the Past in the Nigerian Novel," *Ibadan*, 10 (1960), 27-30.

Ebuh, Stanley Mac. "On the Queston of Theme in Nigerian Literature; A Rejoinder to an Address by Chinua Achebe," *Horizon* (Ibadan), 3, 4 (1966), 14-16. [Reply to "The Role of the Writer in a New Nation" below.]

Echeruo, Michael J. "Incidental Fiction in Nigeria," *African Writer*, 1, 1 (1962), 10-11.

————. "Concert and Theatre in Late Nineteenth Century Lagos." *Nigeria Magazine*, 74 (1962), 68-74.

————. "Traditional and Borrowed Elements in Nigerian Poetry," *Nigeria Magazine*, 89 (1966), 142-55.

————. "Books, Libraries and the Making of a Nigerian Culture," *Nigerian Libraries*, 2 (1966), 24-35.

————. "Publishing and Writing in Nigeria," *Afriscope*, 5, 6 (1975), 42-44, 46-47.

Egudu, Romanus N. "The Nigerian Literary Artist and His Society," *Ufahamu*, 4, 1 (1973), 59-76.

————. "Nigerian Poets and Nigerian Tradition," *West African Religion*, 16, 1 (1975), 1-7.

Ekom, Ernest. "The Development of Theatre in Nigeria 1960-1967," *Journal of the New African Literature and the Arts*, 11/12 (1971), 36-49.

Ekwensi, Cyprian. "Problems of Nigerian Writers," *Nigeria Magazine*, 78 (1963), 217-19.

————. "Literary Influences on a Young Nigerian," *Times Literary Supplement*, 4 June 1964, 475-76.

Ekpenyong, J.O. "The Use of English in Nigeria," *Commonwealth Literature*, ed. John Press (London: Heinemann, 1965), pp. 144-50.

Emenyonu, Ernest. "Igbo Literary Backgrounds," *Conch*, 5 (1973), 43-60.

————. "Post-War Writing in Nigeria," *Ufahamu*, 4, 1 (1973), 77-92; *Issue*, 3, 2 (1973), 49-54; *Studies in Black Literature*, 4, 1 (1973), 17-24.

Esslin, Martin. "Two African Playwrights," *Black Orpheus*, 19 (1966), 33-39; reprinted in *Introduction to African Literature*, ed. Ulli Beier (Evanston: Northwestern University Press, 1967), pp. 255-62.

Ferguson, John. "Nigerian Poetry in English," *English*, 15 (1965), 231-35; *Insight*, 13 (1966), 7-9.

————. "Nigerian Prose Literature in English," *English Studies in Africa*, 9 (1966), 43-60.

————. "Nigerian Drama in English," *Modern Drama*, 11 (1968), 10-26.

Feuser, Willfried F. "A Farewell to the Rising Sun: Post-Civil War Writings from Eastern Nigeria," *Books Abroad*, 49 (1975), 40-49; a longer German version of this essay can be found in *Internationales Afrika Forum*, 11 (1975), 520-32.

Folarin, Tunde. "The Nigerian Theatre," *Beacon* (Ibadan), 1, 8 (1962), 18-21.

Galperina, Y.L. "Under the Sign of Ogun: The Young Writers of Nigeria, 1960-1965," *Africa in Soviet Studies: Annual 1969* (Moscow: Nauka, 1971), pp. 162-83.

Gérard, Albert. "Elégies nigériennes," *Revue Générale Belge*, 91 (1963), 37-49.

_____ . "Nigéria: Naissance d'une littérature moderne," *Congo-Afrique*, 8 (1968), 66-70.

_____ . "Biographies of Eleven Nigerian Writers," *Research in African Literatures*, 5 (1974), 206-12.

Gleason, Judith. "Out of the Irony of Words," *Transition*, 18 (1965), 34-38. [On Achebe and Soyinka.]

Hall, K.G. "Stories of the Nigerian Civil War in *The Insider*," *Bulletin of the Association for Commonwealth Literature and Language Studies* (Kampala), 10 (1972), 71-77. [Stories in an anthology edited by Chinua Achebe.]

Horton, Robin. "Three Nigerian Novelists," *Nigeria Magazine*, 70 (1961), 218-24. [Achebe, Ekwensi, Nzekwu.]

Hossmann, Irmeline. "Le miracle du théâtre nigérien: Un entretien avec Demas Nwoko," *Afrique*, 59 (1966), 36-40.

Irele, Abiola. "Tradition and the Yoruba Writer: D.O. Fagunwa, Amos Tutuola and Wole Soyinka," *Odu*, 11 (1975), 75-100.

Izevbaye, D.S. "Politics in Nigerian Poetry," *Présence Africaine*, 78 (1971), 143-67.

_____ . "Nigeria," *Literatures of the World in English*, ed. Bruce King (London: Routledge & Kegan Paul, 1974), pp. 136-53.

Jahn, Janheinz. "La théâtralité du théâtre nigérien moderne," *Le théâtre négro-africain: Actes du colloque d'Abidjan, 1970* (Paris: Présence Africaine, 1971), pp. 167-71.

_____ . "L'exemple du théâtre anglophone et surtout nigérian," *Le théâtre négro-africain: Actes du colloque d'Abidjan, 1970* (Paris: Présence Africaine, 1971), pp. 219-21.

Jones, Eldred. "Locale and Universe—Three Nigerian Novels," *Journal of Commonwealth Literature*, 3 (1967), 127-31. [Novels by Amadi, Nwapa and Achebe.]

Keszthelyi, T. "Nigéria irodalmi életéröl [On Nigerian literary life]," *Nagyvilag*, 10 (1964), 1544-46.

King, Bruce. "Two Nigerian Writers: Tutuola and Soyinka," *Southern Review,* 6 (1970), 843-48.

————, ed. *Introduction to Nigerian Literature* (New York: Africana Publishing Corp., 1972).

Kinner, Joseph. "With McLuhan in Nigeria, Item I: An Eye for an Ear," *Ufahamu,* 2, 2 (1971), 57-70.

Klima, Vladimír. *Modern Nigerian Novels* (Prague: Academia, 1969).

Kolade, Christopher. "Looking at Drama in Nigeria," *African Forum,* 1 (1966), 77-79.

Larson, Charles R. "Nigerian Drama Comes of Age," *Africa Report,* 13, 5 (1968), 55-57.

Leopold, W. "Chinua Achebe i nardziny powiésci nigeryskiej [Chinua Achebe and the Birth of the Nigerian Novel]," *Przeglad Socjologiczny,* 19, 1 (1965), 192-207.

————. "Powiésci Ibo [Novels by Ibo writers]," *Przeglad Socjologiczny,* 23 (1969), 370-87.

Lindfors, Bernth. "Five Nigerian Novels," *Books Abroad,* 39 (1965), 411-13. [Novels by Okara, Achebe, Nwankwo, Egbuna and Aluko.]

————. "African Vernacular Styles in Nigerian Fiction," *College Language Association Journal,* 9, 3 (1966), 265-73.

————. "Nigerian Novels of 1965," *Africa Report,* 11, 6 (1966), 68-69. [Novels by Soyinka, Nzekwu, Ike and Akpan.]

————. "Nigerian Novels of 1966," *Africa Today,* 14, 5 (1967), 27-31. [Novels by Achebe, Ekwensi, Aluko, Amadi, Munonye and Nwapa.]

————. "Chinua Achebe és a nigériai regény [Chinua Achebe and the Nigerian Novel]," *Helikon,* 16 (1970), 22-32; reprinted in English in *Studies on Modern Black African Literature,* ed. Pál Páricsy (Budapest: Center for Afro-Asian Research, Hungarian Academy of Sciences, 1971), pp. 29-49; and in *Lotus: Afro-Asian Writings,* 15 (1973), 34-51.

————. "Yoruba and Igbo Prose Styles in English," *Black Orpheus,* 2, 7 (1972), 21-30; reprinted in *Common Wealth,* ed. Anna Rutherford (Aarhus: Akademisk Boghandel, 1972), pp. 47-61.

————. *Folklore in Nigerian Literature* (New York: Africana Publishing Corp., 1973).

————. "Popular Literature for an African Elite," *Journal of Modern African Studies,* 12 (1974), 471-86. [Secondary school magazines and univeristy publications.]

————. "Achebe's Followers," *Revue de littérature comparée,* 48 (1974), 569-89. [Igbo novelists.]

————, ed. *Dem-Say: Interviews with Eight Nigerian Writers* (Austin: African and Afro-American Studies and Research Center, University of Texas, 1974).

————. "Shakespeare and Nigerian Drama," *Proceedings of the 6th Congress of the International Comparative Literature Associaiton* (Stuttgart: Kunst and Wissen, Erich Bieber, 1975), pp. 639-41.

————. "Are There Any National Literatures in Sub-Saharan Black Africa Yet?" *English in Africa,* 2, 2 (1975), 1-9.

Laurence, Margaret. *Long Drums and Cannons: Nigerian Dramatists and Novelists, 1952-1966* (London: Macmillan, 1968).

McDowell, Robert E. "Three Nigerian Storytellers: Okara, Tutuola, and Ekwensi," *Ball State University Forum,* 10, 3 (1969), 67-75.

Momodu, A.G.S. "The Problems of Nigeria's Creative Writers," *Radio Times* (Lagos), 20 May 1962, 9.

Moore, Gerald. "Poetry and the Nigerian Crisis," *Black Orpheus,* 2, 3 (1968), 10-13.

Ngugi, James. "Satire in Nigeria: Chinua Achebe, T.M. Aluko and Wole Soyinka," *Protest and Conflict in African Literature,* ed. Cosmo Pieterse and Donald Munro (New York: Africana Publishing Corp.; London: Heinemann, 1969), pp. 56-69.

Ngwube, Anerobi. "Nigerian War Literature," *Indigo,* 2 (1974), 3-4, 6-7.

Nkosi, Lewis. "A Release of Energy: Nigeria, the Arts and Mbari," *New African,* 1, 11 (1962), 10-11.

Nwoga, Donatus. "Nigerian Literature and the Educated Nigerian," *The Muse* (Nsukka), 2, 2 (1965), 14-16.

————. "Onitsha Market Literature," *Transition,* 19 (1965), 26-33.

Obiechina, Emmanuel. *An African Popular Literature: A Study of Onitsha Market Literature* (Cambridge: Cambridge University Press, 1973).

————. *Culture, Tradition and Society in the West African Novel* (Cambridge: Cambridge University Press, 1975).

O'Flinn, J.P. "Towards a Sociology of the Nigerian Novel," *African Literature Today,* 7 (1975), 34-52.

Ogunba, Oyin. "Poetry, Emotion and the Nigerian Public," *Beacon* (Ibadan), 1, 8 (1962), 16-18.

————. "Theatre in Nigeria," *Présence Africaine,* 58 (1966), 65-88.

Ogungbesan, Kolawole. "Nigerian Writers and Political Commitment," *Ufahamu,* 5, 2 (1974), 20-50.

Okonkwo, Juliet N. "Adam and Eve: Igbo Marriage in the Nigerian Novel," *Conch,* 3, 2 (1971), 137-51.

Okpaku, Joseph O. "The Writer in Politics: Christopher Okigbo, Wole Soyinka and the Nigerian Crisis," *Journal of the New African Literature and the Arts,* 4 (1967), 1-13.

Okwu, E.C. "A Language of Expression for Nigerian Literature," *Nigeria Magazine,* 91 (1966), 289-92, 313-15.

O'Malley, P. "Recent Nigerian Fiction," *Nigerian Opinion*, 3, 4 (1967), 190-92.

Omotoso, Kole. "Politics, Propaganda and Prostitution," *Afriscope*, 4, 11 (1974), 45, 47, 49. [Reply to Amadi's essay above.]

Osofisan, Femi. "The Quality of Hurt: A Survey of Recent Nigerian Poetry," *Afriscope*, 4, 7 (1974), 45-48, 51-53; 4, 9 (1974), 46-49, 51, 53-55.

Otenigbagbe, J.A. "The 'Nigerian' Novel," *Horizon* (Ibadan), 1, 3 (1963), 10-11.

Oti, Sonny. "Tragedy's Vocal Audience in Nigeria," *Journal of Commonwealth Literature*, 9, 3 (1975), 53-62.

Parry, J. "Nigerian Novelists," *Contemporary Review*, 200 (1966), 377-81.

Povey, John F. "Changing Themes in the Nigerian Novel," *Journal of the New African Literature and the Arts*, 1 (1966), 3-11.

————. "Wole Soyinka and the Nigerian Drama," *Tri-Quarterly*, 5 (1966), 129-35.

————. "The Nigerian War: The Writer's Eye," *Journal of African Studies*, 1 (1974), 354-60.

Ramsaran, J.A. "African Twilight: Folktale and Myth in Nigerian Literature," *Ibadan*, 15 (1963), 17-19.

Ravenscroft, Arthur. "The Nigerian Civil War in Nigerian Literature," *Commonwealth Literature and the Modern World*, ed. Hena Maes-Jelinek (Brussels: Didier, 1975), pp. 105-13.

Reckord, Barry. "Notes on Two Nigerian Playwrights," *New African*, 4, 7 (1965), 171. [Clark and Soyinka.]

Ricard, Alain. "Nationalisme et littérature au Nigeria: 1960-1967," *L'Afrique Littéraire et Artistique*, 10 (1970), 22-27.

————. "Universités et création artistique au Nigeria," *L'Afrique Littéraire et Artistique*, 22 (1973), 52-60.

————. *Livre et communication au Nigéria: Essai de vue généraliste* (Paris: Présence Africaine, 1975).

————. "Les limites de l'étude d'influence: Théâtre nigérian et théâtre anglais," *Proceedings of the 6th Congress of the International Comparative Literature Association* (Stuttgart: Kunst and Wissen, Erich Bieber, 1975), pp. 635-38.

Richard, R. "Théâtre nigérien anglophone," *Etudes Anglaises*, 25 (1972), 199-206.

Roscoe, Adrian A. *Mother is Gold: A Study in West African Literature* (Cambridge: Cambridge University Press, 1971).

Samsara. "The Future of Nigerian Writing," *Horizon* (Ibadan), 1, 1 (1961), 13-17.

Scheub, Harold. "Two African Women," *Revue des Langues Vivantes*, 37 (1971), 545-58, 664-81. [Amadi's *The Concubine*, Nwapa's *Efuru*.]

Schmidt, Nancy J. "Nigeria: Fiction for the Average Man," *Africa Report*, 10, 8 (1965), 39-41.

_____ . "Nigerian Fiction and the African Oral Tradition," *Journal of the New African Literature and the Arts*, 5/6 (1968), 10-19.

Séverac, Alain. "Aspect du roman africain anglophone: Un roman engagé," *Les Langues Modernes*, 65 (1971), 232-43.

Shelton, Austin J. "Nationalism and Cosmopolitanism as Source-Effect and Motif in Modern Nigerian Literature," *Proceedings of the IVth Congress of the International Comparative Literature Association*, ed. Francois Jost (The Hague: Mouton, 1966), pp. 687-91.

_____ . "The Articulation of Traditional and Modern in Igbo Literature," *Conch*, 1, 1 (1969), 30-52.

Soyinka, Wole. "The Theatre in Nigeria: A Brief Review," *Cultural Events in Africa*, 5 (1965), i supp.

_____ . "Neo-Tarzanism: the Poetics of Pseudo-Tradition," *Transition*, 48 (1975), 38-44. [Reply to essay by Chinweizu et al. above.]

Swados, Harvey. "Chinua Achebe and the Writers of Biafra," *Sarah Lawrence Journal* (Spring 1970), 55-62; *New Letters*, 40 (1973), 5-13.

Taiwo, Oladele. "The Use of Comedy in Nigerian Fiction," *Literary Half-Yearly*, 15, 2 (1974), 107-20.

_____ . "The Link Between Tradition and Modern Experience in the Nigerian Novel," *Studies in Black Literature*, 5, 3 (1974), 11-16.

_____ . *Culture and the Nigerian Novel* (London: Macmillan, 1975).

Thomas, Peter. "Voices from Nsukka: Students and the Art of Poetry," *New African*, 5, 7 (1966), 144-45.

_____ . "The Water Maid and the Dancer: Figures of the Nigerian Muse," *Literature East & West*, 12, 1 (1968), 85-93.

_____ . "Two Voices from the Biafran War," *Concerning Poetry*, 4, 2 (1971), 10-17.

_____ ."Great Plenty to Come: A Personal Reminiscence of the First Generation of Nsukka Poets," *The Muse* (Nsukka), 4 (1972), 5-8.

_____ . "Ibo Poetry in English Since the End of the Nigerian Civil War," *Books Abroad*, 48 (1974), 34-41.

Tucker, Martin. "Three West African Novelists," *Africa Today*, 12, 9 (1965), 10-14. [Tutuola, Ekwensi, Achebe.]

Udoeyop, N.J. *Three Nigerian Poets: A Critical Study of the Poetry of Soyinka, Clark and Okigbo* (Ibadan: Ibadan University Press, 1973).

Uka, Kalu. "Drama in Nigerian Society," *The Hoe* (Enugu), 1, 1 (1973), 23-32; *The Muse* (Nsukka), 5 (1973), 11, 13-15, 36-38.

_____ . "The Place of Drama as Medium of Mass Expression in Nigeria," *The Muse* (Nsukka), 6 (1974), 45-50.

CRITICAL PERSPECTIVES

Vavilov, V. "Nigerian Literature and Reality," *Essays on African Culture/ Essais d'histoire de la culture africaine,* ed. M.A. Korostovtsev (Moscow: Nauka, 1966), pp. 155-63.

————. "Insight on Nigerian Novels," *New World,* 2, 3 (1968), 27.

————. "Nigerija: Roman i vremja," *Voprosy Literatury,* 15, 6 (1971), 164-81.

————. *Proza Nigerii* (Moscow: Nauka, 1973).

Vincent, Theo. "Two Decades of Modern Nigerian Literature," *Oduma,* 2, 2 (1975), 57-67.

Wake, Clive. "Nigeria, Africa and the Caribbean: A Bird's Eye View," *Perspectives on African Literature: Selections from the Proceedings of the Conference on African Literature Held at the University of Ife 1968,* ed. Christopher Heywood (New York: Africana Publishing Corp., 1971), pp. 193-208.

Wren, Robert M. "Anticipation of Civil Conflict in Nigerian Novels: Aluko and Achebe," *Studies in Black Literature,* 1, 2 (1970), 21-32.